International Money & Finance

The Addison-Wesley Series in Economics

Abel/Bernanke
Macroeconomics

Bade/Parkin
Foundations of Economics

Bierman/Fernandez
Game Theory with Economic Applications

Binger/Hoffman
Microeconomics with Calculus

Boyer
Principles of Transportation Economics

Branson
Macroeconomic Theory and Policy

Bruce
Public Finance and the American Economy

Byrns/Stone
Economics

Carlton/Perloff
Modern Industrial Organization

Caves/Frankel/Jones
World Trade and Payments

Chapman
Environmental Economics: Theory, Application, and Policy

Cooter/Ulen
Law and Economics

Downs
An Economic Theory of Democracy

Ehrenberg/Smith
Modern Labor Economics

Ekelund/Tollison
Economics

Fusfeld
The Age of the Economist

Gerber
International Economics

Ghiara
Learning Economics

Gordon
Macroeconomics

Gregory
Essentials of Economics

Gregory/Stuart
Russian and Soviet Economic Performance and Structure

Hartwick/Olewiler
The Economics of Natural Resource Use

Hubbard
Money, the Financial System, and the Economy

Hughes/Cain
American Economic History

Husted/Melvin
International Economics

Jehle/Reny
Advanced Microeconomic Theory

Klein
Mathematical Methods for Economics

Krugman/Obstfeld
International Economics

Laidler
The Demand for Money

Leeds/von Allmen
The Economics of Sports

Lipsey/Courant/Ragan
Economics

Melvin
International Money and Finance

Miller
Economics Today

Miller/Benjamin/North
The Economics of Public Issues

Miller/Benjamin
The Economics of Macro Issues

Mills/Hamilton
Urban Economics

Mishkin
The Economics of Money, Banking, and Financial Markets

Parkin
Economics

Perloff
Microeconomics

Phelps
Health Economics

Riddell/Shackelford/Stamos/Schneider
Economics: A Tool for Critically Understanding Society

Ritter/Silber/Udell
Principles of Money, Banking, and Financial Markets

Rohlf
Introduction to Economic Reasoning

Ruffin/Gregory
Principles of Economics

Sargent
Rational Expectations and Inflation

Scherer
Industry Structure, Strategy, and Public Policy

Schotter
Microeconomics

Stock/Watson
Introduction to Econometrics

Studenmund
Using Econometrics

Tietenberg
Environmental and Natural Resource Economics

Tietenberg
Environmental Economics and Policy

Todaro/Smith
Economic Development

Waldman
Microeconomics

Waldman/Jensen
Industrial Organization

Williamson
Macroeconomics

International Money & Finance

SEVENTH EDITION

Michael Melvin
Arizona State University

Original edition, entitled INTERNATIONAL MONEY AND FINANCE, 7th Edition, by MELVIN, MICHAEL, published by Pearson Education, Inc, publishing as Prentice Hall, Copyright © 2004.

ISBN 978-89-450-1058-2

Contents

Preface

International finance is one of the growth areas of the finance and economics curricula. Today's financial marketplace is truly global. No student of economics or finance can fully understand current developments without some background in international finance. If, after studying this text, a student can pick up *The Wall Street Journal* and understand the international financial news, along with its implications, then I feel that I have succeeded as a teacher. To this end, *International Money and Finance* offers a concise yet comprehensive overview of the subject. The basics of the foreign exchange market and the balance of payments are presented, along with accessible discussions of the most recent research findings related to exchange rate determination. Topics covered range from the nitty-gritty of financing international trade to intuitive discussions of overshooting exchange rates and currency substitution.

The first edition of *International Money and Finance* grew from the lecture notes I used to teach undergraduate students. The notes, as well as the book, summarized the current literature in international finance, with only elementary math as a prerequisite. It was extremely gratifying to find that instructors at other institutions found the earlier editions to be useful texts for undergraduate and MBA students. In fact, the adoption list ranged from the leading MBA schools in the country to small rural four-year colleges. The fact that the text has proved successful with students of varying abilities and backgrounds is a feature that I have strived to retain in preparing this seventh edition.

Users of the sixth edition will find the seventh edition updated and revised to keep pace with the rapidly changing world of international finance. There are several major changes in this edition. Most obvious is the use of euros instead of the legacy European currencies throughout the text. Chapter 3 now has a new section, "The European Monetary System and the Euro," which includes a discussion of the European Central Bank, and a new section on target zones. The currency board section now includes a discussion of Argentina as an example of what can go wrong. Chapter 4 has been streamlined by eliminating the detailed tables of futures and options prices and the accompanying descriptions. Chapter 7 has been thoroughly revised to include expanded coverage of ADRs with a discussion of various types and why foreign firms list their shares in the United States. There is also a new section on "The Globalization of Equity Markets" with a discussion of how countries move from a segmented to a globalized financial market with a consequent reduction in the cost of capital. This section includes a table with the dates of first stock market liberalization for many countries. Chapter 8 now includes a discussion of the real exchange rate. Chapter 9 has been updated to incorporate the latest research on how the effect of devaluations may depend upon what happens to labor costs relative to the cost of capital. Another substantive change in this chapter involved moving the discussion of the monetary approach to the exchange rate to Chapter 10 so that all exchange rate determination material is now located in a single chapter. Chapter 10 also includes a new appendix on technical analysis in the FX market that takes note of the popularity of this approach to exchange rate modeling among practitioners. Chapter 13 now includes an expanded discussion of LIBOR, how it is set, and the contributing banks. A new discussion of early warning indicators of financial crises has been added along with a new section on the role of corruption, its effects on economic growth, and IMF efforts to reduce it. Finally, Chapter 14 reflects two important changes in this edition: a new section, "The New Open-Economy Macroeconomics," that includes a discussion of pricing to market and a new section on "The Open-Economy Multiplier."

The seventh edition has been written in the same spirit as the first six—to provide a concise survey of international finance suitable for undergraduate and MBA classes.

ACKNOWLEDGMENTS

I am grateful to all who have offered comments leading to the revision of *International Money and Finance.* They include countless former students, and instructors at other institutions, who provided informal comments on style and content. Earlier editions were reviewed by Mamadou

K. Diallo of East Stroudsburg University, B.D. Elzas of Erasmus University, Judy L. Klein of Mary Baldwin College, Vibhas Madan of Drexel University, Kiminori Matsuyama of Northwestern University, Thomas Russell of Santa Clara University, Larry J. Sechrest of Sul Ross State University, Robert Sedgwich of Sheffield Hallam University, Darrel Young of St. Edward's University, Carl Beidleman of Lehigh University, Glenn W. Boyle of Louisiana State University, David Ding of Memphis State University, Chen Jia-sheng of the University of Denver, Francis A. Lees of St. Johns University, Chu-Ping Vijverberg of the University of Texas at Dallas, Robert Flood of Northwestern University, Samuel Katz of Georgetown University, Donald P. Stegall of California State University at Fresno, Clas Wihlborg of the University of Southern California, Bernard Gauci of Hollins University, Bang Nam Jeon of Drexel University, Chris Neely of the Federal Reserve Bank of St. Louis, Helen Popper of Santa Clara University, and Felix Rioja of Georgia State University. Reviews of the sixth edition that helped in the preparation of this new edition were provided by Lance Girton of the University of Utah, Bijou Yang Lester of Drexel University, Peter Pedroni of Williams College, Miguel Ramirez of Trinity College, Julie Ryan of Immaculata College, Niloufer Sohrabji of Simmons College, and Mark Wohar of the University of Nebraska. While I could not incorporate all of their thoughtful suggestions, I appreciate their comments and have no doubt that the text has been much improved by their reviews.

Finally, I welcome comments and criticism from users of the seventh edition of *International Money and Finance.* My hope is that the book will evolve over time to best suit your needs.

MICHAEL MELVIN

To the Student

Why Study International Finance?

Why study the subject of international money and finance? One reason is that career goals are paramount to many people, and in this regard the topic of the text is related to a growth area in the labor market. This book provides a background in international finance for those who expect to obtain jobs created by international investment, international banking, and multinational business activity.

Other readers may have a more scholarly concern with "rounding out" their economic education by studying the international relationships between financial markets and institutions. Although a course in principles of economics is the only prerequisite assumed for this text, many students may have already taken intermediate macroeconomics, money and banking, or essentials of finance courses. But for those interested in international economic relationships, such courses often lack a global orientation. The economic models and discussions of the typical money and banking course focus on the *closed economy,* closed in the sense that the interrelationships with the rest of the world are ignored. Here we study the institutions and analysis of an integrated world financial community, thus giving a better understanding of the world in which we live. We will learn that there are constraints as well as opportunities facing the business firm, government, and the individual investor that become apparent only in a worldwide setting.

Finance and the Multinational Firm

A *multinational firm* is a firm with operations that extend beyond its domestic national borders. Such firms have become increasingly sophisticated in international financial dealings because international business poses risk and return opportunities that are not present in purely domestic business operations. A U.S. multinational firm may have accounts payable and receivable that are denominated in U.S. dollars, Japanese yen, British pounds, Mexican pesos, Canadian dollars, and euros. The financial managers of this firm face a different set of problems than the managers of a firm doing business strictly in dollars. It may be true that "a dollar is a dollar," but the dollar value of yen, euros, or pesos can and does change over time. As the dollar value of the yen changes, the value of yen-denominated contracts will change when evaluated in terms of dollars.

Multinational finance responds to this new set of challenges with a tool kit of techniques and market instruments that are used to maximize the return on the firm's investment, subject to an acceptable level of risk. Once we extend beyond the domestic economy, a rich variety of business opportunities exists that must be utilized with the appropriate financial arrangements. This book intends to cover many aspects of these international financial transactions that the financial manager may encounter.

The financial side of international business differs from the study of international trade commonly encountered in international economics courses. Courses in international trade study the determinants of the pattern and volume of world trade—formally referred to as the theory of *comparative advantage.* If country A produces and exports shoes in exchange for country B's food, we say that A has a comparative advantage in shoes and B has a comparative advantage in food. Besides comparative advantage, such courses also examine the movement of factors of production, labor, and capital goods between nations. Obviously, these subjects are important and deserve careful study, but our purpose is to study the monetary consequences of such trade. Although we will not explicitly consider any theories of comparative advantage—such theories are usually developed without referring to the use of money—we will often consider the impact of monetary events on trade in real goods and services. Our discussions range from the effects of the currency used in pricing international trade (Chapter 9) to financing trade in the offshore banking industry (Chapter 13). We will find that monetary events can have real consequences for the volume and pattern of international trade.

The Actors

This course is not simply a study of abstract theories concerning the international consequences of changes in money supply or demand, prices, interest rates, or exchange rates. We also discuss the role and importance of the institutional and individual participants. Most people tend to think immediately of large commercial banks as holding the starring role in the international monetary scene. Because the foreign exchange market is a market where huge sums of national currencies are bought and sold through commercial banks, any text on international finance will include many examples and instances in which such banks play a major part. In fact, Chapter 1 begins with a discussion of the role of banks in the foreign exchange market.

Besides commercial banks, other business firms play a key part in our discussion, since the goods and services they buy and sell internationally effect a need for financing such trade. The corporate treasurer of any multinational firm is well versed in foreign exchange trading and hedging and international investment opportunities. What is hedging? How are international investment opportunities related to domestic opportunities? These are subjects we address in Chapters 4 and 5.

Finally, we examine the role of government. Central banks, such as the Federal Reserve in the United States, are often important actors in our story. Besides their roles of buying, selling, lending, and borrowing internationally, they also act to restrict the freedom of the other actors. The policies of central governments and central banks are crucial to understanding the actual operation of the international monetary system, and each chapter will address the impact of government on the topic being described.

Plan of Attack

This book can be thought of in terms of three main sections. Chapters 1 through 8 identify the key institutions and relationships of the international monetary system. To aid our understanding of the relationships among prices, exchange rates, and interest rates, we will consider existing theories, as well as the current state of research that illuminates their validity. For those students who choose to proceed professionally in the field of international finance, the study of this text should provide both a good reference and a springboard to more advanced work—and ultimately employment.

Chapters 9 and 10 cover the next general area of the determinants of balance of payments and exchange rates. Government and industry devote many resources to trying to forecast the balance of payments and exchange rates. The discussion in these chapters includes the most important recent developments. Although there is some disagreement among economists regarding the relative significance of competing theories, as far as possible in an intermediate-level presentation, the theories are evaluated in light of research evidence. Altogether, these chapters present a detailed summary of the current state of knowledge regarding the determinants of the balance of payments and exchange rates.

Chapters 11 through 13 are devoted to applied topics of interest to the international financial manager. Issues range from the "nuts and bolts" of financing imports and exports to the evaluation of risk in international lending to sovereign governments. The topics covered in these chapters are of practical interest to corporate treasurers and international bankers.

The concluding chapter is an analysis of macroeconomic issues in an open economy. This coverage of open-economy macroeconomics includes the determination of the equilibrium values of key macroeconomic variables and the effects of government monetary and fiscal policy on these variables.

At the beginning of this introduction we asked: Why study international money and finance? I hope that the brief preview provided here will have motivated you to answer this question. International finance is not a dull "ivory tower" subject to be tolerated, or avoided if possible. Instead, it is a subject that involves dynamic real-world events. Since the material covered in this book is emphasized daily in the newspapers and other media, you will soon find that the pages in *International Money and Finance* seem to come to life. To this end, a daily reading of *The Wall Street Journal* or the London *Financial Times* makes an excellent supplement for the text material. As you progress through the book, international financial news will become more and more meaningful and useful. For the many users of this text who do not go on to a career in international finance, the major lasting benefit of the lessons contained here will be the ability to understand the international financial news intelligently and effectively.

M.M.

1

The Foreign Exchange Market

Foreign exchange trading refers to trading one country's money for that of another country. The need for such trade arises because of tourism, the buying and selling of goods internationally, or investment occurring across international boundaries. The kind of money specifically traded takes the form of bank deposits or bank transfers of deposits denominated in foreign currency. The *foreign exchange market,* as we usually think of it, refers to large commercial banks in financial centers, such as New York or London, that trade foreign-currency-denominated deposits with each other. Actual *bank notes* like dollar bills are relatively unimportant insofar as they rarely physically cross international borders. In general, only tourism or illegal activities would lead to the international movement of bank notes.

Spot Rates

Figure 1.1 shows foreign *exchange rate* quotations for a particular day. An exchange rate is the price of one money in terms of another. In the figure we see that on Friday, January 31, 2003, Swiss francs were selling for $0.7332. Note that this exchange rate is quoted at a specific time, 4 P.M., since rates will change throughout the day as supply and demand for the currencies change. Notice also that these exchange rates are quotes based on large trades ($1 million or more), in what is essentially a wholesale

Currency Trading
Exchange Rates

The New York foreign exchange mid-range rates below apply to trading among banks in amounts of $1 million and more, as quoted at 4 P.M. Eastern time by Reuters and other sources. Retail transactions provide fewer units of foreign currency per dollar.

Country	U.S. $ equiv.	Currency per U.S. $
Argentina (Peso)	0.3120	3.2051
Australia (Dollar)	0.5875	1.7021
Bahrain (Dinar)	2.6522	0.3770
Brazil (Real)	0.2854	3.5039
Britain (Pound)	1.6472	0.6071
1 Month Forward	1.6438	0.6083
3 Months Forward	1.6365	0.6111
6 Months Forward	1.6268	0.6147
Canada (Dollar)	0.6572	1.5216
1 Month Forward	0.6564	1.5235
3 Months Forward	0.6545	1.5279
6 Months Forward	0.6514	1.5352
Chile (Peso)	0.001360	735.29
China Renminbi)	0.1208	8.2781
Columbia (Peso)	0.0003393	2,947.2
Czech Republic (Koruna)	—	—
Commercial Rate	0.03417	29.265
Denmark (Krone)	0.1448	6.9061
Ecuador (US Dollar)-e	1.000	1.000
Hong Kong (Dollar)	0.1282	7.8003
Hungary (Forint)	0.004412	226.65
India (Rupee)	0.02092	47.801
Indonesia (Rupiah)	0.0001127	8,873.1
Israel (Shekel)	0.2073	4.8239
Japan (Yen)	0.008341	119.89
1 Month Forward	0.008349	119.77
3 Months Forward	0.008369	119.49
6 Months Forward	0.008396	119.10
Jordan (Dinar)	1.4092	0.7096
Kuwait (Dinar)	3.3450	0.2990
Lebanon (Pound)	0.0006634	1,507.4
Malaysia (Ringitt)-b	0.2632	3.7994
Malta (Lira)	2.5654	0.3898
Mexico (Peso)	0.09165	10.911
New Zealand (Dollar)	0.5448	1.8355

(Continued)

Figure 1.1 Foregin exchange rate quotations for Friday, January 31, 2003. Data were selected from http://online.wsj.com.

Figure 1.1 (Continued)

Norway (Krone)	0.1445	6.9204
Pakistan (Rupee)	0.01723	58.038
Peru (New Sol)	0.2870	3.4843
Philippines (Peso)	0.01858	53.821
Poland (Zloty)	0.2616	3.8226
Russia (Ruble)-a	0.03141	31.837
Saudi Arabia (Riyal)	0.2667	3.7495
Singapore (Dollar)	0.5754	1.7379
Slovak Republic (Koruna)	0.02578	38.790
South Africa (Rand)	0.1175	8.5106
South Korea (Won)	0.0008591	1,164.0
Sweden (Krona)	0.1164	8.5911
Switzerland (Franc)	0.7332	1.3639
1 Month Forward	0.7336	1.3631
3 Months Forward	0.7346	1.3613
6 Months Forward	0.7360	1.3587
Taiwan (Dollar)	0.02882	34.698
Thailand (Baht)	0.02337	42.790
Turkey (Lira)	0.00000061	1,639,344
United Arab (Dirham)	0.2723	3.6724
Uruguay (Peso) Financial	0.03520	28.409
Venezuela (Bolivar)	0.0005200	1,923.1
Euro	1.07650	0.9289

a-Russian Central Bank rate, b-Government rate. d-Floating rate; trading band suspended on 4/11/00. e-Adopted U.S. dollar as of 9/11/00. f-Floating rate, eff. Feb 22.

market for money. The smaller the quantity of foreign exchange purchased, the higher the price. For instance, if you were a U.S. importer buying watches from Switzerland at the dollar price of $10,000, your local bank would sell $10,000 worth of francs to you for more than $0.7332 per franc. Suppose the bank charges you $0.75 per franc. You would then buy SF13,333.33 ($10,000/$0.75) to settle the account with the French exporter. An individual buying even smaller amounts of francs would pay a still higher rate.

In the example just considered, the U.S. importer found that $10,000 was equivalent in value to SF13,333.33. We calculated this by dividing the total dollar value of the purchase ($10,000) by the dollar price of 1 franc ($0.75). Note that the foreign exchange quotations also list quotes in terms of foreign currency units per dollar. In Figure 1.1 we see that on Friday, January 31, the Swiss franc sold for $0.7332. By looking farther to the right, we also see that the dollar was worth SF1.3639. It will always be true that when we know the dollar price of the franc ($/SF), we can find the franc price of the dollar by taking the reciprocal (SF/$). Of course, this relationship works in the opposite direction as well. If the franc price of the dollar is SF1.3639, then the dollar price of the franc is found as the reciprocal (1/1.3639 = 0.7332). In the example of the U.S. watch importer, if the bank is selling francs for $0.75, then what is the implied franc price of the dollar? To find this we simply calculate the reciprocal: 1/0.75 = SF1.3333. Had we initially been given the exchange rate quote in terms of francs per dollar, we could have found the franc equivalent of $10,000 by multiplying $10,000 by the franc price of 1 dollar: 10,000 × 1.3333 = SF13,333. The importer buys this quantity of francs from the bank and actually pays for the watch with a check drawn on the bank (or a foreign associate of the bank).

Note that the exchange rate quotes in Figure 1.1 are mid-range rates. Banks bid to buy foreign exchange at lower rates than they sell, and the difference between the selling and buying rates is called the *spread.* The midrange is the average of the buying and selling rates. Table 1.1 lists the average spreads on Friday, January 31. We see that on this day, the Swiss franc price a bank would pay for dollars was SF1.3571 per dollar. Dollars would be sold for francs by the bank at SF1.3576 per dollar. This spread of less than 1/10 of 1 percent [(1.3576 − 1.3571)/1.3571 = .0004] is indicative of the normal spread in the market for major traded currencies. The existing spread in any currency will vary according to the individual currency trader, the currency being traded, and the trading bank's overall view of conditions in the foreign exchange market. The spread quoted will tend to increase for more thinly traded currencies (i.e., currencies that do not generate a large

Table 1.1 Average Spreads, January 31, 2003

Euro[a]	1.0813–1.0815
British pound[a]	1.6535–1.6543
Canadian dollar	1.5280–1.5285
Japanese yen	119.03–119.09
Swiss franc	1.3571–1.3576

[a]Quotes for the euro and the pound are in terms of U.S. dollars per euro or pound. All other quotes are domestic currency units per U.S. dollar.

Data are from Olsen and Associates (http://www.oanda.com/).

volume of trading) or when the bank perceives that the risks associated with trading in a currency at a particular time are rising.

The large trading banks like Citibank or Deutsche Bank stand ready to "make a market" in a currency by offering buy (bid) and sell (ask) rates on request. Actually, currency traders do not quote all the numbers indicated in Table 1.1. For instance, the table lists the spread on Canadian dollars as C$1.5280 to C$1.5285. In practice, this spread is quoted as C$1.5280–85 or, in words, the Canadian dollar per U.S. dollar rate is one-fifty-two-eighty to eighty-five. The listener then recognizes that the bank is willing to bid C$1.5280 to buy U.S. dollars and will sell U.S. dollars at C$1.5285.

Thus far, we have discussed trading Swiss francs and Canadian dollars using the symbols SF and C$, respectively. Table 1.2 lists the commonly

Table 1.2 International Currency Symbols

Country	Currency	Symbol	ISOCode
Australia	Dollar	A$	AUD
Austria	Euro	€	EUR
Belgium	Euro	€	EUR
Canada	Dollar	C$	CAD
Denmark	Krone	DKr	DKK
Finland	Euro	€	EUR
France	Euro	€	EUR
Germany	Euro	€	EUR
Greece	Euro	€	EUR
India	Rupee	Rs	INR
Iran	Rial	RI	IRR
Italy	Euro	€	EUR
Japan	Yen	¥	JPY
Kuwait	Dinar	KD	KWD
Mexico	Peso	Ps	MXP
Netherlands	Euro	€	EUR
Norway	Krone	NKr	NOK
Saudi Arabia	Riyal	SR	SAR
Singapore	Dollar	S$	SGD
South Africa	Rand	R	ZAR
Spain	Euro	€	EUR
Sweden	Kronar	SKr	SEK
Switzerland	Franc	SF	CHF
United Kingdom	Pound	£	GBP
United States	Dollar	$	USD

used symbols for several currencies along with their international standard (ISO) code. Exchange rate quotations are generally available for all countries where currencies may be freely traded. In the cases where free markets are not permitted, the state typically conducts all foreign exchange trading at an official exchange rate, regardless of current market conditions.

So far we have been discussing the buying and selling of foreign exchange to be delivered on the spot (actually, deposits traded in the foreign exchange market generally take two working days to clear); this is called the *spot market.* In our example of the U.S. watch importer, the importer wanted to buy $10,000 worth of francs for current payment. If the importer purchases the francs in the spot market today, in two days the bank will reduce the importer's checking account balance by $10,000 and wire the SF13,333 to be drawn on a Swiss bank by the exporter (for relatively small transactions, the two-day delay may not be necessary).

In Chapter 4 we will consider the important issues that arise when the trade contract involves payment at a future date. First, however, we should consider in more detail the nature of the foreign exchange market.

Arbitrage

The foreign exchange market is a market where price information is readily available by telephone or computer network. Since currencies are homogeneous goods (a dollar is a dollar regardless of where it is traded), it is very easy to compare prices in different markets. Exchange rates tend to be equal worldwide. If this were not so, there would be profit opportunities for simultaneously buying a currency in one market while selling it in another. This activity, known as *arbitrage,* would raise the exchange rate in the market where it is too low, because this is the market in which you would buy, and the increased demand for the currency would result in a higher price. The market where the exchange rate is too high is one in which you sell, and this increased selling activity would result in a lower price. Arbitrage would continue until the exchange rates in different locales are so close that it is not worth the costs incurred to do any further buying and selling. When this situation occurs, we say that the rates are "transaction costs close." Any remaining deviation between exchange rates will not cover the costs of additional arbitrage transactions, so the arbitrage activity ends.

For instance, suppose Citibank is quoting the Swiss franc/U.S. dollar exchange rate as 1.4445–55 and Dresdner Bank in Frankfurt is quoting 1.4425–35. This means that Citibank will buy dollars for 1.4445 francs and will sell dollars for 1.4455 francs. Dresdner will buy dollars for 1.4425 francs and will sell dollars for 1.4435 francs. This presents an arbitrage opportunity. We could buy \$10 million at Dresdner's ask price of 1.4435 and simultaneously sell \$10 million to Citibank at their bid price of 1.4445 francs. This would earn a profit of SF0.0010 per dollar traded, or SF10,000 would be the total arbitrage profit.

If such a profit opportunity existed, the demand to buy dollars from Dresdner would cause them to raise their ask price above 1.4435, while the increased interest in selling dollars to Citibank at their bid price of 1.4445 francs would cause them to lower their bid. In this way, arbitrage activity pushes the prices of different traders to levels where no arbitrage profits are earned. Suppose the prices moved to where Citibank is quoting the Swiss franc/dollar exchange rate at 1.4440–50 and Dresdner is quoting 1.4430–40. Now there is no arbitrage profit possible. The ask price at Dresdner of 1.4440 is equal to the bid price at Citibank. The difference between the bid and ask prices of each bank is equal to the spreads of SF0.001. In the wholesale banking foreign exchange market, the bid-ask spread is the only transaction cost. Therefore, when the quotes of two different banks differ by no more than the spread being quoted in the market by these banks, there is no arbitrage opportunity.

Arbitrage could involve more than two currencies. When we consider that the bulk of foreign exchange trading involves the U.S. dollar, we note the role of comparing dollar exchange rates for different currencies to determine if the implied third exchange rates are in line. Since banks quote foreign exchange rates with respect to the dollar (the dollar is said to be the "numeraire" of the system), such comparisons are readily made. For instance, if we know the dollar price of pounds (\$/£) and the dollar price of Swiss francs (\$/SF), we can infer the corresponding pound price of francs (£/SF). From now on we will explicitly write the units of our exchange rates to avoid the confusion that can easily arise. For instance, \$/£ = \$2.00 is the exchange rate in terms of dollars per pound.

To simplify the analysis of arbitrage involving three currencies, let's temporarily ignore the bid-ask spread and assume that we can either buy or sell at one price. Suppose that in London \$/£ = \$2.00, while in New York \$/SF = \$0.40. The corresponding *cross rate* is the £/SF rate. Simple algebra shows that if \$/£ = \$2.00 and \$/SF = 0.40, then £/SF = (\$/SF)/(\$/£) = 0.40/2.00 = 0.2. If we observe a market where one of the three exchange rates—\$/£, \$/SF, £/SF—is out of line with the other two, there is an arbitrage opportunity. Suppose that in Frankfurt the exchange rate is £/SF = 0.2, while in New York \$/SF = 0.40, but in London \$/£ = \$1.90. Astute traders in the foreign exchange market would observe the discrepancy, and quick action would be rewarded. The trader could start with dollars and buy £1 million in London for \$1.9 million since \$/£ = \$1.90. The pounds could be used to buy francs at £/SF = 0.2, so that £1,000,000 = SF5,000,000. The SF5 million could then be used in New York to buy dollars at \$/SF = \$0.40, so that SF5,000,000 = \$2,000,000. Thus the initial \$1.9 million could be turned into \$2 million with the *triangular arbitrage* action earning the trader \$100,000 (costs associated with the transaction should be deducted to arrive at the true arbitrage profit).

As in the case of the two-currency arbitrage covered earlier, a valuable product of this arbitrage activity is the return of the exchange rates to internationally consistent levels. If the initial discrepancy was that the dollar price of pounds was too low in London, the selling of dollars for pounds in London by the arbitragers will make pounds more expensive, raising the price from \$/£ = \$1.90 back to \$2.00. (Actually, the rate would not return to \$2.00, because the activity in the other markets would tend to raise the pound price of francs and lower the dollar price of francs, so that a dollar price of pounds somewhere between \$1.90 and \$2.00 would be the new equilibrium among the three currencies.)

Table 1.3 gives the cross rates for several currencies in New York on January 31, 2003. Effective arbitrage will ensure that by knowing any two exchange rates, we will be able to infer a third. For instance, we find that £/\$ = 0.6071 by looking across the U.S.\$ row for the £ column, which happens to be the first column. To find the dollar price of euros, we glance across the euro row for the \$ column and notice that \$/€ = 1.0765; the implied cross

Table 1.3 Foreign Exchange Cross Rates, January 31, 2003

	£	\$	€	¥
U.K. pound (£)	1	1.6472	1.5301	196.12
U.S. dollar (\$)	0.6071	1	0.9289	119.06
European euro (€)	0.6535	1.0765	1	128.17
Japanese yen (¥)	0.0050	0.0083	0.0077	1

Note: Exchange rates are units of the currency listed in the top row per unit of the currency listed in the left-hand column.

rate for £/€ is determined by multiplication: £/€ = (£/$)($/€) = 0.6071 × 1.0765 = 0.6535. We can look at the € row and the £ column to see the cross rate of 0.6535.

Since there is active trading between the dollar and other currencies, we can look to any two exchange rates involving dollars to infer the cross rates. So even if there is limited direct trading between, for instance, Mexican pesos and yen, by using pesos/$ and $/¥, we can find the implied pesos/¥ rate. Since transaction costs are higher for lightly traded currencies, the depth of foreign exchange trading that involves dollars often makes it cheaper to go through dollars to get from some currency *X* to another currency *Y* when *X* and *Y* are not widely traded. Thus, if a business firm in small country *X* wants to buy currency *Y* to pay for merchandise imports from small country *Y*, it may well be cheaper to sell *X* for dollars and then use dollars to buy *Y* rather than try to trade currency *X* for currency *Y* directly.

The Intradaily Activity

Although arbitrage will tend to equalize exchange rate quotes worldwide, we must remember that the different financial centers operate in different time zones. Therefore, it only makes sense to compare quotations at a time when the markets overlap. As Figure 1.2 indicates, we could not compare $/£ quotes in late afternoon in New York with those in London because the London market is closed by then. Figure 1.2 illustrates the 24-hour dimension of the foreign exchange market. We can determine the local hours of major trading activity in each location by the country bars at the top of the figure. Time is measured as Greenwich Mean Time (GMT) at the bottom of the figure. For instance, in New York 7 A.M. is 1200 GMT and 3 P.M. is 2000 GMT. Since London trading has ended by 4 P.M. London time, or 1600 GMT (11 A.M. in New York), active arbitrage involving comparisons of New York and London exchange rate quotes would end around 1600 GMT. Figure 1.2 shows that there is a small overlap between European trading and Asian trading, and there is no overlap between New York trading and Asian trading.

Dealers in foreign exchange publicize their willingness to deal at certain prices by posting quotes on news services such as Reuters. When a dealer at a bank posts a quote on a news service, that quote then appears on computer monitors sitting on the desks of other foreign exchange market participants worldwide. This posted quote is like an advertisement, telling the rest of the market the prices at which the quoting dealer is ready to deal.

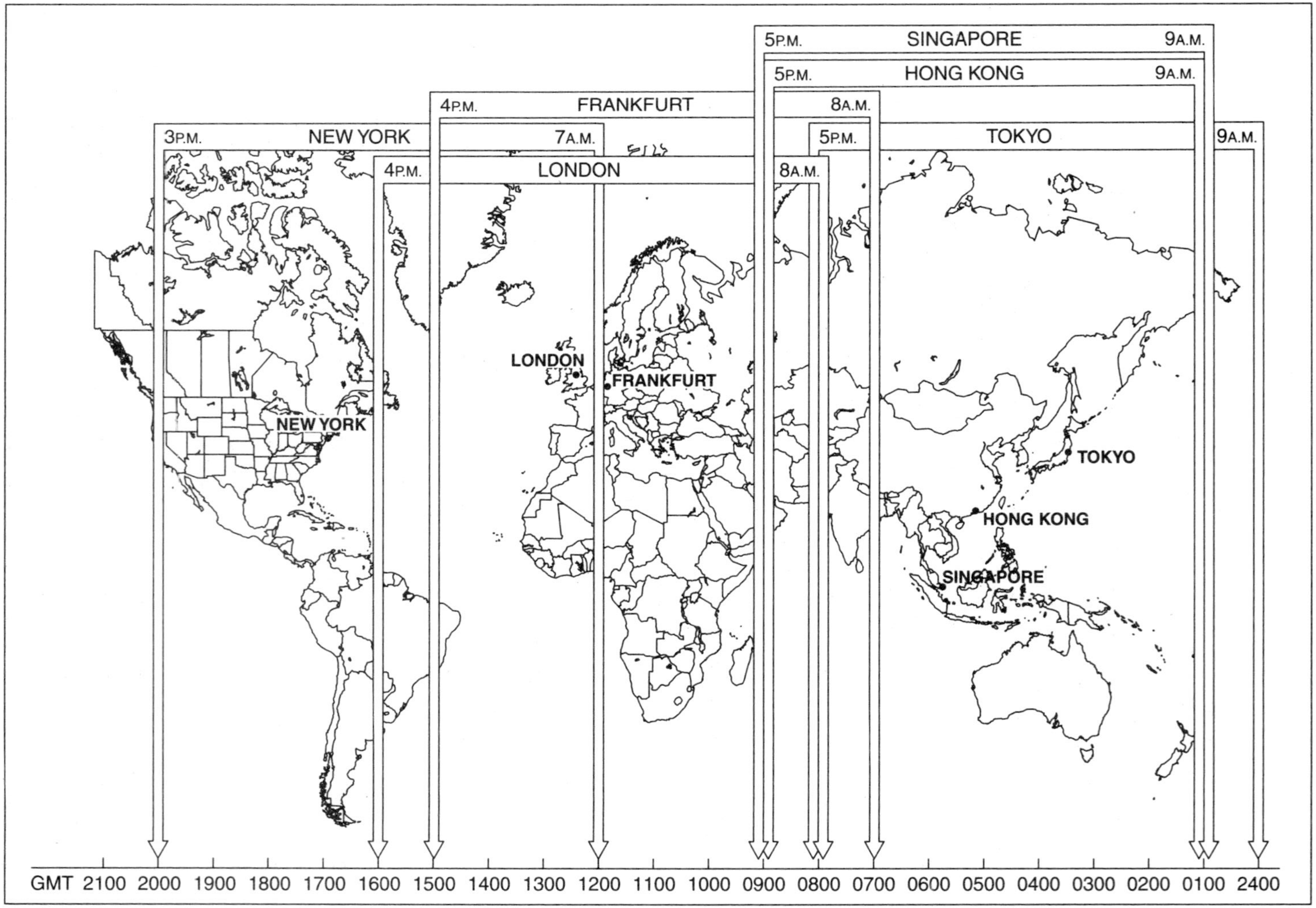

Figure 1.2 The world of foreign exchange dealing.

The actual prices at which transactions are carried out will have narrower spreads than the bid and ask prices quoted on the news service screens. These transaction prices are proprietary information and are known only by the two participants in a transaction. The quotes on the news service screens are the best *publicly* available information on the current prices in the market.

Figure 1.3 provides another view of the 24-hour nature of the foreign exchange market. This figure shows the average number of quotes on the Japanese yen/U.S. dollar posted to the Reuters news service screen devoted to foreign exchange. Figure 1.3 reports the hourly average number of quotes over the business week. Weekends are excluded since there is little trading outside of normal business hours. The vertical axis measures the average number of quotes per hour, and the horizontal axis shows the hours of each weekday measured in GMT. A clear pattern emerges in the figure—every business day tends to look the same. Trading in the yen starts each business day in Asian markets with a little more than 20 quotes per hour being entered on the Reuters screen. Quoting activity rises and falls through the

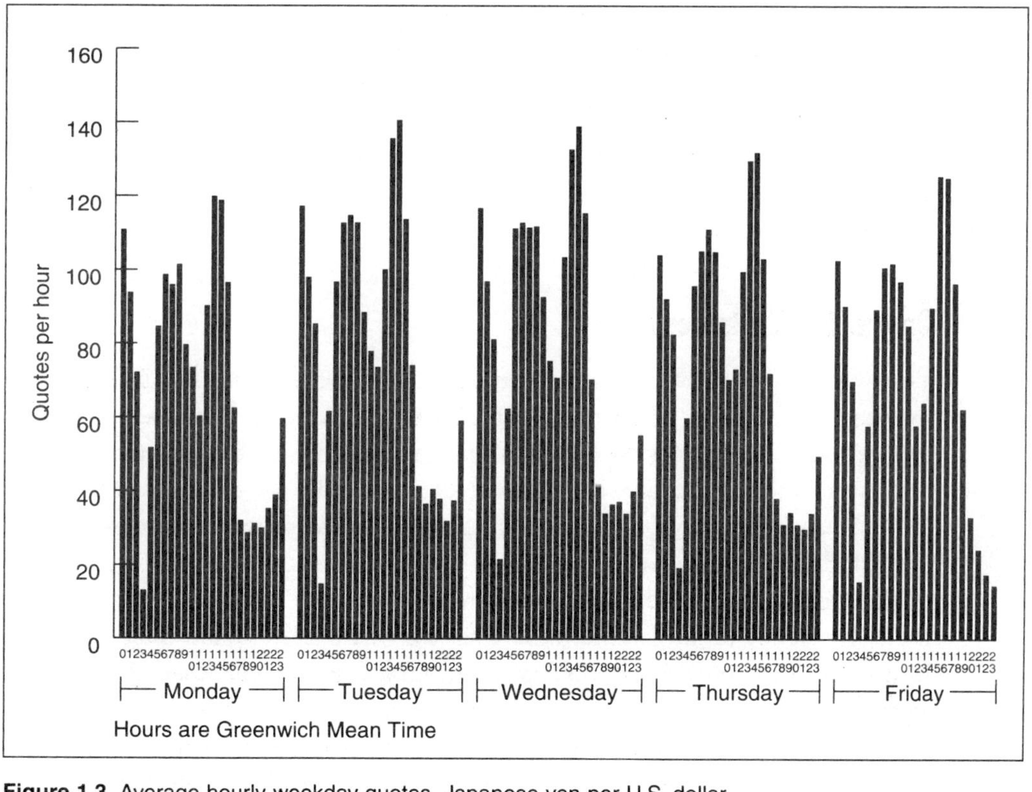

Figure 1.3 Average hourly weekday quotes, Japanese yen per U.S. dollar.

Asian morning until reaching a daily low at lunch time in Tokyo (3–4:30 GMT). This lull in trading during the Tokyo lunch hour was initially the result of a Japanese regulation prohibiting trading during this time. Since December 22, 1994, trading has been permitted in Tokyo during lunch time, but there still is a pronounced drop in activity because many traders take a lunch break.

Following the Tokyo lunch break, market activity picks up in the Asian afternoon and rises substantially as European trading begins around 0700 GMT. There is another decrease in trading activity associated with lunch time in Europe, 12 to 13. Trading rises again when North American trading begins around 1300 GMT, and hits a daily peak when London and New York trading overlap. Trading drops substantially with the close of European trading, and then rises again with the opening of Asian trading the next day.

Note that every weekday has this same pattern, as the pace of the activity in the foreign exchange market follows the opening and closing of business hours around the world. While it is true that the foreign exchange market is a 24-hour market with continuous trading possible, the amount of trading follows predictable patterns. This is not to say that there are not days that differ substantially from this average daily number of quotes. If some surprising event occurs that stimulates trading, some days may have a much different pattern. Later in the text we consider the determinants of exchange rates and study what sorts of news would be especially relevant to the foreign exchange market.

Central Bank Intervention

Thus far we have not explicitly introduced government into the foreign exchange market but, of course, central banks and national treasuries play a large role in the market. Since the exchange rate is the price of one money in terms of another, changes in exchange rates affect the prices of goods and services traded internationally and also account for the official intervention in the foreign exchange market. Central banks, such as the Federal Reserve in the United States, buy and sell currencies to drive the value of their domestic money to levels other than what the free market would establish. In the case of a depreciating domestic currency, central banks can sell foreign currencies in exchange for domestic currency to halt the depreciation.

Official institutions appear in the foreign exchange markets for reasons other than intervening in the determination of exchange rates. In the course of the normal operations of government, it is often necessary to use the foreign exchange market to facilitate the transfer of goods and services internationally. The role of the various central banks is to conduct foreign exchange operations for central governments.

We can use a familiar diagram from principles of economics courses—the supply and demand diagram—to illustrate how central bank intervention works. Figure 1.4 illustrates the market for the yen/dollar exchange rate. Think of the demand for dollars as coming from the Japanese demand for U.S. goods or financial assets (they must buy dollars in order to purchase U.S. goods). The downward-sloping demand curve illustrates that the higher the yen price of the dollar, the more expensive U.S. goods are to Japanese buyers, so the smaller the quantity of dollars demanded. The supply curve is the supply of dollars to the yen/dollar market and comes from U.S. buyers of Japanese goods or financial assets. The upward-sloping supply curve indicates that as U.S. residents receive more yen per dollar, they will buy more from Japan and will supply a larger quantity of dollars to the market.

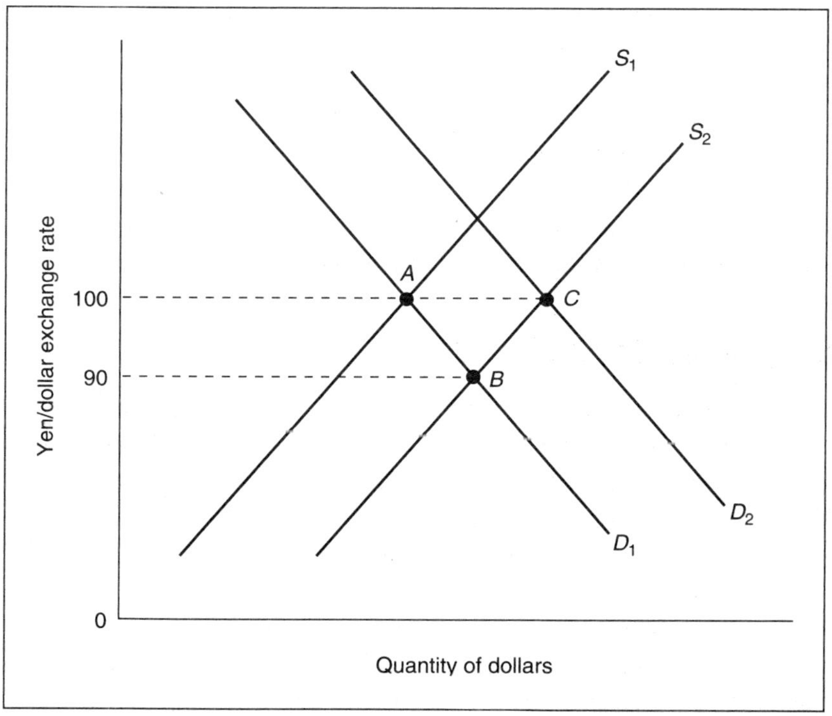

Figure 1.4 Central bank intervention to offset a dollar depreciation.

The initial equilibrium exchange rate is at point *A*, where the exchange rate is 100 yen per dollar. Now suppose there is an increase in U.S. demand for Japanese products so that the supply of dollars increases from S_1 to S_2. The equilibrium exchange rate will now change to 90 yen per dollar at point *B* as the dollar depreciates in value against the yen. This dollar depreciation makes Japanese goods more expensive to U.S. buyers, so the Bank of Japan may desire to halt the dollar depreciation by buying dollars. As the demand for dollars increases, the demand curve shifts from D_1 to D_2 and a new equilibrium is established at point *C*, back at the initial exchange rate of 100 yen per dollar. The Bank of Japan's purchase of U.S. dollars maintains the exchange rate at the level desired by the central bank and offsets the free market's push to yen appreciation. Later in the text we investigate the effectiveness of central bank intervention. We shall see that there are circumstances that may render some interventions less effective than others in bringing about change in an exchange rate.

Typically, the central bank's activities are not publicly known because they are conducted in a secretive manner. While central banks have the ability to influence foreign exchange rates, this ability comes largely through making policy announcements to change private market behavior. The central banks command large resources, but when \$1 trillion a day are traded in the foreign exchange market, it takes a huge commitment of central bank resources to change the direction of a currency by simply buying or selling without an accompanying policy signal to the financial community. The central bank is able to get maximum "bang per buck" by making its current policies known to the public. If private traders believe that the central bank is supporting a currency depreciation, they will be more reluctant to bet on an appreciation.

Black Markets and Parallel Markets

So far, we have discussed the foreign exchange market as a market where currencies are bought and sold openly by individuals, business firms, and governments. For the major developed countries, this is an accurate description. However, some developing countries do not permit free markets in foreign exchange and impose many restrictions on foreign currency transactions. These restrictions take many forms, such as government licensing requirements, limiting the amounts of foreign currency that may be purchased, limiting the time following the receipt of foreign currency before it must be sold to the central bank, or even outright prohibitions of foreign currency use by private concerns.

As a result of government restrictions or legal prohibitions on foreign exchange transactions, illegal markets in foreign exchange develop to satisfy trader demand. These illegal markets are known as *black markets.* In many countries such illegal markets exist openly, with little or no government enforcement of legal prohibitions. In other countries foreign exchange laws are strictly enforced, and lawbreakers receive harsh sentences when caught.

Often the government sets an official exchange rate that deviates widely from that which the free market would establish. If the government will purchase foreign exchange only at the official rate, but private citizens are willing to pay the market-determined rate, there will be a steady supply of foreign exchange to the black market. Obviously, government policy creates the black market. The demand arises because of legal restrictions on buying foreign exchange, and the supply exists because government-mandated official exchange rates offer less than the free market rate. Ironically, governments defend the need for foreign exchange restrictions based on conserving scarce foreign exchange for high-priority uses. But such restrictions work to reduce the amount of foreign exchange that flows to the government as traders turn to the black market instead.

In many countries facing economic hardship, the illegal markets have allowed normal economic activities to continue through a steady supply of foreign exchange. Some governments have unofficially acknowledged the benefits of a black market by allowing the market to exist openly. For instance, Guatemala had an artificially low official exchange rate of one quetzale per dollar for more than three decades; however, a black market where the exchange rate fluctuated daily with market conditions was allowed to flourish openly in front of the country's main post office. In many Latin American countries, the post office is a center for black market trading since relatives living in the United States send millions of dollars in checks and money orders home. In Guatemala, the government allowed such activity openly, and foreign currency traders often called out to people leaving the post office, offering to buy dollars. This sort of government-tolerated alternative to the official exchange market is referred to as a *parallel market.*

While many other anecdotes could be included, the point is that foreign exchange trading has a dimension beyond the open trading and single exchange rate that exist for the major developed countries. In developing countries, foreign exchange transactions are generally strictly regulated activities. In many countries, the official exchange rate has no relation to current economic reality, so we should expect black markets or parallel markets to flourish.

Foreign Exchange Trading Volume

The foreign exchange market is the largest financial market in the world. In April 2001, the Bank for International Settlements (BIS) conducted a survey of trading volume around the world and found that the average amount of currency traded each business day was $1,210 billion. In terms of individual currencies, the U.S. dollar is by far the most important currency, being involved in over 90 percent of all trades. Since foreign exchange trading involves pairs of currencies, it is useful to know which currency pairs dominate the market.

Table 1.4 reports the share of spot market activity taken by different currencies. The largest volume occurs in dollar/euro trading, accounting for 30 percent of the total. The next closest currency pair, the dollar/yen, involves roughly 2/3 as much spot trading as the dollar/euro. After these two currency pairs, the volume drops off dramatically.

In terms of the geographic pattern of foreign exchange trading, a small number of locations account for the majority of trading. Table 1.5 reports the average daily volume of foreign exchange trading in different countries. The United Kingdom and the United States account for half of

Table 1.4 The Share of Foreign Exchange Trading Volume by Currency Pairs (Spot Transactions)

Currency pair	Percent of total
U.S. dollar/euro	30
U.S. dollar/Japanese yen	20
U.S. dollar/U.K. pound	11
U.S. dollar/Swiss franc	5
U.S. dollar/Canadian dollar	4
U.S. dollar/Australian dollar	4
U.S. dollar/Other	17
euro/Japanese yen	3
euro/U.K. pound	2
euro/Swiss franc	1
euro/Other	2
Other	2

Source: Table created from data found in Bank for International Settlements, *Central Bank Survey of Foreign Exchange and Derivatives Market Activity,* Basle, October 2001.

Table 1.5 Foreign Exchange Market Trading Volume in Different Countries (daily averages)

Country	Total volume (billions of dollars)	Percent share
United Kingdom	504	31
United States	254	16
Japan	147	9
Singapore	101	6
Germany	88	5
Switzerland	71	4
Hong Kong	67	4
Australia	52	3
France	48	3
Canada	42	3

Source: Bank for International Settlements, *Central Bank Survey of Foreign Exchange and Derivatives Market Activity,* Basle, October 2001.

total world trading. The United Kingdom has long been the leader in foreign exchange trading. In 2001, it accounted for 31 percent of total world trading volume. While it is true that foreign exchange trading is a round-the-clock business, with trading taking place somewhere in the world at any point in time, the peak activity occurs during business hours in London, New York, and Tokyo.

Summary

1. The foreign exchange market is a global market where foreign currency deposits are traded. Trading in actual currency notes is generally limited to tourism or illegal activities.
2. Arbitrage ensures that exchange rates are transaction costs close in all markets.
3. Central banks intervene in the foreign exchange market in order to change exchange rates.
4. Black markets or parallel markets in foreign exchange arise because of government regulation of the foreign exchange market.
5. The dollar/euro currency pair dominates foreign exchange trading volume, and the United Kingdom is the largest trading location.

Exercises

1. If the euro is selling for $0.98 in New York and the Japanese yen is selling for $0.0077, what is the cross rate between the euro and yen?
2. Suppose ¥1 = $0.0077 in London, $1 = SF2.00 in New York, and SF1 = ¥65 in Paris.
   a. If you begin by holding 10,000 yen, how could you make a profit from these exchange rates?
   b. Find the arbitrage profit per yen initially traded. (Ignore transaction costs.)
3. a. What is meant by "official intervention" in the foreign exchange market?
   b. What is the rationale behind this intervention?
   c. If the exchange rate changes from ¥/$ = 100 to ¥/$ = 97, and the Japanese government wants to keep the exchange rate fixed, then how does the Japanese government operate in the foreign exchange market? Illustrate by using a diagram.
   d. How might the credibility of central banks influence the future value of domestic currencies? Comment.
4. a. Compare and contrast black markets and parallel markets.
   b. Can you find real-world examples that would fit the description of these markets?
5. Suppose Mitsubishi Bank quotes the ¥/$ exchange rate as 110.30–.40 and Tokai Bank quotes 110.40–.50. Is there an arbitrage opportunity? If so, explain how you would profit from these quotes. If not, explain why not.
6. What is the cross-rate implied by the following quotes?
   a. C$/$ = 1.5613, $/€ = 1.0008
   b. ¥/$ = 124.84, $/£ = 1.5720
   c. SF/$ = 1.4706,1 C$/$ = 1.5613

References

Bank for International Settlements, *Central Bank Survey of Foreign Exchange and Derivatives Market Activity,* Basle: BIS. October 2001.

The Basics of Foreign Trade and Exchange, Federal Reserve Bank of New York, http://www.newyorkfed.org/pihome/educator/fx.

Galati, Gabriele, "Why Has Global FX Turnover Declined? Explaining the 2001 Triennial Survey," *BIS Quarterly Review,* December 2001, 39–47.

Olsen and Associates, "Changes in the Foreign Exchange Market," *Currency Forecasts Euromoney,* Supplement, September 1995, 2–5.

APPENDIX 1A: Exchange Rate Indexes

Suppose we want to consider the value of a currency. One measure is the bilateral exchange rate—say, the yen value of the dollar. However, if we are interested in knowing how a currency is performing globally, we need a broader measure of the currency's value against many other currencies. This is analogous to looking at a consumer price index to measure how prices in an economy are changing. We could look at the price of shoes or the price of a loaf of bread, but such single-good prices will not necessarily reflect the general inflationary situation—some prices may be rising while others are falling.

In the foreign exchange market it is common to see a currency rising in value against one foreign money while it depreciates relative to another. As a result, exchange rate indexes are constructed to measure the average value of a currency relative to several other currencies. An *exchange rate index* is a weighted average of a currency's value relative to other currencies, with the weights typically based on the importance of each currency to international trade. If we want to construct an exchange rate index for the United States, we would include the currencies of the countries that are the major trading partners of the United States.

If half of U.S. trade was with Canada and the other half was with Mexico, then the percentage change in the trade-weighted dollar exchange rate index would be found by multiplying the percentage change in both the Canadian dollar/U.S. dollar exchange rate and the Mexican peso/U.S. dollar exchange rate by one-half and summing the result. Table 1A.1 lists two popular exchange rate indexes and their weighting schemes. The indexes listed are the Federal Reserve Board (BOG) and the Federal Reserve Bank of Atlanta (FRBA).

Since the different indexes are constructed using different currencies, should we expect them to tell a different story? It is entirely possible for a currency to be appreciating against some currencies while it depreciates against others. Therefore, the exchange rate indexes will not all move identically, but they will all show the same general trends. Figure 1A.1 plots the movement of the various indexes over time.

Figure 1A.1 indicates that the value of the dollar generally rose in the early 1980s and fell in the late 1980s—a conclusion we draw regardless of the exchange rate index used. Differences arise when we want to measure the amount of dollar appreciation or depreciation. From January 1993 to January 1994, the dollar rose in value by 3.7 percent according to the FRBA index, or by 0.2 percent according to the BOG index. This suggests that, for discerning broad trends in the value of a currency, all indexes tell much the same story. Yet for shorter-term movements, where the magnitude of the change is important, there can be large differences across exchange rate indexes. Since different indexes assign a different importance to each foreign currency, this is not surprising. For instance, if we look at the weights

Table 1A.1 Percentage Weights Assigned to Major Currencies in Two U.S. Dollar Exchange Rate Indexes

Country	Exchange rate index	
	BOG	FRBA
Euro countries	28.7	16.6
Japan	25.6	15.6
United Kingdom	8.0	5.1
Canada	30.3	24.6
Sweden	1.6	—
Switzerland	3.2	1.3
Australia	2.6	1.3
South Korea	—	4.1
Mexico	—	11.0
China	—	5.5
Taiwan	—	4.2
Singapore	—	3.0
Malaysia	—	2.3
Hong Kong	—	2.1
Brazil	—	1.9
Saudi Arabia	—	1.4
Total	100.0	100.0

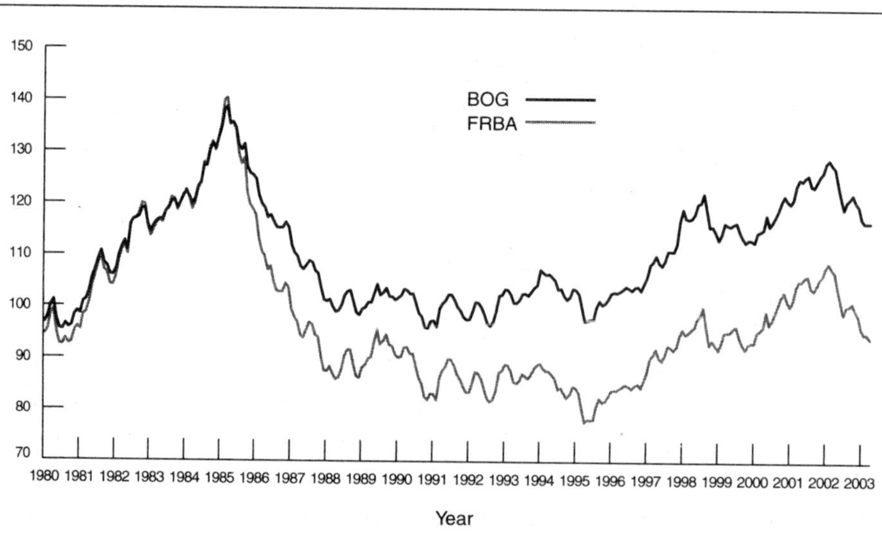

Figure 1A.1 The value of the dollar as measured by exchange rate indexes.

in Table 1A.1, then a period in which the dollar appreciated rapidly against the Mexican peso relative to other currencies would have to use the BOG index to record a smaller dollar appreciation relative to the FRBA index. This is true because the peso accounts for 11 percent of the FRBA index, but zero for the BOG.

Exchange rate indexes are commonly used analytical tools in international economics. When changes in the average value of a currency are important, bilateral exchange rates (between only two currencies) are unsatisfactory. Neither economic theory nor practice gives a clear indication of which exchange rate index is best. In fact, for some questions there is little to differentiate one index from another. In many cases, however, the best index to use will depend on the question addressed.

APPENDIX 1B: The Top Foreign Exchange Dealers

Foreign exchange trading is dominated by large commercial banks with worldwide operations. The market is very competitive, since each bank tries to maintain its share of the corporate business. *Euromoney* magazine provides some interesting insights into this market by publishing periodic surveys of information supplied by the treasurers of the major multinational firms.

When asked to rank the factors that determined who got their foreign exchange business, the treasurers responded that the following factors were the most important: The speed with which a bank makes foreign exchange quotes was ranked third. A second-place ranking was given to competitiveness of quotes. The most important factor was the firm's relationship with the bank. A bank that handles the other banking needs of a firm is also likely to receive its foreign exchange business.

The significance of competitive quotes is indicated by the fact that treasurers often contact more than one bank to get several quotes before placing a deal. Another implication is that the market will be dominated by the big banks, because only the giants have the global activity to allow competitive quotes on a large number of currencies. Table 1B.1 gives the rankings of the *Euromoney* survey. According to the rankings, Citigroup receives more business than any other bank.

It appears that a smaller bank can "carve a niche" for itself by specializing in a minor currency. When the treasurers were asked to identify banks with expertise in a particular minor currency, they often named banks based in the particular region, as shown in Table 1B.2.

What makes Citigroup the world's best foreign exchange dealer? Many factors have kept Citigroup on top of the heap. An important factor is simply

Table 1B.1 The Top 20 Foreign Exchange Dealers

1	Citigroup
2	UBS Warburg
3	Deutsche Bank
4	Goldman Sachs
5	JP Morgan Chase
6	Credit Suisse First Boston
7	Morgan Stanley
8	ABN Amro
9	S-E-Banken
10	Barclays Capital
11	Bank of America
12	HSBC
13	Royal Bank of Scotland
14	Dresdner Kleinwort Wasserstein
15	Royal Bank of Canada
16	BNP Paribas
17	Nordea
18	Bank One
19	Svenska Handelsbanken
20	State Street Bank and Trust

Rankings as reported in *Euromoney,* May 2002, p. 58.

Table 1B.2 Which Banks, Which Currency?[a]

Currency	Banks
Australian dollar, NZ dollar	Citigroup, Westpac Banking Group, ANZ Banking Group
Canadian dollar	Royal Bank of Canada, Citigroup, Bank of Nova Scotia
Indian rupee	Citigroup, HSBC, Standard Chartered Bank
Singapore dollar	HSBC, Citigroup, Deutsche Bank

[a]*Note:* Treasurers were asked to name banks they preferred for certain currencies. Banks scored on the number of mentions they received.

As reported in *Euromoney,* May 2002, pp. 64–66.

sheer size. Citigroup holds the bank accounts for many corporations, giving it a natural advantage in foreign exchange trading.

Foreign exchange trading has emerged as an important center for bank profitability. Since each trade generates revenue for the bank, the volatile foreign exchange markets of recent years have often led to frenetic activity in the market with a commensurate revenue increase for the banks.

2

The Balance of Payments

We have all heard of the balance of payments. Unfortunately, common usage does not allow us to discuss *the* balance of payments because there are several ways to measure the balance, and the press often blurs the distinctions among these various measures. In general, the *balance of payments* records a country's trade in goods, services, and financial assets with the rest of the world. Such trade is divided into useful categories that provide summaries of a nation's trade. A distinction is made between private (individuals and business firms) and official (government) transactions. Balance of payments data are reported quarterly for most developed countries. Figure 2.1 presents the balance of payments as reported by the U.S. Department of Commerce. This rather imposing document is of great use to economists, but it provides more detail than we need be concerned with here. To identify the popular summary measures of the balance of payments, we are interested only in broad definitions. We must be aware that although the several broad measures have their uses, they also have drawbacks, as will be pointed out in the following discussion.

The balance of payments is an accounting statement based on double-entry bookkeeping. Every transaction is entered on both sides of the balance sheet, as a credit and as a debit. Credit entries are those entries that will bring foreign exchange into the country, whereas debit entries record items that would mean a loss of foreign exchange. In Figure 2.1, debit entries are recorded as a negative value. For instance, suppose we record

Line	(Credits +; debits −)	1960	1970	1980	1990	2000
1	Exports of goods, services, and income	30,556	68,387	343,241	652,936	1,417,236
2	Merchandise, adjusted, excluding military	19,650	42,469	224,269	389,550	771,994
3	Services	6,290	14,171	47,584	133,295	292,245
4	Transfers under U.S. military agency sales contracts	2,030	4,214	9,029	9,899	13,981
5	Travel	919	2,331	10,588	40,579	82,267
6	Passenger fares	175	544	2,591	12,251	20,760
7	Other transportation	1,607	3,125	11,618	22,407	30,137
8	Royalties and license fees	837	2,331	7,085	15,291	39,607
9	Other private services	570	1,294	6,276	32,173	104,707
10	U.S. Government miscellaneous services	153	332	398	695	786
11	Income receipts	—	—	—	—	352,997
11a	Compensation of employees	—	—	—	—	2,341
11b	Income receipts on U.S. assets abroad	4,616	11,748	71,388	130,091	350,656
12	Direct investment receipts	3,621	8,169	37,146	54,444	149,677
13	Other private receipts	646	2,671	31,680	65,702	197,133
14	U.S. Government receipts	349	907	2,562	9,945	3,846
15	Imports of goods, services, and income	−23,670	−59,901	−333,774	−722,730	−1,774,135
16	Merchandise, adjusted, excluding military	−14,758	−39,866	−249,750	−497,665	−1,224,417
17	Services	−7,674	−14,520	−41,491	−106,919	−218,503
18	Direct defense expenditures	−3,087	−4,855	−10,851	−17,119	−13,560
19	Travel	−1,750	−3,980	−10,397	−38,671	−64,788
20	Passenger fares	−513	−1,215	−3,607	−8,963	−24,306
21	Other transportation	−1,402	−2,843	−11,790	−23,463	−41,598
22	Royalties and license fees	−74	−224	−724	−2,644	−16,115
23	Other private services	−593	−827	−2,909	−13,819	−55,253
24	U.S. Government miscellaneous services	−254	−576	−1,214	−2,240	−2,883
25	Income payments	—	—	—	—	−331,215
25a	Compensation of employees	—	—	—	—	−8,210
25b	Income payments on foreign assets in the United States	−1,238	−5,515	−42,532	−118,146	−323,005
26	Direct investment payments	−394	−875	−8,635	−1,782	−60,815
27	Other private payments	−511	−3,617	−21,214	−78,494	−179,217
28	U.S. Government payments	−332	−1,024	−12,684	−37,870	−82,973

(Continued)

Figure 2.1 U.S. International transactions (millions of dollars).
Source: Bureau of Economic Analysis, www.bea.doc.gov/bea/international/bp_web

Figure 2.1 (Continued)

Line	(Credits +; debits −)	1960	1970	1980	1990	2000
29	Unilateral transfers, net	−4,062	−6,156	−8,349	−22,329	−53,442
30	U.S. Government grants	−3,367	−4,449	−5,486	−17,486	−16,821
31	U.S. Government pensions and other transfers	−273	−611	−1,818	−2,947	−4,705
32	Private remittances and other transfers	−423	−1,096	−1,044	−1,896	−31,916
33	U.S. assets abroad, net (increases/capital outflow (−))	−4,099	−9,337	−86,118	−57,706	−606,489
34	U.S. official reserve assets, net	2,145	2,481	−8,155	−2,158	−290
35	Gold	1,703	787	—	—	—
36	Special drawing rights	—	−851	−16	−192	−722
37	Reserve position in the International Monetary Fund	442	389	−1,667	731	2,308
38	Foreign currencies	—	2,156	−6,472	−2,697	−1,876
39	U.S. Government assets, other than official reserve assets, net	−1,100	−1,589	−5,162	2,976	−941
40	U.S. credits and other long-term assets	−1,214	−3,293	−9,860	−7,319	−5,182
41	Repayments on U.S. credits and other long-term assets, net	642	1,721	4,456	10,327	4,265
42	U.S. foreign currency holdings and U.S. short-term assets, net	−528	−16	242	−32	−24
43	U.S. private assets, net	−5,144	−10,229	−72,802	−58,524	−605,258
44	Direct investment	−2,940	−7,590	−19,222	−33,437	−178,294
45	Foreign securities	−663	−1,076	−3,568	−28,476	−127,502
46	U.S. claims on unaffiliated foreigners reported by U.S. nonbanking concerns	−394	−596	−3,174	−1,944	−150,805
47	U.S. claims reported by U.S. banks, not included elsewhere	−1,148	−967	−46,838	5,333	−148,657
48	Foreign assets in the United States, net (increase/capital inflow (+))	2,294	6,359	58,112	86,303	1,015,986
49	Foreign official assets in the United States, net	1,473	6,908	15,497	32,425	37,640
50	U.S. Government securities	655	9,439	11,895	29,310	30,676
51	U.S. Treasury securities	655	9,411	9,708	28,643	−10,233
52	Other	—	28	2,187	667	40,909
53	Other U.S. Government liabilities	215	−456	615	1,703	−1,909
54	U.S. liabilities reported by U.S. banks, not included elsewhere	603	−2,075	−159	2,998	5,746
55	Other foreign official assets	—	—	3,145	−1,586	3,127

(Continued)

Figure 2.1 (Continued)

Line	(Credits +; debits −)	1960	1970	1980	1990	2000
56	Other foreign assets in the United States, net	821	−550	42,615	53,879	978,346
57	Direct investment	315	1,464	16,918	37,213	307,747
58	U.S. Treasury securities	−364	81	2,645	1,131	−76,965
59	U.S. securities other than U.S. Treasury securities	282	2,189	5,457	1,781	455,213
60	U.S. liabilities to unaffiliated foreigners reported by U.S. nonbanking concerns	−90	2,014	6,852	3,779	174,251
61	U.S. liabilities reported by U.S. banks not included elsewhere	678	−6,298	10,743	9,975	116,971
62	Allocations of special drawing rights	—	867	1,152	—	—
63	Statistical discrepancy (sum of above items with sign reversed)	−1,019	−219	25,736	63,526	844
	Memoranda:					
64	Balance on merchandise trade (lines 2 and 16)	4,892	2,603	−25,481	−108,115	−452,423
65	Balance on services (lines 3 and 17)	−1,385	−349	6,093	26,376	73,742
66	Balance on goods and services (lines 64 and 65)					−378,681
67	Balance on income (lines 11 and 25)	3,379	6,233	28,856	11,945	21,782
68	Balance on goods, services, and income (lines 1 and 15 or lines 66 and 67)	6,886	8,486	9,467	−69,794	−356,899
69	Unilateral transfers, net (line 29)	−4,062	−6,156	−8,349	−22,329	−53,442
70	Balance on current account (lines 1, 15, and 29 or lines 68 and 69)	2,824	2,331	1,119	−92,123	−410,341

the sale of a machine from a U.S. manufacturer to a French importer and the manufacturer allows the buyer 90 days credit to pay. The machinery export is recorded as a credit in the merchandise account, whereas the credit extended to the foreigner is a debit to the capital account. The capital we speak of is financial capital. Thus, credit extended belongs in the same broad account with stocks, bonds, and other financial instruments of a short-term nature. If, for any particular account, the value of the credit entries exceeds the debits, we say a *surplus* exists. On the other hand, where the debits exceed the credits, a *deficit* exists. Note that a surplus or deficit can apply only to a particular area of the balance of payments, since the sum of the credits and debits on all accounts will always be equal; in other words, the balance of payments always balances. This will become apparent in the following discussion.

Let us consider some of the popular summary measures of the balance of payments.

Current Account

The *current account* is defined as including the value of trade in merchandise, services, investment income, and unilateral transfers. Merchandise is the obvious trade in tangible commodities. *Services* refers to trade in the services of factors of production: land, labor, and capital. Included in this category are travel and tourism, royalties, transportation costs, and insurance premiums. The payment for the services of physical capital, or the return on investments, is recorded in the investment income account. The amounts of interest and dividends paid internationally are large and are growing rapidly as the world financial markets become more integrated.

The final component of the balance of payments includes unilateral transfers, like U.S. foreign aid, gifts, and retirement pensions. The United States always records a large deficit on these items, except for 1991 when several foreign countries transferred large sums of money to the United States to help pay for the expense of the war in the Mideast.

Figure 2.2 illustrates how the various account balances have changed over time. The merchandise and current account deficits of the 1980s were unprecedented at the time, but have since been dwarfed by the deficits of recent years. In Figure 2.1, line 70 shows that there was a current account surplus of $2,824 million in 1960 and a deficit of $410,341 million in 2000. The $410 billion current account deficit of 2000 is the sum of a $452 billion merchandise trade deficit, a $73 billion services surplus, a $21 billion investment income surplus, and a $53 billion transfers deficit. From 1955 to 1970, the United States ran a merchandise trade surplus. Following a $2 billion deficit in 1971, the merchandise account has been in deficit every year since, except 1973 and 1975. Even with this persistent merchandise trade deficit, U.S. earnings from foreign investments have had sizable surpluses so that the current account realized a surplus in the periods from 1973 to 1976 and from 1980 to 1981.

The balance of payments in Figure 2.1 actually ends at line 63. Lines 64 to 70 are summaries drawn from lines 1 to 63. We can draw a line in the balance of payments to sum the debit and credit items above that line. If we draw the line at the current account balance items ending with unilateral

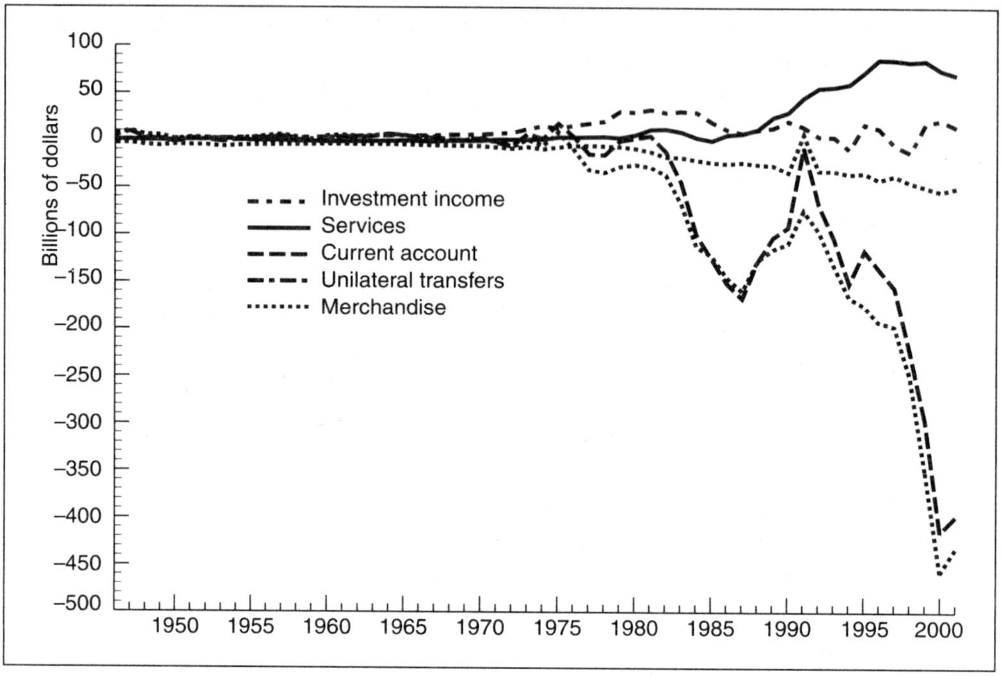

Figure 2.2 The current account and its components.

transfers (line 32), all the entries below that line account for financing the merchandise, services, investment income, and unilateral transfers (gifts); thus, the current account indicates whether a country is a net borrower from, or lender to, the rest of the world. A current account surplus implies that a country is running a net deficit below the line and that the country is a net lender to the rest of the world.

The current account excludes capital account transactions—purchases and sales of financial assets. Since the items below the line of the current account must be equal in value (but opposite in sign) to the current account balance, we can see how the current account balance indicates financial activity (below the line) as well as the value of trade in merchandise, services, and unilateral transfers that are recorded above the line. In a period (year or quarter) during which a current account deficit is recorded, the country must borrow from abroad an amount sufficient to finance the deficit.

Since the balance of payments always balances, the massive current account deficits of recent years are matched by massive capital account surpluses. This means that foreign investment in U.S. securities has been at very high levels. Some analysts have expressed concern over the growing foreign indebtedness of the United States. The next section reviews the issue.

Financing the Current Account

Large current account deficits imply large capital account surpluses. The capital account transactions are recorded below the current account items in the balance of payments. Referring back to Figure 2.1, lines 33 through 62 record capital account transactions. We see that capital account transactions include both official and private transactions. For ease of understanding, Table 2.1 provides a summary of U.S. capital account transactions since 1961. In this table, the debit and credit items are entered separately so that we can identify the sources of changes in net capital flows (capital inflows less capital outflows). For instance, in 2001 we see that U.S. security purchases abroad totaled $94,662 million. This is a capital account debit entry because it involves foreign exchange leaving the United States. Security purchases in the United States by foreigners totaled $399,983 million in 2001. This is a credit item in the capital account since it brings foreign exchange to the United States. We can interpret the other capital account items in a similar manner.

Before interpreting the recent history of U.S. international capital flows, we should consider the definitions of the individual capital account items.

> *Direct investment:* Private financial transactions that result in the ownership of 10 percent or more of a business firm.
>
> *Security purchases:* Private sector net purchases of equity (stock) and debt securities.
>
> *Bank claims and liabilities:* Claims include loans, collections outstanding, acceptances, deposits abroad, claims on affiliated foreign banks, foreign government obligations, and foreign commercial and finance paper; liabilities include deposits, certificates of deposit, liabilities to affiliated foreign banks, and other liabilities.
>
> *U.S. government assets abroad:* Changes in U.S. official reserve assets (gold, SDRs, foreign currency holdings, and reserve position in the IMF).
>
> *Foreign official assets in the United States:* Net purchases of U.S. government securities, obligations of U.S. government corporations and agencies, securities of U.S. state and local governments, and changes in liabilities to foreign official agencies reported by U.S. banks.

Some capital account transactions are a direct result of trade in merchandise and services. For instance, many goods are sold using trade credit.

Table 2.1 **U.S. Capital Account Transactions (capital flows, in millions of dollars)**

Year	Direct investment abroad	Direct investment in U.S.	Security purchases abroad	Security purchases in U.S.	Bank claims on foreigners	Bank liabilities to foreigners	U.S. government assets abroad	Foreign official assets in U.S.
1961	2,653	311	762	475	1,261	928	303	765
1964	3,760	322	677	–231	2,505	1,818	1,509	1,660
1967	4,805	698	1,308	881	495	1,765	2,370	3,451
1970	7,590	1,464	1,076	2,270	967	–6,298	–892	6,908
1973	11,353	2,800	671	3,825	5,980	4,702	2,486	6,026
1976	11,949	4,347	8,885	4,067	21,368	10,990	6,772	17,693
1979	25,222	11,877	4,726	6,311	26,213	32,607	4,879	–13,665
1982	–991	12,464	7,983	13,112	111,070	65,633	11,096	3,593
1985	14,065	20,010	7,481	71,395	1,323	41,045	6,679	–1,119
1988	16,175	57,278	7,846	46,592	53,927	63,744	945	39,758
1991	31,369	22,004	45,673	53,970	610	3,994	–8,674	17,389
1994	75,214	44,592	60,309	91,245	4,200	104,338	–5,735	39,583
1997	121,843	93,449	87,981	343,555	147,439	148,059	1,184	15,817
1998	142,644	179,045	136,135	184,896	35,572	39,769	–7,205	–19,903
1999	188,901	289,954	128,436	254,337	76,263	54,232	11,497	43,666
2000	178,294	307,747	127,502	378,248	148,657	116,971	–1,231	37,640
2001	127,840	130,796	94,662	399,983	128,705	110,667	–5,397	5,224

The exporter allows the importer a period of time—typically 30, 60, or 90 days—before payment is due. This sort of financing will generally be reflected in bank claims and liabilities, because such transactions are handled by the exporter's bank. Other capital account items are a result of portfolio management by international investors. Security purchases would fall in this category. Official transactions involve governments and are motivated by a host of economic and political considerations.

One implication of capital account transactions is the change in the net creditor or debtor status of a nation. A net debtor owes more to the rest of the world than it is owed, while a net creditor is owed more than it owes. The United States became a net international debtor in 1985 for the first time since World War I. The high current account deficits of the 1980s were matched by high capital account surpluses. This rapid buildup of foreign direct investment and purchases of U.S. securities led to a very rapid drop from being a net creditor of $147 billion in 1982 to net debtor status by 1985. Once again, we see that the current account is a useful measure because it summarizes the trend with regard to the net debtor position of a country. For this reason, international bankers focus on the current account trend as one of the crucial variables to consider when evaluating loans to foreign countries.

Additional Summary Measures

So far we have focused on the current account of the balance of payments. In terms of practical importance to economists, government policymakers, and business firms, this emphasis on the current account is warranted. However, there are other summary measures of balance of payments phenomena. Within the current account categories, the balance on merchandise trade is often cited in the popular press (because it is reported on a monthly basis by the United States). The *balance of trade* (line 2 plus line 16 in Figure 2.1) records a surplus when merchandise exports exceed imports. Domestic business firms and labor unions often use the balance of trade to justify a need to protect the domestic market from foreign competition. When a country is running a large balance of trade deficit, local industries that are being hurt by import competition will argue that the trade balance reflects the harm done to the economy. Because of the political sensitivity of the balance of trade, it is a popularly cited measure.

The *official settlements balance* (lines 34 and 49 in Figure 2.1) measures changes in financial assets held by foreign monetary agencies and official reserve asset transactions. The official settlements balance serves as a measure of potential foreign exchange pressure on the dollar, in that official institutions may not want to hold increasing stocks of dollars but would rather sell them, which would drive down the foreign exchange value of the dollar. Yet if there is a demand for the dollar, official stocks of dollars may build without any foreign exchange pressure. Furthermore, in the modern world it is not always clear whether official holdings are what they seem to be, since (as we will see in a later chapter) the Eurodollar market allows central banks to turn official claims against the United States into private claims. Still, monetary economists have found the official settlements account to be useful because changes in international reserves are one element on which the nation's money supply depends.

The foreign monetary agency holdings of the liabilities of most countries are trivial, so that the official settlements balance essentially measures international reserve changes. In the case of the United States, the official settlements balance primarily records changes in short-term U.S. liabilities held by foreign monetary agencies. This demand for dollar-denominated short-term debt by foreign central banks is what allows the United States to finance current account deficits largely with dollars. Other countries must finance deficits by selling foreign currency, and, as a result, they face a greater constraint on their ability to run deficits as they eventually deplete their stocks of foreign currency.

Transactions Classifications

So far we have defined the important summary measures of the balance of payments and have developed an understanding of the various categories included in a nation's international transactions. The actual classification of transactions is often confusing to those first considering such issues. To aid in understanding these classification problems, we will analyze six transactions and their placement in a simplified U.S. balance of payments.

First, we must remember that the balance of payments is a balance sheet, so, at the bottom line, total credits equal total debits. This means that we use double-entry bookkeeping—every item involves two entries, a credit and a debit, to the balance sheet. The credits record items leading to inflows of payments. Such items are associated with a greater demand for domestic currency or supply of foreign currency to the foreign exchange market. The debits record items that lead to payments outflows. These are associated with a greater supply of domestic currency or demand for foreign currency in the foreign exchange market. Now consider the following six hypothetical transactions and their corresponding entries in Table 2.2.

Table 2.2 Balance of Payments

	Credit (+)	Debit (–)	Net balance
Merchandise	$1,000,000 (2) 100,000 (5)		
Services		$10,000 (4)	
Investment income	10,000 (3)		
Unilateral transfers		100,000 (5)	
Current account			+$1,000,000
Official capital	$50,000,000 (6)	$50,000,000 (6)	
Private capital	1,000,000 (1) $10,000 (4)	1,000,000 (1) 1,000,000 (2) $10,000 (3)	
Total	$52,120,000	$52,120,000	

Note: The numbers in parentheses refer to the six transactions we have analyzed.

1. *A U.S. bank makes a loan of $1 million to a Romanian food processor. The loan is funded by creating a $1 million deposit for the Romanian firm in the U.S. bank.* The loan represents a private capital outflow and is recorded as a debit to private capital. The new deposit is recorded as a credit to private capital, since an increase in foreign-owned bank deposits in U.S. banks is treated as a capital inflow.

2. *A U.S. firm sells $1 million worth of wheat to the Romanian firm. The wheat is paid for with the bank account created in (1).* The wheat export represents a merchandise export of $1 million, and thus we credit merchandise $1 million. Payment using the deposit results in the decrease of foreign-owned deposits in U.S. banks; this is treated as a capital outflow, leading to a $1 million debit to private capital.

3. *A U.S. resident receives $10,000 in interest from German bonds she owns. The $10,000 is deposited in a German bank.* Earnings on international investments represent a credit to the investment income account. The increase in U.S.-owned foreign bank deposits is considered a capital outflow and is recorded by debiting private capital in the amount of $10,000.

4. *A U.S. tourist travels to Europe and spends the $10,000 German deposit.* Tourist spending is recorded in the services account. U.S. tourist spending abroad is recorded as a $10,000 debit to the services account. The decrease in U.S.-owned foreign deposits is considered a private capital inflow and is recorded by a $10,000 credit to private capital.

5. *The United States government gives $100,000 worth of grain to Nicaragua.* The grain export is recorded as a $100,000 credit to the merchandise account. Since the grain was a gift, the balancing entry is unilateral transfers; in this case, there is a debit of $100,000 to unilateral transfers.

6. *The Treasury Department of the government of Japan buys $50 million worth of U.S. government bonds paid for with a deposit in a U.S. bank.* Foreign government purchases of U.S. government securities are recorded as an official capital inflow so we credit official capital $50 million. The reduction in foreign-owned deposits in U.S. banks is treated as a capital outflow; but, since the deposit was owned by a foreign government, there is a $50 million debit to official capital.

Note that the current account balance is the sum of the merchandise, services, investment income, and unilateral transfers accounts. Summing the credits and debits, we find that the credits sum to $1,110,000, whereas the debits sum to $110,000, so that there is a positive, or credit, balance of $1 million on the current account.

The capital entries are typically the most confusing, particularly those relating to changes in bank deposits. For instance, the third transaction we analyzed recorded the deposit of $10,000 in a German bank as a debit to the private capital account of the United States. The fourth transaction recorded the U.S. tourist's spending of the $10,000 German bank deposit as a credit to the private capital account of the United States. This may seem confusing because early in the chapter it was suggested that credit items are items that bring foreign exchange into a country, while debit items involve foreign exchange leaving the country. But neither of these transactions affected bank deposits in the United States, just foreign deposits. The key is to think of the deposit of $10,000 in a German bank as money that had come from a U.S. bank account. Increases in U.S.-owned deposits in foreign banks are debits whether or not the money was ever in the United States. What matters is not whether the money is ever physically in the United States, but the country of residence of the owner. Similarly, decreases in U.S.-owned foreign deposits are recorded as a credit to private capital, whether or not the money is actually brought from abroad to the United States.

The item called "statistical discrepancy" (line 63) in Figure 2.1 is not the result of not knowing where to classify some transactions. The international transactions that are recorded are simply difficult to measure accurately. Taking the numbers from customs records and surveys of business firms will not capture all of the trade actually occurring. Some of this may be due to illegal or underground activity, but in the modern dynamic economy we would expect sizable measurement errors even with no illegal activity. It is simply impossible to observe every transaction, so we must rely on a statistically valid sampling of international transactions.

Balance of Payments Equilibrium and Adjustment

So far we have focused on the accounting procedures and definitions that apply to the balance of payments. Now we want to consider the economic implications of the balance of payments. For instance, since merchandise exports earn foreign exchange while imports involve outflows of foreign exchange, we often hear arguments for policy aimed at maximizing the trade or current account surplus. Is this in fact desirable? First, it must be realized that, because one country's export is another's import, it is impossible for everyone to have surpluses. On a worldwide basis the total value of exports equals the total value of imports—that is, there is globally balanced trade. Actually, the manner in which trade data are collected imparts a surplus bias to trade balances. Exports are recorded when goods are shipped, while imports are recorded upon receipt. Because there are always goods in transit from the exporter to the importer, if we sum the balance of trade for all nations we would expect a global trade surplus. However, the global current account balance has summed to a deficit in recent years. The problem seems to involve the difficulty of accurately measuring international financial transactions. Merchandise trade can be measured fairly accurately, and the global sum of trade balances is roughly zero; but, service transactions are more difficult to observe, and investment income flows seem to be the major source of global current account discrepancies. The problem arises because countries receiving capital inflows (the debtors) more accurately record the value received than the resident countries of the creditors. For instance, if an investor in Singapore bought shares of stock in Mexico, the government of Mexico is more likely to observe accurately the transaction than is the government of Singapore. Yet even with these bookkeeping problems facing government statisticians, the essential economic point of one country's deficit being another's surplus is still true.

Since one country must always have a trade deficit if another has a trade surplus, is it necessarily true that surpluses are good and deficits bad and that one country benefits at another's expense? In one sense, it would seem that imports should be preferred to exports. In terms of current consumption, merchandise exports represent goods that will be consumed by foreign importers no longer available for domestic consumption. As we learn from studying international trade theory, the benefits of free international trade are more efficient production and increased consumption. Imports allow countries to realize a higher living standard than they could by just having domestic production. Children have more toys at Christmas because of imports from China. Bananas and pineapples are readily available due to trade with tropical countries. If trade between nations is voluntary, then it is difficult to argue that deficit countries are harmed while surplus countries benefit by trade.

In general, it is not obvious whether a country is better or worse off if it runs payments surpluses rather than deficits. Consider the following simple example of a world with two countries, *A* and *B*. Country *A* is a wealthy creditor country that has extended loans to poor country *B*. In order for country *B* to repay these loans, *B* must run trade surpluses with *A* to earn the foreign exchange required for repayment. Would you rather live in rich country *A* and experience trade deficits or in poor country *B* and experience trade surpluses? Although this is indeed a simplistic example, there are real-world analogues of rich creditor countries with trade deficits and poor debtor nations with trade surpluses. The point here is that you cannot analyze the balance of payments apart from other economic considerations. Deficits are not inherently bad, nor are surpluses necessarily good.

Balance of payments equilibrium is often thought of as a condition in which exports equal imports or credits equal debits on some particular subaccount, like the current account or the official settlements account. In fact, countries can have an equilibrium balance on the current account that is positive, negative, or zero, depending upon what circumstances are sustainable over time. For instance, a current account deficit is the equilibrium for the United States if the rest of the world wants to accumulate U.S. financial assets. This involves a U.S. capital account surplus as U.S. financial assets are sold to foreign buyers, which will be matched by a current account deficit. So equilibrium need not be a zero balance. However, to simplify the next analysis, let's assume that equilibrium is associated with a zero balance. In this sense, if we had a current account equilibrium, then the nation would find its net creditor or debtor position unchanging since there is no need for any net financing—the current account export items are just balanced by the current account import items. Equilibrium on the official settlements basis would mean no change in short-term capital held by foreign monetary agencies and reserve assets. For most countries, this would simply mean that their stocks of international reserves would be unchanging.

What happens if there is a disequilibrium in the balance of payments—say the official settlements basis? Now there will be reserve asset losses from deficit countries and reserve accumulation by surplus countries. International reserve assets comprise gold, IMF *special drawing rights* (a credit issued by the IMF and allocated to countries on the basis of their level of financial support for the IMF), and foreign exchange. To simplify matters (although this is essentially the case for most countries), let us consider foreign exchange alone. The concept of balance of payments equilibrium may be linked to the supply and demand diagram presented in Chapter 1. Figure 2.3 depicts the hypothetical supply and demand diagram for the Japanese yen/U.S. dollar foreign exchange market. To further simplify matters, let's assume that Japan and the United States are the only two countries in the world.

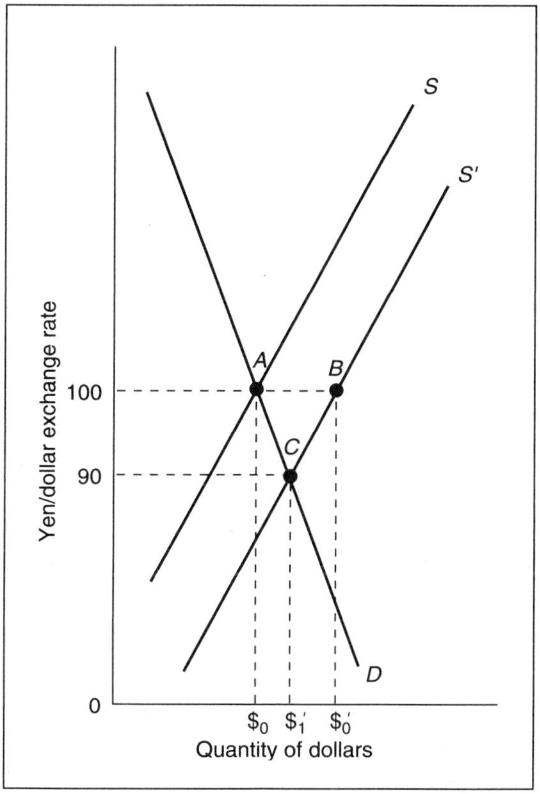

Figure 2.3 Balance of payments disequilibrium as reflected in the foreign exchange market.

Initially there is an official settlements balance of payments equilibrium and foreign exchange market equilibrium at point *A* in Figure 2.3. At this point the yen price of the dollar is 100, and quantity $\$_0$ (we don't care about a specific number here) is bought and sold. Notice that the demand is a familiar downward-sloping demand curve. In this case, the demand for dollars comes from the Japanese demand for U.S. goods or financial assets. The higher the yen price of the dollar, the more expensive are U.S. goods and the smaller the quantity of dollars demanded. The supply curve is the supply of dollars to this market from U.S. buyers of Japanese goods or financial assets. The upward-sloping supply curve reflects the fact that, as the dollar appreciates in value (and the exchange rate, ¥/$, rises), Japanese products are cheaper to U.S. buyers and more dollars will be supplied to this market.

Suppose the initial equilibrium at point *A* is disturbed by a change in market preferences for Japanese goods. For instance, suppose U.S. buyers now believe that Japanese automobiles are of higher quality and demand more auto imports from Japan. The supply of dollars to this market will shift right to S' so that more dollars are offered for yen at every level of the exchange rate. In terms of the Japanese balance of trade, there is now a surplus resulting from the higher U.S. demand for Japanese cars. The United States, on the other hand, now has a balance of payments deficit.

Figure 2.3 suggests an obvious way to restore equilibrium to the foreign exchange market and the balance of payments: let the dollar depreciate to 90 yen per dollar. At ¥/$ = 90, equilibrium is restored at point *C*. A new equilibrium quantity of dollars ($\$'_1$) is traded at the new exchange rate. With the appreciation of the yen, Japanese buyers are willing to buy more from the United States to balance the increased purchases of Japanese autos by U.S. buyers. In this case of *flexible exchange rates,* where the exchange rate is determined by free market supply and demand, balance of payments equilibrium is restored by the operation of the free market.

As we will learn in Chapter 3, exchange rates are not always free to adjust to changing market conditions. With *fixed exchange rates,* central banks set exchange rates at a particular level. If the exchange rate is fixed at 100, then after the shift in the supply curve, the dollar will be overvalued, there will be an excess supply of dollars ($\$'_0 - \$_0$) on the foreign exchange market, and the United States will run a balance of trade deficit while Japan runs a surplus. The central banks must now finance the trade imbalance by international reserve flows. Specifically, the Federal Reserve (or the Bank of Japan) must sell yen for dollars to support the deficit. In this case, the U.S. deficit could continue only as long as the U.S. stock of yen lasts. Once the United States has depleted its stock of foreign exchange, the dollar would have to be devalued to 90 yen per dollar, at which time the trade imbalance would end and there would again be equilibrium in the foreign exchange market.

Besides these methods of adjusting a balance of payments disequilibrium, countries sometimes use direct controls on international trade, such as government-mandated quotas or prices, to shift the supply and demand curves and induce balance of payments equilibrium. Such policies are particularly popular in developing countries where chronic shortages of international reserves do not permit financing the free-market-determined trade disequilibrium at the government-supported exchange rate.

The mechanism of adjustment to balance of payments disequilibrium is one of the most important practical problems in international economics. The discussion here is but an introduction; much of the analysis of Chapters 9 and 10 is related to this issue as well.

Summary

1. If the value of the credit items on a particular balance of payments account exceeds (is less than) that of the debit items, a surplus (deficit) exists.
2. The current account is the sum of the merchandise, services, investment income, and unilateral transfers accounts.
3. Current account deficits are offset by capital account surpluses.
4. The United States became a net international debtor in 1985.
5. Merchandise exports minus imports equal the balance of trade.
6. The official settlements balance is equal to changes in financial assets held by foreign monetary agencies and official reserve asset transactions.
7. Increases (decreases) in U.S.-owned deposits in foreign banks are debits (credits) to U.S. capital. Increases (decreases) in foreign-owned deposits in U.S. banks are credits (debits) to capital.
8. Deficits are not necessarily bad, nor are surpluses necessarily good.
9. With floating exchange rates, balance of payments equilibrium is restored by exchange rate changes.
10. With fixed exchange rates, central banks must finance deficits, allow a devaluation, or use trade restrictions to restore equilibrium.

Exercises

1. Under what circumstances could a country simultaneously have a balance of trade surplus and a capital account deficit?

2. Classify the following transactions in the German balance of payments:
   a. A U.S. tourist travels to Frankfurt and spends €1,000 on bratwurst and beer. He pays with a check drawn on a Tulsa, Oklahoma, bank.
   b. Mercedes-Benz sells €400,000 of its cars to a U.S. distributor, allowing 90 days' trade credit until payment is due.
   c. Herr Schmidt in Bonn, Germany, sends his grandson in New York €10 as a high school graduation present.
   d. A resident in Sun City, Arizona, receives a €4,000 dividend check from a German corporation and deposits it in a local bank.
   e. The U.S. Treasury buys €10,000,000 worth of German government bonds paid for with a deposit in a German bank.
3. What is the value of the current account in the preceding problem?
4. If a country has a current account deficit, is it a net lender or borrower to the rest of the world? Should a country necessarily be concerned if it experiences a current account deficit?
5. What is a balance of payments disequilibrium? Can a country run a balance of payments deficit indefinitely? Explain how balance of payments disequilibria are self-correcting.
6. Use the information in the following table on Mexico's 1996 international transactions to answer the questions (amounts are U.S. dollar values in millions):

Merchandise imports	\$89,469
Merchandise exports	\$96,000
Services exports	\$10,901
Services imports	\$10,819
Investment income receipts	\$ 4,032
Investment income payments	\$17,099
Unilateral transfers	\$ 4,531

   a. What is the balance of trade?
   b. What is the current account?
   c. Did Mexico become a larger international net debtor during 1996?

References

Bergin, Paul, "Should We Worry about the Large U.S. Current Account Deficit?" *Federal Reserve Bank of San Francisco Economic Letter,* December 22, 2000.

Glick, Reuven, "The Largest Debtor Nation," *Federal Reserve Bank of San Francisco Weekly Letter,* February 14, 1986.

Gonelli, Adam, *The Basics of Foreign Trade and Exchange,* Federal Reserve Bank of New York, 1993.

Marquez, Jaime, and Lisa Workman, *Modeling the IMF's Statistical Discrepancy in the Global Current Account,* International Finance Division, Federal Reserve Board, July 2000.

Motala, John, "Statistical Discrepancies in the World Current Account," *Finance and Development,* March 1997, 24–25.

3

Past and Present International Monetary Arrangements

Like most areas of public policy, international monetary relations are subject to frequent proposals for change. Fixed exchange rates, floating exchange rates, and commodity-backed currency all have their advocates. Before considering the merits of alternative international monetary systems, we should understand the background of the international monetary system. Although an international monetary system has existed since monies have been traded, it is common for most modern discussions of international monetary history to start in the late nineteenth century. It was during this period that the gold standard began.

The Gold Standard: 1880 to 1914

Although an exact date for the beginning of the gold standard cannot be pinpointed, we know that it started during the period from 1880 to 1890. Under a *gold standard,* currencies are valued in terms of their gold equivalent (an ounce of gold was worth \$20.67 in terms of the U.S. dollar over the gold standard period). The gold standard is an important beginning for a discussion of international monetary systems because when each currency is defined in terms of its gold value, all currencies are linked in a system of fixed exchange rates. For instance, if currency *A* is worth 0.10 ounce of gold, whereas currency *B* is worth 0.20 ounce of gold, then 1 unit of currency *B* is worth twice as much as 1 unit of *A,* and thus the exchange rate of 1 currency *B* = 2 currency *A* is established.

Maintaining a gold standard requires a commitment from participating countries to be willing to buy and sell gold to anyone at the fixed price. To maintain a price of $20.67 per ounce, the United States had to buy and sell gold at that price.

Gold was used as the monetary standard because it is a homogeneous commodity (could you have a fish standard?) worldwide that is easily storable, portable, and divisible into standardized units like ounces. Since gold is costly to produce, it possesses another important attribute—governments cannot easily increase its supply. A gold standard is a *commodity money standard.* Money has a value that is fixed in terms of the commodity gold.

One aspect of a money standard that is based on a commodity with relatively fixed supply is long-run price stability. Since governments must maintain a fixed value of their money relative to gold, the supply of money is restricted by the supply of gold. Prices may still rise and fall with swings in gold output and economic growth, but the tendency is to return to a long-run stable level. Figure 3.1 illustrates graphically the relative stability of U.S. and U.K. prices over the gold standard period as compared to later years. Since currencies were convertible into gold, national money supplies were constrained by the growth of the stock of gold. As long as the gold stock grew at a steady rate, prices would also follow a steady path. New discoveries of gold would generate discontinuous jumps in the price level, but the period of the gold standard was marked by a fairly stable stock of gold.

People today often look back on the gold standard as a "golden era" of economic progress. It is common to hear arguments supporting a return to the gold standard. Such arguments usually cite the stable prices, economic growth, and development of world trade during this period as evidence of the benefits provided by such an orderly international monetary system. Others have suggested that the economic development and stability of the world economy in those years did not necessarily reflect the existence of the gold standard but, instead, the absence of any significant real shocks such as war. Although we may disagree on the merits of returning to a gold standard, it seems fair to say that the development of world trade was encouraged by the systematic linking of national currencies and the price stability of the system.

Since gold is like a world money during a gold standard, we can easily understand how a balance of payments disequilibrium may be remedied. A country running a balance of payments (official settlements) deficit would find itself with net outflows of gold, which would reduce its money supply and, in turn, its prices. A surplus country would find gold flowing in

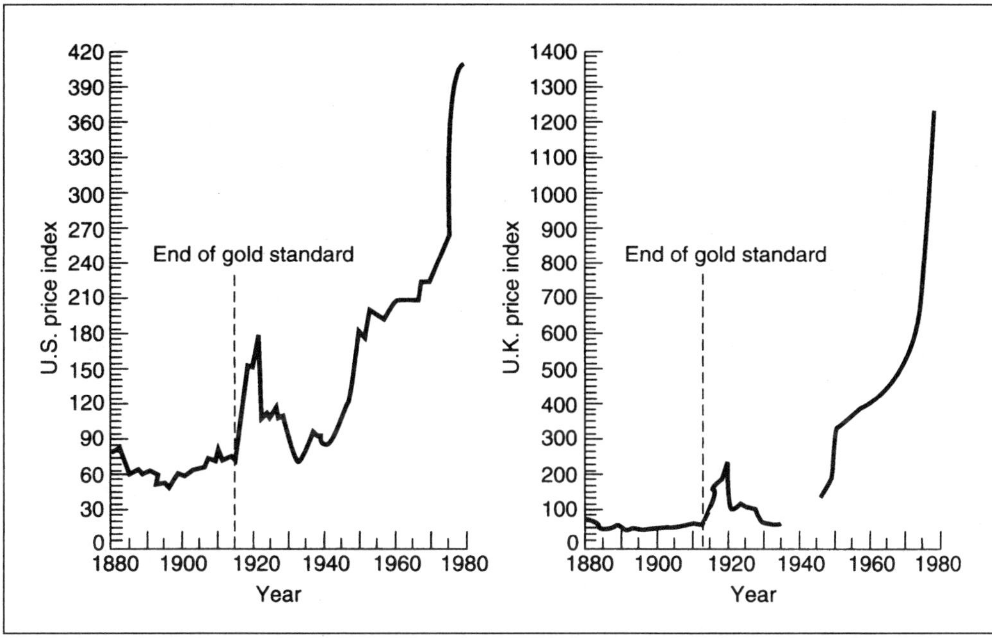

Figure 3.1 U.S. and U.K. wholesale price indexes from 1880 to 1976. Data are missing for World War II years in the United Kingdom.
Source: Roy W. Jastram, *The Golden Constant,* New York: Wiley, 1977.

and expanding its money supply, so that prices rose. The fall in price in the deficit country would lead to greater net exports (exports minus imports), and the rise in price in the surplus country would reduce its net exports, so that balance of payments equilibrium would be restored.

In practice, actual flows of gold were not the only, or even necessarily the most important, means of settling international debts during this period. Since London was the financial center of the world, and England the world's leading trader and source of financial capital, the pound also served as a world money. International trade was commonly priced in pounds, and trade that never passed through England was often paid for with pounds.

The Interwar Period: 1918 to 1939

World War I ended the gold standard. International financial relations are greatly strained by war, because merchants and bankers must be concerned about the probability of countries suspending international capital flows. At the beginning of the war both the patriotic response of each nation's citizens and legal restrictions stopped private gold flows. Since wartime financing required the hostile nations to manage international reserves very carefully, private gold exports were considered unpatriotic. Central governments encouraged (and sometimes mandated) that private holders of gold and foreign exchange sell these holdings to the government.

Because much of Europe experienced rapid inflation during the war and in the period immediately following it, it was not possible to restore the gold standard at the old exchange values. However, the United States had experienced little inflation and thus returned to a gold standard by June 1919. The war ended Britain's financial preeminence, since the United States had risen to the status of the world's dominant banker country. In the immediate postwar years the pound fluctuated freely against the dollar in line with changes in the price level of each country.

In 1925, England returned to a gold standard at the old prewar pound per gold exchange rate, even though prices had risen since the prewar period. As John Maynard Keynes had correctly warned, the overvalued pound hurt U.K. exports and led to a deflation of British wages and prices. By 1931, the pound was declared inconvertible because of a run on British gold reserves (a large demand to convert pounds into gold), and so ended the brief U.K. return to a gold standard. Once the pound was no longer convertible into gold, attention centered on the U.S. dollar. A run on U.S. gold at the end of 1931 led to a 15 percent drop in U.S. gold holdings. Although this did not lead to an immediate change in U.S. policy, by 1933 the United States abandoned the gold standard.

The depression years were characterized by international monetary warfare. In trying to stimulate domestic economies by increasing exports, country after country devalued, so that the early to mid-1930s may be characterized as a period of competitive devaluations. Governments also resorted to foreign exchange controls in an attempt to manipulate net exports in a manner that would increase GDP (gross domestic product). Of course, with the onslaught of World War II, the hostile countries utilized foreign exchange controls to aid the war-financing effort.

The Gold Exchange Standard: 1944 to 1970

Memories of the economic warfare of the interwar years led to an international conference at Bretton Woods, New Hampshire, in 1944. At the close of World War II there was a desire to reform the international monetary system to one based on mutual cooperation and freely convertible currencies.

The Bretton Woods agreement required that each country fix the value of its currency in terms of gold (this established the "par" value of each currency and was to ensure parity across currencies). The U.S. dollar was the key currency in the system, and \$1 was defined as being equal in value to 1/35 ounce of gold. Since every currency had a defined gold value, all currencies were linked in a system of fixed exchange rates.

Nations were committed to maintaining the parity value of their currencies within ± 1 percent of parity. The various central banks were to achieve this goal by buying and selling their currencies (usually against the dollar) on the foreign exchange market. When a country was experiencing difficulty maintaining its parity value because of balance of payments disequilibrium, it could turn to a new institution created at the Bretton Woods Conference: *the International Monetary Fund* (*IMF*). The IMF was created to monitor the operation of the system and provide short-term loans to countries experiencing temporary balance of payments difficulties. Such loans are subject to IMF conditions regarding changes in domestic economic policy aimed at restoring balance of payments equilibrium. In the case of a fundamental disequilibrium, when the balance of payments problems are not of a temporary nature, a country was allowed to devalue its currency, making a permanent change in the parity rate of exchange. Table 3.1 summarizes the history of exchange rate adjustments over the Bretton Woods period for the major industrial countries.

We notice, then, that the Bretton Woods system, although essentially a fixed, or pegged, exchange rate system, allowed for changes in exchange rates when economic circumstances warranted such changes. In actuality, the system is best described as an *adjustable peg*. The system may also be described as a gold exchange standard because the key currency, the dollar, was convertible into gold for official holders of dollars (such as central banks and treasuries).

The Bretton Woods system worked well through the 1950s and part of the 1960s. In 1960, there was a dollar crisis because the United States had run large balance of payments deficits in the late 1950s. Concern over large foreign holdings of dollars led to an increased demand for gold. Central bank cooperation in an international gold pool managed to stabilize gold prices at the official rate, but still the pressures mounted. Although the problem of chronic U.S. deficits and Japanese and European surpluses could have been remedied by revaluing the undervalued yen, mark, and franc, the surplus countries argued that it was the responsibility of the United States to restore balance of payments equilibrium.

Table 3.1 Exchange Rates of the Major Industrial Countries over the Period of the Bretton Woods Agreement

Country	Exchange rates[a]
Canada	Floated until May 2, 1962, then pegged at C$1.081 = $1. Floated again on June 1, 1970.
France	No official IMF parity value after 1948 (although the actual rate hovered around FF350 = $1) until December 29, 1958, when rate fixed at FF493.7 = $1 (old francs). One year later, rate was FF4.937 = $1 when new franc (one new franc was equal to 100 old francs) was created. Devaluation to FF5.554 = $1 on August 10, 1969.
Germany	Revalued on March 6, 1961, from DM4.20 = $1 to DM4.0 = $1. Revalued to DM3.66 = $1 on October 26, 1969.
Italy	Pegged at Lit625 = $1 from March 30, 1960, until August 1971.
Japan	Pegged at ¥360 = $1 until 1971.
Netherlands	Pegged at F13.80 = $1 until March 7, 1961, when revalued at F13.62 = $1.
United Kingdom	Devalued from $2.80 = £1 to $2.40 = £1 on November 11, 1967.

[a]Relative to the U.S. dollar.

The failure to realign currency values in the face of fundamental economic change spelled the beginning of the end for the gold exchange standard of the Bretton Woods agreement. By the late 1960s the foreign dollar liabilities of the United States were much larger than the U.S. gold stock. The pressures of this "dollar glut" finally culminated in August 1971, when President Nixon declared the dollar to be inconvertible and provided a close to the Bretton Woods era of fixed exchange rates and convertible currencies.

The Transition Years: 1971 to 1973

In December 1971, an international monetary conference was held to realign the foreign exchange values of the major currencies. The *Smithsonian agreement* provided for a change in the dollar per gold exchange value from $35 to $38.02 per ounce of gold. At the same time that the dollar was being devalued by about 8 percent, the surplus countries saw their currencies revalued upward. After the change in official currency values the system was to operate with fixed exchange rates under which the central banks would buy and sell their currencies to maintain the exchange rate within ±2.25 percent of the stated parity.

Although the realignment of currency values provided by the Smithsonian agreement allowed a temporary respite from foreign exchange crises, the calm was short-lived. Speculative flows of capital began to put downward pressure on the pound and lira. In June 1972, the pound began to float according to supply and demand conditions. The countries experiencing large inflows of speculative capital, such as Germany and Switzerland, applied legal controls to slow further movements of money into their countries.

Although the gold value of the dollar had been officially changed, the dollar was still inconvertible into gold, and thus the major significance of the dollar devaluation was with respect to the foreign exchange value of the dollar, not to official gold movements. The speculative capital flows of 1972 and early 1973 led to a further devaluation of the dollar in February 1973, when the official price of an ounce of gold rose from $38 to $42.22. Still, the speculative capital flows persisted from the weak to the strong currencies. Finally, in March 1973, the major currencies began to float.

Floating Exchange Rates: 1973 to the Present

Although we refer to the exchange rate system in existence since 1973 as a floating rate system, exchange rates have not been determined solely by the free market forces of supply and demand. The system as operated is best described as a *managed float,* wherein central banks intervene at times to obtain a politically desirable exchange rate apart from that which would be determined by free market supply and demand. Such managed floating does not apply to all countries and currencies, as we observe several different exchange rate policies followed by countries today. Table 3.2 lists the exchange rate practices of the IMF member countries. We observe some currencies, such as the U.S. dollar, to be freely floating, whereas others choose to maintain a fixed value (or peg) relative to a single currency and still others choose to peg to a composite or basket of currencies. There are several reasons for choosing a basket peg. If trade is not heavily concentrated with the United States but is instead diversified across several countries, then it may make more sense to alter the currency value relative to a weighted average of foreign currencies rather than any single currency.

Note that some countries listed under "exchange arrangements with no separate legal tender" in Table 3.2 have no unique national money. This would include some countries like Ecuador or El Salvador that have adopted the U.S. dollar as their money. Other countries are members of a *currency union* like the CFA franc zone of Africa, the 12 European countries that use the euro, or the Caribbean countries that belong to the East Caribbean currency union.

Table 3.2 Exchange Rate Practices of IMF Member Countries

Crawling pegs (4)	Exchange rates within crawling bands (6)	Managed floating with no preannounced path for exchange rate (42)	Independently floating (40)
Bolivia	Belorus	Algeria	Afghanistan
Costa Rica	Honduras	Angola	Albania
Nicaragua	Israel	Azerbaijan	Argentina
Solomon Islands	Romania	Burundi	Armenia
	Uruguay	Cambodia	Australia
	Venezuela	Croatia	Brazil
		Dominican Rep.	Canada
		Ethiopia	Chile
		Ghana	Colombia
		Guatemala	Congo, Dem. Rep. of the
		Guinea	Czech Rep.
		Guyana	Gambia, The
		India	Georgia
		Indonesia	Haiti
		Iraq	Iceland
		Jamaica	Japan
		Kazakhstan	Korea
		Kenya	Liberia
		Kyrgyz Republic	Madagascar
		Lao P.D.R.	Mexico
		Mauritania	Moldova
		Mauritius	Mozambique
		Mongolia	New Zealand
		Myanmar	Norway
		Nigeria	Papua New Guinea
		Pakistan	Peru
		Paraguay	Philippines
		Russia	Poland
		Rwanda	Sierra Leone
		São Tomé and Príncipe	Somalia
		Singapore	South Africa
		Slovak Rep.	Sweden
		Slovenia	Switzerland
		Sri Lanka	Tajikistan
		Thailand	Tanzania
		Trinidad and Tobago	Turkey
		Tunisia	Uganda
		Ukraine	United Kingdom
		Uzbekistan	United States
		Vietnam	Yemen
		Yugoslavia	
		Zambia	

Exchange arrangements with no separate legal tender (40)	Currency board arrangements (7)	Other conventional fixed peg arrangements (including de facto peg arrangements under managed floating) (44)	Exchange rates within horizontal bands (5)
Another currency as legal tender	Bosnia and Herzegovina	*Against a single currency (31)*	*Within a cooperative arrangement ERM II*
Ecuador	Brunei Darusalam	Aruba	Denmark
El Salvador	Bulgaria	Bahamas	*Other band arrangements*
Kiribati	Djibouti	Bahrain	Cyprus
Marshall Islands	Estonia	Bangladesh	Egypt
Micronesia	Hong Kong SAR	Barbados	Hungary
Palau	Lithuania	Belize	Tonga
Panama		Bhutan	
San Marino		Cape Verde	
CFA franc zone		China	
WAEMU		Comoros	
Benin		Eritea	
Burkina Faso		Iran, Islamic Rep. of	
Côte d'Ivoire		Jordan	
Guinea-Bissau		Lebanon	
Mali		Lesotho	
Niger		Macedonia, FYR	
Senegal		Malaysia	
Togo		Maldives	
CAEMC		Namibia	
Cameroon		Nepal	
Central African Rep.		Netherlands Antilles	
Chad		Oman	
Congo, Rep. of		Qatar	
Equatorial Guinea		Saudi Arabia	
Gabon		Sudan	
Euro Area		Suriname	
Austria		Swaziland	
Belgium		Syrian Arab Republic	
Finland		Turkmenistan	
France		United Arab Emirates	
Germany		Zimbabwe	
Greece		*Against a composite (13)*	
Ireland		Botswana	
Italy		Burundi	
Luxembourg		Fiji	
Netherlands		Kuwait	
Portugal		Latvia	
Spain		Malta	
ECCU		Morocco	
Antigua and Barbuda		Myanmar	
		Samoa	

(Continued)

Table 3.2 *(Continued)*

Exchange arrangements with no separate legal tender (40)	Currency board arrangements (7)	Other conventional fixed peg arrangements (including de facto peg arrangements under managed floating) (44)	Exchange rates within horizontal bands (5)
Dominica		Seychelles	
Grenada		Solomon Islands	
St. Kitts and Nevis		Tonga	
St. Lucia		Vanuatu	
St. Vincent and the Grenadines			

Source: International Monetary Fund, *Annual Report,* 2002.

Finally, some countries have chosen an intermediate path between floating and pegging. A *crawling peg* is a system wherein the exchange rate is held fixed in the short run but is adjusted at regular intervals to reflect supply and demand pressures.

The various headings in Table 3.2 indicate quite a variety of exchange rate arrangements. We provide a brief description of each:

Crawling pegs The exchange rate is adjusted periodically in small amounts at a fixed, preannounced rate or in response to certain indicators (such as inflation differentials against major trading partners).

Crawling bands The exchange rate is maintained within certain fluctuation margins around a central rate that is periodically adjusted at a fixed, preannounced rate or in response to certain indicators.

Managed floating The monetary authority (usually the central bank) influences the exchange rate through active foreign exchange market intervention with no preannounced path for the exchange rate.

Independently floating The exchange rate is market determined, and any intervention is aimed at moderating fluctuations rather than determining the level of the exchange rate.

No separate legal tender Either another country's currency circulates as the legal tender, or the country belongs to a monetary union where the legal tender is shared by the members (like the euro).

Currency board A fixed exchange rate is established by a legislative commitment to exchange domestic currency for a specified foreign currency at a fixed exchange rate. New issues of domestic currency are typically backed in some fixed ratio (like one-to-one) by additional holdings of the key foreign currency.

Fixed peg The exchange rate is fixed against a major currency or some basket of currencies. Active intervention may be required to maintain the target pegged rate.

Horizontal bands The exchange rate fluctuates around a fixed central target rate. Such target zones allow for a moderate amount of exchange rate fluctuation while tying the currency to the target central rate.

The Choice of an Exchange Rate System

Perfectly fixed or pegged exchange rates would work much as a gold standard does. All currencies would fix their exchange rate in terms of another currency, say, the dollar, and thereby would fix their rate relative to every other currency. Under such an arrangement each country would have to follow the monetary policy of the key currency in order to experience the same inflation rate and keep the exchange rate fixed.

Flexible or floating exchange rates occur when the exchange rate is determined by the market forces of supply and demand. As the demand for a currency increases relative to supply, that currency will appreciate, whereas currencies in which the quantity supplied exceeds the quantity demanded will depreciate.

Economists do not all agree on the advantages and disadvantages of a floating as opposed to a pegged exchange rate system. For instance, some would argue that a major advantage of flexible rates is that each country can follow domestic macroeconomic policies independent of the policies of other countries. To maintain fixed exchange rates, countries have to share a common inflation experience, which was often a source of problems under the post–World War II system of fixed exchange rates. If the dollar, which was the key currency for the system, was inflating at a rate faster than, say, Japan desired, then the lower inflation rate followed by the Japanese led to pressure for an appreciation of the yen relative to the dollar. Thus the existing pegged rate could not be maintained. Yet with flexible rates, each country can choose a desired rate of inflation and the exchange rate will adjust accordingly. Thus, if the United States chooses 8 percent inflation and Japan chooses 3 percent, there will be a steady depreciation of the dollar relative to the yen (absent any relative price movements). Given the different political environment and cultural heritage existing in each country, it is reasonable to expect different countries to follow different monetary policies. Floating exchange rates allow for an orderly adjustment to these differing inflation rates.

Still there are those economists who argue that the ability of each country to choose an inflation rate is an undesirable aspect of floating exchange rates. These proponents of fixed rates indicate that fixed rates are useful in providing an international discipline on the inflationary policies of countries. Fixed rates provide an anchor for countries with inflationary tendencies. By maintaining a fixed rate of exchange to the dollar (or some other currency), each country's inflation rate is "anchored" to the dollar, and thus will follow the policy established for the dollar.

Critics of flexible exchange rates have also argued that flexible exchange rates would be subject to destabilizing speculation. By *destabilizing speculation* we mean that speculators in the foreign exchange market will cause exchange rate fluctuations to be wider than they would be in the absence of such speculation. The logic suggests that, if speculators expect a currency to depreciate, they will take positions in the foreign exchange market that will cause the depreciation as a sort of self-fulfilling prophecy. But speculators should lose money when they guess wrong, so that only successful speculators will remain in the market, and the successful players serve a useful role by "evening out" swings in the exchange rate. For instance, if we expect a currency to depreciate or decrease in value next month, we could sell the currency now, which would result in a current depreciation. This will lead to a smaller future depreciation than would occur otherwise. The speculator then spreads the exchange rate change more evenly through time and tends to even out big jumps in the exchange rate. If the speculator had bet on the future depreciation by selling the currency now and the currency appreciates instead of depreciates, then the speculator loses and will eventually be eliminated from the market if such mistakes are repeated.

Research has shown that there are systematic differences between countries choosing to peg their exchange rates and those choosing floating rates. One very important characteristic is country size in terms of economic activity or GDP. Large countries tend to be more independent and less willing to subjugate domestic policies with a view toward maintaining a fixed rate of exchange with foreign currencies. Since foreign trade tends to constitute a smaller fraction of GDP the larger the country is, it is perhaps understandable that larger countries are less attuned to foreign exchange rate concerns than are smaller countries.

The openness of the economy is another important factor. By openness, we mean the degree to which the country depends on international trade. The greater the fraction of tradable (i.e., internationally tradable) goods in GDP, the more open the economy will be. A country with little or no international trade is referred to as a *closed economy.* As previously mentioned, openness is related to size. The more open the economy, the greater the weight of tradable goods prices in the overall national price level, and therefore the greater the impact of exchange rate changes on the national price level. To minimize such foreign-related shocks to the domestic price level, the more open economy tends to follow a pegged exchange rate.

Countries that choose higher rates of inflation than their trading partners will have difficulty maintaining an exchange rate peg. We find, in fact, that countries whose inflation experiences are different from the average follow floating rates, or a crawling-peg-type system in which the exchange rate is adjusted at short intervals to compensate for the inflation differentials.

Countries that trade largely with a single foreign country tend to peg their exchange rate to that country's currency. For instance, since the United States accounts for the majority of Barbados trade, by pegging to the U.S. dollar, Barbados imparts to its exports and imports a degree of stability that would otherwise be missing. By maintaining a pegged rate between the Barbados dollar and the U.S. dollar, Barbados is not unlike another state of the United States as far as pricing goods and services in United States–Barbados trade. Countries with diversified trading patterns will not find exchange rate pegging so desirable.

The evidence from previous studies indicates quite convincingly the systematic differences between peggers and floaters, which is summarized in Table 3.3. But there are exceptions to these generalities because neither all peggers nor all floaters have the same characteristics. We can safely say that, in general, the larger the country is, the more likely it is to float its exchange rate; the more closed the economy is, the more likely the country will float; and so on. The point is that economic phenomena, and not just political maneuvering, ultimately influence foreign exchange rate practices.

There is also concern about how the choice of an exchange rate system affects the stability of the economy. If the domestic policy authorities seek to minimize unexpected fluctuations in the domestic price level, then they will choose an exchange rate system that best minimizes such fluctuations. For instance, the greater the foreign tradable goods price fluctuations are, the more likely there will be a float, since the floating exchange rate helps to insulate the domestic economy from foreign price disturbances. The

Table 3.3 Characteristics Associated with Countries Choosing to Peg or Float

Peggers	Floaters
Small size	Large size
Open economy	Closed economy
Harmonious inflation rate	Divergent inflation rate
Concentrated trade	Diversified trade

greater the domestic money supply fluctuations are, the more likely there will be a peg, since international money flows serve as shock absorbers that reduce the domestic price impact of domestic money supply fluctuations. With a fixed exchange rate, an excess supply of domestic money will cause a capital outflow because some of this excess supply is eliminated via a balance of payments deficit. With floating rates, the excess supply of money is contained at home and reflected in a higher domestic price level and depreciating domestic currency. Once again, the empirical evidence supports the notion that real-world exchange rate practices are determined by such economic phenomena.

Optimum Currency Areas

The *optimum currency area* is the best area within which exchange rates are fixed and between which exchange rates are flexible. Looking at the real world, we might suggest that North America and Western Europe appear to be likely currency areas given the geographic proximity of Canada, Mexico, and the United States, as well as the geographic position of the Western European nations. Since exchange rates between U.S. and Canadian dollars and the Mexican peso seem closely linked (certainly the peso and the U.S. dollar had a long history of fixed exchange rates), we might expect these three countries to maintain pegged exchange rates with each other and to float versus the rest of the world. Western Europeans, in fact, have explicitly adopted such a regional optimum currency area arrangement with the euro.

One theory suggests that the optimum currency area is the region characterized by relatively costless mobility of the factors of production (labor and capital). As an illustration of this theory, suppose we have two countries, A and B, producing computers and cotton, respectively. Suddenly there is a change in tastes resulting in a shift of demand from computers to cotton. Country A will tend to run a deficit balance of trade and have an excess supply of labor and capital since the demand for computers has fallen, whereas country B will run a surplus and have an excess demand for labor and capital because of the increase in demand for its cotton. What are the possibilities for international adjustment to these changes?

1. Factors of production could move from A to B and thereby establish new equilibrium wages and prices in each region.
2. Prices in A could fall relative to those in B, and the relative price change would eliminate the balance of trade disequilibrium if labor and capital cannot move between the countries. (We are ignoring the capital account now in order to assume zero capital flows.)
3. The exchange rate could adjust and bring about the required change in relative prices if A and B have different currencies.

Now we can understand why the optimum currency area is characterized by mobile factors of production. If factors can freely and cheaply migrate from an area lacking jobs to an area where labor is in demand, then the mobility will restore equilibrium since the unemployment in one area is remedied by migration. Thus, fixed exchange rates within the area will be appropriate because relative price movements are not the only means for restoring equilibrium.

When factors are immobile so that equilibrium is restored solely through relative price change, then there is an advantage to flexible exchange rates. If the monetary authorities in each country tend to resist any price changes, then the easiest way to adjust is with flexible exchange rates, because the adjustment can go largely through the exchange rate rather than through prices.

The European Monetary System and the Euro

The optimum currency area literature suggests that in a regional setting like Western Europe a system of fixed exchange rates might be appropriate. While the establishment of the common euro currency may be viewed as a kind of permanently fixed exchange rate, prior to the euro, a system to link currencies and limit exchange rate flexibility had been in place since the late 1970s. The European Monetary System (EMS) was established in March 1979. The EMS committed the member countries to maintaining small exchange rate fluctuations among themselves, while allowing for large fluctuations against outside currencies. The EMS worked quite well through the 1980s and led to optimism that the member nations eventually could evolve into a system with one European central bank and one money. It was in this spirit that the Maastricht Treaty was signed in December 1991 and a timetable for the evolution of the system was spelled out. The treaty called for:

- The immediate removal of restrictions on European flows of capital and greater coordination of monetary and fiscal policy.
- The establishment of a European Monetary Institute (EMI) in January 1994 to coordinate monetary policies of the individual central banks and make technical preparations for a single monetary policy.
- The irrevocable fixing of exchange rates among all member countries, with a common currency and a European Central Bank in January 1997, at the earliest, and by January 1999, at the latest.

This last step did not occur until January 1999. The countries that moved to this last step of monetary union required their macroeconomic policy to converge to that of the other EMS countries. Convergence was defined as occurring when (a) the country's inflation rate did not exceed the average of the lowest three member country rates by more than 1.5 percentage points; (b) its interest rate on long-term government bonds did not exceed those of the three lowest-inflation members by more than 2 percentage points; and (c) the country's government budget deficit did not exceed 3 percent of GDP, and outstanding government debt did not exceed 60 percent of GDP.

The new European currency, the euro, made its debut on January 1, 1999. The symbol is €, and the ISO code is EUR. Euro notes and coins began to circulate on January 1, 2002. In the transition years of 1999 to 2001, people used the euro as a unit of account, denominating financial asset values and transactions in euro amounts. Bank accounts were available in euros and credit transactions were denominated in euros. However, actual cash transactions were not made with euros until euro cash started circulating in 2002.

Prior to the beginning of the euro, the value of each of the "legacy currencies" of the euro-area countries was fixed in terms of the euro. Table 3.4 gives the exchange rates at which each of the old currencies was fixed in terms of the euro. For instance, 1 euro is equal to 40.3399 Belgian francs or 1.95583 German marks. Of course, the prior monies of each of the euro-area countries no longer are used, having been replaced by the euro.

Table 3.4 Exchange Rates of Old National Currencies Replaced by the Euro

Former Currency	1 euro =
Belgian franc	BEF40.3399
German mark	DEM1.95583
Spanish peseta	ESP166.386
Finnish markka	FIM5.94753
French franc	FRF6.55957
Greek drachma	GRD340.750
Irish pound	IEP0.787564
Italian lira	ITL1936.27
Luxembourg franc	LUF40.3399
Netherlands guilder	NLG2.20371
Austrian schilling	ATS13.7603
Portuguese escudo	PTE200.482

One money requires one central bank, and the euro is no exception. The European Central Bank (ECB) began operations on June 1, 1998, in Frankfurt, Germany, and now conducts monetary policy for the euro-area countries. The national central banks like the Bank of Italy or the German Bundesbank are still operating and perform many of the functions they had prior to the ECB, such as regulating and supervising banks and facilitating payments systems in each nation. In some sense they are like the regional banks of the Federal Reserve System in the United States. Monetary policy for the euro-area countries is conducted by the ECB in Frankfurt just as monetary policy for the United States is conducted by the Federal Reserve in Washington, D.C. Yet the national central banks of the euro-area play an important role in each of the respective countries. The entire network of national central banks and the ECB are called the *European System of Central Banks.* Monetary policy for the euro-area is determined by the *Governing Council* of the ECB. This council is comprised of the heads of the national central banks of the euro-area countries plus the members of the ECB *Executive Board.* The board is made up of the ECB president and vice-president and four others chosen by the heads of the governments of the euro-area nations.

Currently, three member countries of the European Union have not adopted the euro and still maintain their own currencies and monetary policies. The three countries are Denmark, Sweden, and the United Kingdom. It remains to be seen when, and if, these countries become part of "euroland."

Target Zones

Exchange rate arrangements like the old EMS, where there was limited flexibility around some central fixed value, are sometimes called *target zones*. In this setting, the exchange rate is allowed to change with changes in the fundamental determinants of exchange rates like money supplies, incomes, and prices, but the amount of change allowed is limited by the width of the bands permitted by the target zone arrangement.

Figure 3.2 illustrates the essentials of a target zone system. For purposes of example, let's assume that the United States and the United Kingdom have agreed on a target zone for the dollar/pound exchange rate where the exchange rate will be kept between 2.04 and 1.96 dollars per pound. The vertical axis of Figure 3.2 measures the exchange rate in dollars per pound. The upper bound of the target zone is shown in the figure as $E_{max} = 2.04$. The lower bound is shown as $E_{min} = 1.96$. The horizontal axis measures the value of the "fundamentals" like the net effect of money supply, income, prices, and any other fundamental determinants of exchange rates.

If instead of a target zone there were a fixed exchange rate at $2 per pound, what would that look like in the figure? A fixed exchange rate would be represented by one point in the figure at the origin where $E = 2$. This means that, as other fundamentals change, the central banks change the money supply to offset the effects of the other fundamentals so that the exchange rate is left unchanged.

If instead of a target zone there were a flexible exchange rate system, what would that look like in the figure? A flexible exchange rate would be represented by the 45 degree line. This indicates that the exchange rate changes match changes in the fundamentals as the central banks do not attempt to offset the effects of the fundamentals. Also, note that a flexible exchange rate may rise or fall without bounds if pushed by the fundamentals.

With the target zone system, the central banks are committed to intervening so that the exchange rate rises no higher than $E = 2.04$ and falls no lower than $E = 1.96$. If people believe that this zone will be enforced by the government authorities, then the exchange rate will lie along the S-shaped line in Figure 3.2. Note that this line is flatter than the 45 degree line of the flexible exchange rate. This S-shape is due to the fact that the closer the exchange rate gets to the upper or lower limit, the greater the probability of

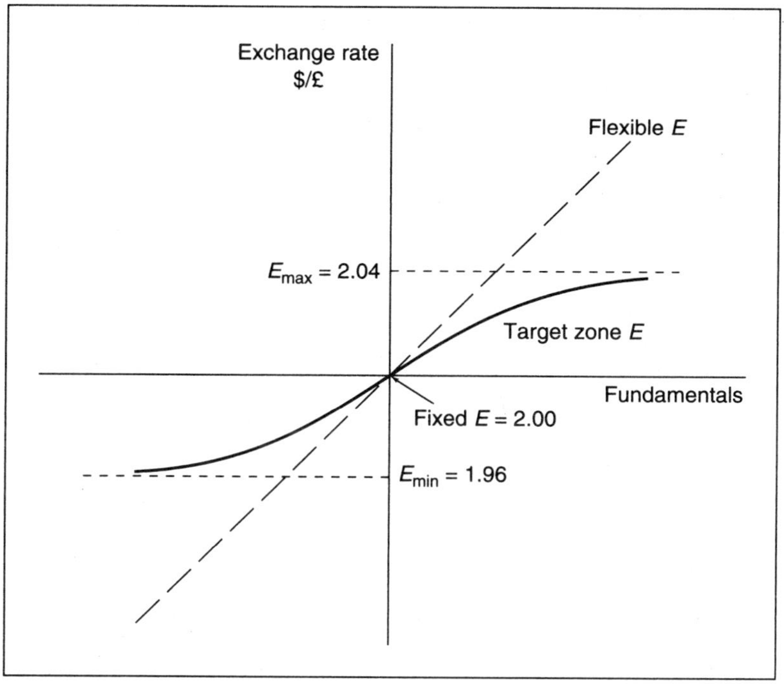

Figure 3.2 An exchange-rate target zone.

intervention. For instance, suppose the exchange rate is rising and approaches the upper limit of 2.04. The probability of a central bank intervention is increased so that people will expect a greater probability of the exchange rate dropping with the intervention rather than continuing to rise. As a result, the exchange rate line flattens to give the top of the *S*-shape. Continued increases in the fundamentals result in smaller and smaller dollar depreciation as the threat increases of central bank intervention aimed at dollar appreciation. In this sense, a target zone backed by credible government policies helps to stabilize the exchange rate relative to a floating exchange rate.

Currency Boards

Developing countries with a long history of unstable exchange rates often find it difficult to convince the public that government policy will maintain stable exchange rates in the future. This lack of credibility on the part of a government can be overcome if some sort of constraint is placed on the discretionary policy-making ability of the authorities with control over monetary and exchange rate policy. One such form of constraint is a *currency board.* A currency board is a government institution that exchanges domestic currency for foreign currency at a fixed rate of exchange.

The typical demise of a fixed exchange rate system comes when the central bank runs out of foreign currency to exchange for domestic currency and ends up devaluing the domestic currency. Currency boards achieve a credible fixed exchange rate by holding a stock of the foreign currency equal to 100 percent of the outstanding currency supply of the nation. As a result of such foreign currency holdings, people believe that the board will always have an adequate supply of foreign currency to exchange for domestic currency at the fixed rate of exchange. Critics of currency boards point to such reserve holdings as a cost of operating a currency board. However, since the board holds largely short-term, interest-bearing securities denominated in the foreign currency rather than actual non-interest-bearing currency to back its own currency, these interest earnings tend to make currency boards profitable.

During the Asian financial crisis in 1997 to 1998, the debate over currency boards was heightened by a proposed currency board for Indonesia. The Indonesian government wanted to introduce a currency board to buy credibility for the rupiah and halt a rapid rupiah depreciation. Critics emphasized several potential problems with a currency board that eventually led to the abandonment of the Indonesian plan. Critics emphasized that a currency board can only succeed if a sustainable fixed rate of exchange between the domestic currency and the U.S. dollar is chosen. An obvious problem is what exchange rate is correct? If the exchange rate overvalues the domestic currency, then the currency board would be "attacked" by speculators exchanging domestic currency for dollars, betting on a devaluation of the domestic currency. Because the currency board has a finite supply of dollars, an exchange rate fixed at unsustainable levels would eventually lead to a large loss of dollar reserves so that the currency board collapses and the exchange rate is eventually devalued. Another problem related to a currency board is that the requirement to maintain foreign currency backing for the domestic currency would constrain the central bank from responding to a domestic financial crisis where the central bank might act as a "lender of last resort" to financial institutions. Because the central bank cannot create domestic currency to lend to domestic institutions facing a "credit crunch," the financial crisis could potentially erupt into a national economic crisis with a serious recession.

It is important to remember that boards do not engage in the monetary policy actions typical of central banks like the Federal Reserve in the United States. Their sole function is to provide for a fixed exchange rate between the domestic currency and some major currency like the U.S. dollar. To promote public confidence in the banking system, some currency board countries also have central banks that simultaneously provide supervision of the domestic banking system and act as lenders of last resort to troubled banks. However, such central banks have no discretionary authority to influence the exchange rate; if they did, the public would likely doubt the government's commitment to maintaining the fixed exchange rate.

Table 3.2 shows that there are currency boards in seven countries. The choice of fixed versus floating exchange rates is often a difficult one for governments. In the case of developing countries that have made a choice for fixed rates, but face a skeptical public due to past policy mistakes, a currency board may be a reasonable way to establish a credible exchange rate system. The recent experience of Argentina shows that a currency board is no guarantee of success.

For a decade, Argentina maintained a currency board arrangement that supported an exchange rate of 1 peso per U.S. dollar. However, large fiscal deficits resulted in the essential insolvency of the government. At the same time that the government amassed large debts denominated in U.S. dollars, economic fundamentals were consistent with peso devaluation. The fixed exchange rate of the currency board was no longer consistent with the economic realities created by the expansionary fiscal policy, and an economic crisis erupted in late 2001 and early 2002 that resulted in a run on dollars as people tried to exchange pesos for dollars at the obviously overvalued exchange rate of 1 peso per dollar. The crisis in Argentina saw rioting in the streets, the resignations of two presidents in quick succession, a freeze on bank deposit withdrawals, and a break with the fixed exchange rate. Once the currency board arrangement was ended, the peso quickly fell in value from one-to-one parity with the U.S. dollar to a level of 3 pesos per dollar. The Argentine case serves as a warning that currency boards are not a guarantee of forever-fixed exchange rates. If government policy is inconsistent with the fixed exchange rate, the currency board cannot last.

International Reserve Currencies

International reserves are the means of settling international debts. Under the gold standard, gold was the major component of international reserves.

Following World War II, we had a gold exchange standard in which international reserves included both gold and a reserve currency, the U.S. dollar. The reserve currency country was to hold gold as backing for the outstanding balances of the currency held by foreigners. These foreign holders of the currency were then free to convert the currency into gold if they wished. However, as we observed with the dollar, once the convertibility of the currency becomes suspect, or once large amounts of the currency are presented for gold, the system tends to fall apart.

This appears to describe the dollar following World War II. At the end of the war, and throughout the 1950s, the world demanded dollars for use as an international reserve. During this time, U.S. balance of payments deficits provided the world with a much-needed source of growth for international reserves. As the rest of the world developed and matured, over time U.S. liabilities to foreigners greatly exceeded the gold reserve backing these liabilities. Yet as long as the increase in demand for these dollar reserves equalled the supply, the lack of gold backing was irrelevant. Through the late 1960s, U.S. political and economic events began to cause problems for the dollar's international standing, and the continuing U.S. deficits were not matched by a growing demand, so that pressure to convert dollars into gold resulted in the dollar being declared officially no longer exchangeable for gold in August 1971.

Table 3.5 illustrates the diversification of the currency composition of foreign exchange reserves since the mid-1970s. There was a trend of a falling share devoted to U.S. dollars along with a rising share devoted to the mark and yen until the early 1990s when the trend reversed.

At first glance it may appear very desirable to be the reserve currency and have other countries accept your balance of payments deficits as a necessary means of financing world trade. The difference between the cost to the reserve country of creating new balances and the real resources the reserve country is able to acquire with the new balances is called *seigniorage.* Seigniorage then is a financial reward accruing to the reserve currency as a result of the use of the currency as a world money.

The seigniorage return for being the dominant money must be quite low since the United States, and the United Kingdom before it, have not produced very high quality reserve money. The seigniorage return to the United Kingdom was probably eroded by the dollar's growing dominance through the twentieth century, so that the United Kingdom did not have much to lose by following a domestic policy of high and variable inflation and thereby losing the international dominance of the pound. Likewise, the

Table 3.5 Share of National Currencies in Total Identified Official Holdings of Foreign Exchange (In Percentages)

	1977	1981	1985	1989	1993	1997	2001
All countries							
U.S. dollar	80.3	73.1	65.1	51.4	55.6	68.4	68.3
Pound sterling	1.8	2.2	3.2	2.3	2.9	3.7	4.0
Deutsche mark	9.3	13.4	15.5	17.8	14.0	12.9	—
French franc	1.3	1.4	1.2	1.4	2.2	1.4	—
Swiss franc	2.3	2.8	2.4	1.4	1.1	0.7	0.7
Netherlands guilder	0.9	1.2	1.0	1.1	0.6	0.4	—
Japanese yen	2.5	4.3	7.6	7.2	7.7	5.2	4.9
Unspecified currencies	1.6	1.4	3.9	6.6	7.3	8.4	9.0
ECUs	—	—	—	10.8	8.6	5.0	—
Euro	—	—	—	—	—	—	13.0
Industrial countries							
U.S. dollar	89.4	78.7	63.2	47.9	49.9	57.9	74.5
Pound sterling	0.9	0.7	2.0	1.1	2.0	1.9	1.8
Deutsche mark	5.5	13.1	19.2	20.4	16.2	15.9	—
French franc	0.3	0.5	0.5	1.1	2.5	0.9	—
Swiss franc	0.8	1.8	1.8	1.1	0.3	0.1	0.4
Netherlands guilder	0.6	0.8	1.0	1.1	0.4	0.2	—
Japanese yen	1.8	3.7	8.5	7.4	7.7	5.8	5.5
Unspecified currencies	0.7	0.7	3.9	4.5	5.8	6.4	8.1
ECUs	—	—	—	15.3	15.2	10.9	—
Euro	—	—	—	—	—	—	9.7
Developing countries							
U.S. dollar	70.9	67.1	67.5	59.8	63.1	66.2	64.1
Pound sterling	2.8	3.8	4.7	5.3	4.0	5.1	5.5
Deutsche mark	13.3	13.9	10.9	11.4	11.1	10.3	—
French franc	2.3	2.5	2.1	2.1	1.9	1.8	—
Swiss franc	3.9	3.9	3.1	2.2	2.2	1.1	0.9
Netherlands guilder	1.2	1.6	1.1	0.9	0.9	0.6	—
Japanese yen	3.2	5.0	6.5	6.6	7.6	4.7	4.5
Unspecified currencies	2.5	2.2	4.0	11.7	9.3	10.2	9.6
Euro	—	—	—	—	—	—	15.3

United States in the late 1960s and 1970s depreciated some of the dollar's international standing by a relatively high and variable U.S. inflation. At any rate, the fact that we have not observed countries competing for reserve currency status indicates that the seigniorage return is likely to be quite small.

Table 3.5 indicates that the dollar is still, by far, the dominant reserve currency. Since the U.S. international position has been somewhat eroded in the past few decades, the question arises as to why we did not see the German mark, Japanese yen, or Swiss franc emerge as the dominant reserve currency. Although the mark, yen, and Swiss franc have been popular currencies, the respective governments in each country have resisted a greater international role for their monies. Besides the apparently low seigniorage return to the dominant international money, there is another reason for these countries to resist. The dominant money producer (country) finds that international shifts in the demand for its money may have repercussions on domestic operations. For a country the size of the United States, domestic economic activity is large relative to international activity, so international capital flows of any given magnitude have a much smaller potential to disrupt U.S. markets than would be the case for Japanese, German, or Swiss markets, where foreign operations are much more important. In this sense, it is clear why these countries have withstood the movement of the yen, mark, and franc to reserve currency status. Over time, we may find that the euro emerges as a dominant reserve currency as the combined economies of the euro-area countries provide a very large base of economic activity. However, Table 3.5 shows that the euro only accounts for 13 percent of total international reserves, so it is not close to the 68 percent share taken by the dollar.

In domestic monetary theory, economists often identify three roles of money. Money is said to serve as (1) a unit of account, (2) a medium of exchange, and (3) a store of value. Likewise, in an international context we can explain the choice of a reserve currency according to criteria relevant for each role.

Table 3.6 summarizes the roles of a reserve currency. First, the role of the international unit of account results from information costs. We find that primary goods like coffee, tin, or rubber are quoted in terms of dollars worldwide. Since these goods are homogeneous, at least relative to manufactured goods, information regarding their value is conveyed more quickly when prices are quoted in terms of one currency worldwide. The private use as an invoicing currency in international trade contracts arises from the reserve currency's informational advantage over other currencies. Besides being a unit of account for private contracts, the reserve currency also serves as a base currency to which other currencies peg exchange rates.

A currency's role as an international medium of exchange is the result of transaction costs. In the case of the U.S. dollar, the dollar is so widely traded that it is often cheaper to go from currency *A* to dollars to currency

Table 3.6 Roles of a Reserve Currency

Function	Resulting from	Private role	Official role
1. International unit of account	Information costs	Invoicing currency	Pegging currency
2. International medium of exchange	Transaction costs	Vehicle currency	Intervention currency
3. International store of value	Stable value	Banking currency	Reserve currency

B, than directly from currency *A* to currency *B.* Thus, it is efficient to use the dollar as an international medium of exchange, and the dollar serves as the vehicle for buying and selling nondollar currencies. The private (mainly interbank) role as a vehicle currency means that the dollar (or the dominant reserve currency) will also be used by central banks in foreign exchange market intervention aimed at achieving target levels for exchange rates.

Finally, a currency's role as an international store of value results from the stability of its value. In other words, certainty of future value enhances a currency's role as a store of purchasing power. The U.S. dollar's role in this area was diminished in the 1970s, and it seems likely that further instability in U.S. monetary policy would contribute to a further fall. The private market use of the dollar for denominating international loans and deposits indicates the role of the dominant reserve currency in banking. In addition, countries will choose to hold their official reserves largely in the dominant reserve currency.

As the preceding discussion indicates, market forces determine a currency's international role and not a government's decree. It is important to realize, however, that just as the market chooses to elevate a currency like the U.S. dollar to reserve currency status, it can also take away some of that status, which happened to the U.K. pound earlier in this century and has happened to the dollar to a lesser extent since the 1970s.

Multiple Exchange Rates

Most countries conduct all foreign exchange transactions at a single exchange rate. But some countries maintain multiple exchange rates. A typical arrangement is a dual exchange rate system, with a free-market-determined floating exchange rate for capital account transactions and a fixed exchange rate overvaluing the domestic currency for current account transactions. Some countries have much more complex arrangements, involving three or more exchange rates applied to various transactions.

The IMF has generally sought to unify exchange rates in countries where multiple rates exist. The argument is that multiple exchange rates harm both the countries that impose them as well as other countries. With different exchange rates for different types of transactions, domestic relative prices of internationally traded goods tend to differ from international relative prices. This results in distorted decision making in consumption, production, and investment as domestic residents respond to artificial relative prices rather than the true prices set on world markets. Multiple exchange rates are also costly in that people devote resources to finding ways to profit from the tiered exchange rates (like having transactions classified to the most favorable exchange rate category). Finally, the maintenance of a multiple exchange rate system requires a costly administrative structure.

Research has generally found that multiple exchange rates are a form of protectionism, originally introduced to improve a country's balance of payments. The elimination of a multiple exchange rate system could simply involve allowing all transactions to occur at the market-determined rate. If a unified fixed exchange rate is desired, the floating rate will suggest an appropriate level for the new fixed rate. Of course, after the fixed rate is established, monetary and fiscal policy must be consistent with the maintenance of the new exchange rate.

Summary

1. Under a gold standard, currencies are convertible into gold at fixed exchange rates.
2. The IMF and a system of fixed exchange rates were created at the Bretton Woods Conference in 1944.
3. In March 1973, the major developed countries began floating their exchange rates.
4. Countries with floating exchange rates tend to have large, closed economies, with inflation rates that differ from those of their trading partners and trade diversified across many countries.
5. The optimum currency area is characterized by mobile factors of production.

6. Reserve currencies serve as an international unit of account, a medium of exchange, and a store of value.
7. Multiple exchange rates are used to encourage exports and discourage imports.

Exercises

1. What is seigniorage? Does the United States possess an unfair advantage in world commerce due to seigniorage?
2. With a gold standard, is it feasible for a country to continuously change the value of its currency in terms of gold to achieve faster and faster money supply growth?
3. How does a gold standard eliminate the possibility of continuous balance of payments disequilibria?
4. When did the euro begin? What countries are in the euro-area and which currencies were replaced by the euro?
5. Discuss the common economic arguments germane to whether, in general, exchange rates should float or be fixed.
6. How did the Bretton Woods international monetary system differ from the gold standard? What was the primary purpose of the IMF under Bretton Woods? Why did the Bretton Woods agreement finally break down?
7. How can a target zone help create a more stable exchange rate?
8. Where is the European Central Bank located ? In what way is the European System of Central Banks like the Federal Reserve System?

References

Alesina, Alberto, and Robert J. Barro, *Currency Unions.* Stanford: Hoover Institution Press, 2001.

Bordo, Michael David, "The Classical Gold Standard: Lessons from the Past," in Michael B. Connolly, ed., *The International Monetary System: Choices for the Future.* New York: Praeger, 1982.

Dowd, Kevin, and David Greenaway, "Currency Competition, Network Externalities and Switching Costs: Towards an Alternative View of Optimum Currency Areas," *Economic Journal,* September 1993.

Edison, Hali J., and Michael Melvin, "The Determinants and Implications of the Choice of an Exchange Rate System," in William S. Haraf and Thomas D. Willett, eds., *Monetary Policy for a Volatile Global Economy.* Washington, D.C.: The AEI Press, 1990.

Hartmann, Philipp, Michele Manna, and Andres Manzanares, "The Microstructure of the Euro Money Market," *Journal of International Money and Finance,* November 2001.

Hau, Harold, William P. Killeen, and Michael Moore, "The Euro as an International Currency: Explaining Puzzling First Evidence from the Foreign Exchange Markets," *Journal of International Money and Finance,* June 2002.

Levin, Jay H., *A Guide to the Euro.* Boston: Houghton Mifflin, 2002.

Masson, Paul R., and Mark P. Taylor, *Policy Issues in the Operation of Currency Unions.* Cambridge: Cambridge University Press, 1993.

McKinnon, Ronald I., "Optimum Currency Areas," *American Economic Review,* September 1963.

Savvides, Andreas, "Real Exchange Rate Variability and the Choice of Exchange Rate Regime by Developing Countries," *Journal of International Money and Finance,* December 1990.

Tower, Edward, and Thomas Willett, *The Theory of Optimum Currency Areas and Exchange Rate Flexibility,* International Finance Section, No. 11, Princeton University, 1976.

4

Forward-Looking Market Instruments

In Chapter 1 we considered the problem of a U.S. importer buying Swiss watches. Since the exporter requires payment in Swiss francs, the transaction requires an exchange of U.S. dollars for francs. The discussion in Chapter 1 was related to the *spot market*—exchanging dollars for francs today at the current spot exchange rate.

Suppose we return to the example of the U.S. watch importer. Earlier, the importer purchased francs in the spot market to settle a contract payable now. Yet much international trade is contracted in advance of delivery and payment. It would not be unusual for the importer to place an order for Swiss watches for delivery at a future date. For instance, suppose the order calls for delivery of the goods and payment of the invoice in three months. Specifically, let's say that the order is for SF100,000.

What options does the importer have with respect to payment? One option is to wait three months and then buy the francs. A disadvantage of this strategy is that the exchange rate could change over the next three months in a way that makes the deal unprofitable. Looking at Figure 4.1, we see that the current spot rate is \$0.7332 = SF1, or SF100,000 = 73,320. But there is no guarantee that this exchange rate (and the consequent dollar value of the contract) will prevail in the future. If the dollar were to *depreciate* against the franc, then it would take more dollars to buy any given quantity of francs. For instance, suppose the future spot rate (which is currently unknown) is \$0.75 = SF1. Then it would take

The New York foreign exchange mid-range rates below apply to trading among banks in amounts of $1 million and more, as quoted at 4 P.M. Eastern time by Reuters and other sources. Retail transactions provide fewer units of foreign currency per dollar.

Country	U.S. $ equiv.	Currency per U.S. $
Argentina (Peso)	0.3120	3.2051
Australia (Dollar	0.5875	1.7021
Bahrain (Dinar)	2.6522	0.3770
Brazil (Real)	0.2854	3.5039
Britain (Pound)	1.6472	0.6071
1 Month Forward	1.6438	0.6083
3 Months Forward	1.6365	0.6111
6 Months Forward	1.6268	0.6147
Canada (Dollar)	0.6572	1.5216
1 Month Forward	0.6564	1.5235
3 Months Forward	0.6545	1.5279
6 Months Forward	0.6514	1.5352
Chile (Peso)	0.001360	735.29
China (Renminbi)	0.1208	8.2781
Colombia (Peso)	0.0003393	2,947.2
Czech Republic (Koruna)		
Commercial Rate	0.03417	29.265
Denmark (Krone)	0.1448	6.9061
Ecuador (US Dollar)-e	1.0000	1.0000
Hong Kong (Dollar)	0.1282	7.8003
Hungary (Forint)	0.004412	226.65
India (Rupee)	0.02092	47.801
Indonesia (Rupiah)	0.0001127	8,873.1
Israel (Shekel)	0.2073	4.8239
Japan (Yen)	0.008341	119.89
1 Month Forward	0.008349	119.77
3 Months Forward	0.008369	119.49
6 Months Forward	0.008396	119.10
Jordan (Dinar)	1.4092	0.7096
Kuwait (Dinar)	3.3450	0.2990
Lebanon (Pound)	0.0006634	1,507.4
Malaysia (Ringitt)-b	0.2632	3.7994
Malta (Lira)	2.5654	0.3898
Mexico (Peso)	0.09165	10.911
New Zealand (Dollar)	0.5448	1.8355
Norway (Krone)	0.1445	6.9204
Pakistan (Rupee)	0.01723	58.038
Peru (New Sol)	0.2870	3.4843
Philippines (Peso)	0.01858	53.821

(Continued)

Figure 4.1 Foreign exchange rate quotations for January 31, 2003.

Figure 4.1 (Continued)

Poland (Zloty)	0.2616	3.8226
Russia (Ruble)-a	0.03141	31.837
Saudi Arabia (Riyal)	0.2667	3.7495
Singapore (Dollar)	0.5754	1.7379
Slovak Republic (Koruna)	0.02578	38.790
South Africa (Rand)	0.1175	8.5106
South Korea (Won)	0.0008591	1,164.0
Sweden (Krona)	0.1164	8.5911
Switzerland (Franc)	0.7332	1.3639
1 Month Forward	0.7336	1.3631
3 Months Forward	0.7346	1.3613
6 Months Forward	0.7360	1.3587
Taiwan (Dollar)	0.02882	34.698
Thailand (Baht)	0.02337	42.790
Turkish (Lira)	0.00000061	1,639,344
United Arab (Dirham)	0.2723	3.6724
Uruguay (Peso) Financial	0.03520	28.409
Venezuela (Bolivar)	0.0005200	1,923.1
Special Drawing Rights	1.3727	0.7285
Euro	1.07650	0.9289

Special Drawing Rights (SDR) are based on exchange rates for the U.S.,German, British, French, and Japanese currencies. Source: International Monetary Fund.

a-Russian Central Bank rate. b-Government rate. e-Adopted U.S. dollar as of 9/11/00.

Source: Reuters.

$75,000 to purchase SF100,000, and the watch purchase would not be as profitable for the importer. Of course, if the dollar were to *appreciate* against the franc, then the profits would be larger. As a result of this uncertainty regarding the dollar/franc exchange rate in the future, the importer may not want to choose the strategy of waiting three months to buy francs.

An alternative is to buy the francs now and hold or invest them for three months. This alternative has the advantage that the importer knows exactly how many dollars are needed now to buy SF100,000. But the importer is faced with a new problem of coming up with cash now and investing the francs for three months. Another alternative that ensures a certain dollar price of francs is using the *forward exchange market.* As will be shown in Chapter 5, there is a close relationship between the forward market and the former alternative of buying francs now and investing them for three months. For now, we will focus on the operation of the forward market.

Forward Rates

The forward exchange market refers to buying and selling currencies to be delivered at a future date. Figure 4.1 includes forward exchange rates for the major traded currencies, including the Swiss franc. Note that the three-month or 90-day forward rate on the franc is \$0.7346 = SF1. To buy francs for delivery in 90 days would cost \$0.7346 per franc. Note that a one-month and six-month forward rate is also quoted.

The advantage of the forward market is that we have established a set exchange rate between the dollar and the franc and do not have to buy the francs until they are needed in 90 days. This may be preferred to buying francs now and investing them for three months, because it is neither necessary to part with any funds now nor to have knowledge of investment opportunities in francs. (However, the selling bank may require that the importer hold "compensating balances" until the 90-day period is up—that is, leave funds in an account at the bank, allowing the bank to use the money until the forward date.) With a forward rate of \$0.7346 = SF1, SF100,000 will sell for \$73,460. The importer now knows with certainty how many dollars the watches will cost in 90 days.

If the forward exchange price of a currency exceeds the current spot price, that currency is said to be selling at a *forward premium.* A currency is selling at a *forward discount* when the forward rate is less than the current spot rate. The forward rates in Figure 4.1 indicate that the British pound is selling at a discount against the dollar, but the Japanese yen is selling at a premium. The implications of a currency selling at a discount or premium will be explored in coming chapters. In the event that the spot and forward rates are equal, the currency is said to be *flat.*

Swaps

Commercial banks rarely use forward exchange contracts for interbank trading; instead, swap agreements are arranged. A *foreign exchange swap* is a trade involving two currencies. For example, suppose Citibank wants pounds now. They could borrow the pounds, arranging to repay in three months. Then they could buy pounds in the forward market to ensure a certain price to be paid when the pounds are needed in three months. Alternatively, Citibank could enter into a swap agreement wherein they trade dollars for pounds now and pounds for dollars in three months. The terms of the arrangement are obviously closely related to conditions in the forward market, since the swap rates will be determined by the discounts or premiums in the forward exchange market.

Suppose Citibank wants pounds for three months and works a swap with Lloyds. Citibank will trade dollars to Lloyds and in return will receive pounds. In three months the trade is reversed. Citibank will pay out pounds to Lloyds and receive dollars (of course, there is nothing special about the three-month period used here—swaps could be for any period). Suppose the spot rate is \$/£ = \$2.00 and the three-month forward rate is \$/£ = \$2.10, so that there is a \$0.10 premium on the pound. These premiums or discounts are actually quoted in basis points when serving as swap rates (a *basis point* is $^1/_{100}$ percent, or 0.0001). Thus the \$0.10 premium converts into a swap rate of 1,000 points, which is all the swap participants are interested in; they do not care about the actual spot or forward rate since only the difference between them matters for a swap.

Swap rates are usefully converted into percent per annum terms to make them comparable to other borrowing and lending rates (remember a swap is the same as borrowing one currency while lending another currency for the duration of the swap period). The swap rate of 1,000 points or 0.1000 was for a three-month period. To convert this into annual terms, we find the percentage return for the swap period and then multiply this by the reciprocal of the fraction of the year for which the swap exists. The percentage return for the swap period is equal to the

$$\text{Premium (discount)} \div \text{spot rate} = 0.10/\$2.00 = 0.05$$

The fraction of a year for which the swap exists is

$$3 \text{ months}/12 \text{ months} = \frac{1}{4}$$

And the reciprocal of the fraction is

$$1/(\tfrac{1}{4}) = 4$$

Thus the percent per annum premium (discount) or swap rate = $0.05 \times 4 = 0.20$. This swap, then, yields a return of 20 percent per annum, which can be compared to the other opportunities open to the bank.

We have been discussing *foreign exchange swaps,* in which there is a simultaneous exchange of two currencies on a specific date at a rate agreed at the time of the contract, and a reverse exchange of the same two currencies at a date further in the future at a rate agreed at the time of the contract. An alternative swap agreement is a *currency swap.* A currency swap is a contract in which two counterparties exchange streams of interest payments in different currencies for an agreed period of time and then exchange principal amounts in the respective currencies at an agreed exchange rate at maturity.

Currency swaps allow firms to obtain long-term foreign currency financing at lower cost than they can by borrowing directly. Suppose a Canadian firm wants to receive Japanese yen today with repayment in five years. If the Canadian firm is not well known to Japanese banks, the firm will pay a higher interest rate than firms that actively participate in Japanese financial markets. The Canadian firm may approach a bank to arrange a currency swap that will reduce its borrowing costs. The bank will find a Japanese firm desiring Canadian dollars. The Canadian firm is able to borrow Canadian dollars more cheaply than the Japanese firm, and the Japanese firm is able to borrow yen more cheaply than the Canadian firm. The intermediary bank will arrange for each firm to borrow its domestic currency and then swap the domestic currency for the desired foreign currency. The interest rates paid on the two currencies will reflect the forward premium in existence at the time the swap is executed. When the swap agreement matures, the original principal amounts are traded back to the source firms. Both firms benefit by having access to foreign funds at a lower cost than they could obtain directly.

Swaps are an efficient way to meet the firm's need for foreign currencies because they combine two separate transactions into one. We will learn later that the firm avoids any foreign exchange risk by matching the liability created by borrowing foreign currencies with the asset created by lending domestic currency, both to be repaid at the known future exchange rate. This is known as *hedging* the foreign exchange risk.

Table 4.1 presents data on the volume of activity in the foreign exchange market. About 33 percent of the transactions reported by the banks surveyed were spot transactions. Swaps constitute 56 percent of the business, and forwards account for around 11 percent. Swaps do 5 times the volume of outright forward purchases or sales of currency.

In foreign exchange dealing, banks do not always trade directly with one another but often use someone in the middle—a *broker.* If a bank wants to buy a particular currency, several other banks could be contacted for quotes, or the bank representative could input an order with an electronic broker where many banks participate and the best price at the current time among the participating banks is revealed. While trading in the broker's market is in progress, the names of the banks making bids and offers are not

Table 4.1 Foreign Exchange Market Turnover

Type of transaction	Average daily turnover (Billions of U.S. Dollars)
Spot	387
Swaps	656
Forwards	131
	1,174

Source: Bank for International Settlements, *Central Bank Survey of Foreign Exchange and Derivatives Market Activity,* Basle, October 2001.

known until a deal is reached. This anonymity may be very important to the trading banks, because it allows banks of different sizes and market positions to trade on an equal footing. The broker's reward, the commission, is split by the buyer and seller and is usually less than 0.01 percent of the selling price.

In the electronic brokers market, computer programs take offers to buy and sell from different agents and match them. In addition to the electronic brokers, there are electronic dealing systems. Rather than talking directly over the telephone dealer-to-dealer, computer networks allow for trades to be executed electronically. The use of electronic broker systems varies greatly across countries. Approximately 54 percent of trading in the United States goes through such networks, compared to 66 percent in the United Kingdom and 48 percent in Japan.

Futures

The foreign exchange market we have discussed (spot, forward, and swap transactions) is a global market. Commercial banks, business firms, and governments in various locations buy and sell using telephone and computer systems with no centralized geographical market location. However, there exist additional institutions that have not yet been covered, one of which is the foreign exchange futures market. The *futures market* is a market where foreign currencies may be bought and sold for delivery at a future date. The futures market differs from the forward market in that only a few currencies are traded; moreover, trading occurs in standardized contracts and in a specific geographic location, such as the International Monetary Market (IMM) of the Chicago Mercantile Exchange (CME), which is the largest currency futures market.

CME futures are traded on the British pound, Canadian dollar, Japanese yen, Swiss franc, Australian dollar, Mexican peso, and euro. The contracts involve a specific amount of currency to be delivered at specific maturity dates. Contracts mature on the third Wednesday of March, June, September, and December. In the forward market, contracts are typically 30, 90, or 180 days long and are maturing every day of the year. Forward market contracts are written for any amount agreed upon by the parties involved. In the futures market the contracts are written for fixed amounts: GBP62,500, CAD100,000, JPY12,500,000, CHF125,000, MXP500,000, and EUR125,000.

Futures markets provide a hedging facility for firms involved in international trade, as well as a speculative opportunity. Speculators will profit when they accurately forecast a future price for a currency that differs significantly (by more than the transaction cost) from the current contract price. For instance, if we believe that in September the pound will sell for \$1.60, and the September futures contract is currently priced at \$1.6670, we would sell a September contract. Then, at maturity we will receive \$1.6670 per pound, or \$104,187.50 for £62,500 as the futures contract specifies. If the actual price of the pound falls below \$1.6670, we will realize a profit (less transaction costs). Suppose the actual price in March is \$1.60. We could then buy 62,500 pounds for \$100,000 (1.60 × 62,500). The difference of \$104,187.50 − \$100,000 = \$4,187.50, less transaction costs, will be our profit.

Futures contracts are for smaller amounts of currency than are forward contracts, and therefore serve as a useful hedging vehicle for relatively small firms. Forward contracts are within the realm of wholesale banking activity and are typically used only by large financial institutions and other large business firms that deal in very large amounts of foreign exchange.

Options

Besides forward and future contracts, there is an additional market where future foreign currency assets and liabilities may be hedged; it is called the *options market.* A foreign currency option is a contract that provides the right to buy or sell a given amount of currency at a fixed exchange rate on or before the maturity date (these are known as "American" options; "European" options may be exercised only at maturity). A *call option* gives the right to buy currency and a *put option* gives the right to sell. The price at which currency can be bought or sold is the *strike price* or *exercise price.*

The use of options for hedging purposes is straightforward. Suppose a U.S. importer is buying equipment from a Swiss manufacturer, with a SF1 million payment due in December. The importer can hedge against a franc appreciation by buying a call option that confers the right to purchase francs over the next three months, until the December maturity, at a specified price. Specifically, assume that the current spot exchange rate is $0.70 per franc. At this exchange rate, SF1 million would cost $700,000. If the franc appreciated to $0.75 over the next three months, then using the spot market in three months would change the value of the imports to $750,000 (0.75 × SF1,000,000), an increase in the price of the imports of $50,000. The call option will provide insurance against such change.

Foreign currency options have been traded only since December 1982, when the Philadelphia Stock Exchange offered a market. The Philadelphia exchange offers contracts for AUD50,000, GBP31,250, CAD50,000, EUR62,500, JPY6,250,000, and CHF62,500.

An option is said to be "in the money" if the strike price is less than the current spot rate for a call or greater than the current spot rate for a put. Returning to our example of the U.S. importer buying SF1 million of equipment to be paid for in December, the current spot rate is $0.7084 per SF. At this rate SF1 million is equal to $708,400. To hedge against unexpected exchange rate change, the importer could buy a December option. Suppose he wants a strike price of $0.71, so that the upper bound on the value of the imports is $710,000. Suppose a December option with a strike price of 71 sells for $0.0178 per franc, so one contract for SF62,500 costs $1,112.50. To cover SF1 million, the importer must buy 16 contracts (16 × 62,500 = 1,000,000) at a cost of $17,800. If the franc appreciates above $0.71, the option will be exercised. For instance, if the December spot price is $0.75, then using the spot market would mean a cost of $750,000 for the imports. Exercising the option contracts ensures a price of $710,000, so that the firm saves $40,000 less the $17,800 premium, compared to an unhedged position. If the franc does not appreciate to the level of the strike price, then the option is allowed to expire. For instance, if the December spot price is $0.70, then using the spot market would mean a cost of $700,000 for the imports. This is $10,000 less than the cost using the option contracts. In this case the firm is out the $17,800 it paid for the options.

Aside from trading options on organized exchanges like the Philadelphia Exchange, large multinational firms often buy options directly from banks. Such custom options may be for any size or date agreed to and therefore provide greater flexibility than is possible on organized exchanges.

If we knew with certainty what the future exchange rate would be, there would be no market for options, futures, or forward contracts. In an uncertain world, risk-averse traders willingly pay to avoid the potential loss associated with adverse movements in exchange rates. An advantage of options over futures or forwards is greater flexibility. A futures or forward contract is an obligation to buy or sell at a set exchange rate. An option offers the right to buy or sell if desired in the future and is not an obligation.

Recent Practices

The growth of options contracts since the early 1980s has stimulated the development of new products and techniques for managing foreign exchange assets and liabilities. One recent development combines the features of a forward contract and an option contract. Terms such as *break forward, participating forward,* or *FOX* (forward with option exit) refer to forward contracts with an option to break out of the contract at a future date. In this case, the forward exchange rate price includes an option premium for the right to break the forward contract. The incentive for such a contract comes from the desire of customers to have the insurance provided by a forward contract when the exchange rate moves against them and yet not lose the potential for profit available with favorable exchange rate movements.

One might first wonder whether a break-forward hedge could not be achieved more simply by using a straight option contract. There are several attractive features of the break-forward contract that do not exist with an option. For one thing, an option requires an up-front premium payment. The corporate treasurer may not have a budget for option premiums or may not have management approval for using options. The break forward hides the option premium in the forward rate. Since the price at which the forward contract is broken is fixed in advance, the break forward may be treated as a simple forward contract for tax and accounting purposes, whether the contract is broken or not.

One of the more difficult problems in hedging foreign exchange risk arises in bidding on contracts. The bidder submits a proposal to perform some task for the firm or government agency that will award a contract to the successful bidder. Since there may be many other bidders, the bidding firms face the foreign exchange risk associated with the contract only if they are, in fact, awarded the contract. Suppose a particular bidder assesses that it has only a 20 percent chance of winning the contract. Should that bidder buy a forward contract or option today to hedge the foreign exchange risk it faces in the event it is the successful bidder? If substantial foreign exchange risk is involved for the successful bidder, then not only the bidders but also the contract awarder face a dilemma. The bids will not be as competitive in light of the outstanding foreign exchange risk as they would be if the exchange rate uncertainty were hedged.

One approach to this problem is the *Scout* contract. Midland Bank developed the Scout (share currency option under tender) as an option that is sold to the contract awarder, who then sells it to the successful bidder. The awarding agency now receives more competitive, and perhaps a greater number of, bids because the bidders now know that the foreign exchange hedge is arranged.

Over time, we should expect a proliferation of new financial market products aimed at dealing with future transactions involving foreign exchange. If there is a corporate interest in customizing an option or a forward arrangement to a specific type of transaction, an innovative bank will step in and offer a product. The small sample of new products discussed in this section is intended to suggest the practical use of these financial innovations.

Summary

1. The forward exchange market is composed of commercial banks buying and selling foreign currency for delivery at a future date.
2. If the forward price of a currency is greater than (less than) the spot price, the currency is said to sell at a forward premium (discount).
3. Swap contracts allow participants to borrow the currency of a market where they receive favorable credit terms and then trade for another currency required for financing activities.
4. Foreign currency futures are standardized contracts traded on established exchanges for delivery of currencies at a specified future date.
5. Foreign currency options are contracts for the right to buy or sell currencies on or before a certain date.
6. Futures and options are traded on exchanges and are available on a customized basis from commercial banks.

Exercises

1. Use Figure 4.1 to determine whether each of the currencies listed here is selling at a forward premium or discount against the dollar:
   a. Pound
   b. Swiss franc
   c. Yen
   d. Canadian dollar
2. Calculate the per annum premium (discount) of a one-month forward contract on Canadian dollars based on the information in Figure 4.1.
3. List at least three ways in which a futures contract differs from a forward contract.
4. Assume U.S. corporation XYZ needs to arrange to have £10,000 in 90 days. Discuss the alternatives available to the corporation in meeting this obligation. What factors are important in determining which strategy is best?
5. Suppose you are the treasurer of a large U.S. multinational firm that wants to hedge the foreign exchange risk associated with a payable of 1,000,000 Australian dollars due in 90 days? How many futures contracts would cover your risk? How many options contracts would cover the risk? What would determine whether you use a futures or options contract?
6. Suppose you are the treasurer of a U.S. multinational firm that wants to hedge the foreign exchange risk associated with your firm's sale of equipment to a Swiss firm worth SF1,000,000. The receivable is due in six months. You want to ensure that Swiss francs are worth at least $0.70 when the francs are received so you want a strike price of $0.70. How many options contracts do you need to hedge this risk? Do you want a call or put on Swiss francs? When will you exercise the options? When will you let the options expire?

References

Broll, Udo, and Itzhak Zilcha, "Exchange Rate Uncertainty, Futures Markets and the Multinational Firm," *European Economic Review,* May 1992.

Géczy, Christopher, Bernadette A. Minton, and Catherine Schrand, "Why Firms Use Currency Derivatives," *Journal of Finance,* September 1997, 1323–1354.

Lien, Donald, and Kit Pong Wang, "Optimal Bidding and Hedging in International Markets," *Journal of International Money and Finance,* forthcoming.

Smith, Clifford W., Jr., Charles W. Smithson, and Lee M. Wakeman, "The Evolving Market for Swaps," *Midland Corporate Finance Journal,* Winter 1986, 20–32.

5

Exchange Rates, Interest Rates, and Interest Parity

International trade occurs in both goods and financial assets. Exchange rates change in a manner to accommodate this trade. In this chapter, we study the relationship between interest rates and exchange rates, and consider how exchange rates adjust to achieve equilibrium in financial markets.

Interest Parity

The interest parity relationship results from profit-seeking arbitrage activity, specifically *covered interest arbitrage*. Let us go through an example of how covered interest arbitrage works. For expositional purposes

$i_\$$ = interest rate in the United States
$i_£$ = interest rate in the United Kingdom
F = forward exchange rate (dollars per pound)
E = spot exchange rate (dollars per pound)

Where the interest rates and the forward rate are for assets with the same term to maturity (e.g., three months or one year), the investor in the United States can earn $(1 + i_\$)$ at home by investing \$1 for 1 period (for instance, one year). Alternatively, the U.S. investor can invest in the United Kingdom by converting dollars to pounds and then investing the pounds. Here, \$1 is equal to $1/E$ pounds (where E is the dollar price of pounds). Thus, by investing in the United Kingdom, the U.S. resident can earn $(1 + i_£)/E$. This is the quantity of pounds resulting from the \$1 invested. Remember, \$1 buys $1/E$ pounds, and £1 will return $1 + i_£$ after 1 period. Thus, $1/E$ pounds will return $(1 + i_£)/E$ after 1 period.

Since the investor is a resident of the United States, the investment return will ultimately be converted into dollars. But since future spot exchange rates are not known with certainty, the investor can eliminate the uncertainty regarding the future dollar value of $(1 + i_£)/E$ by *covering* the £ currency investment with a forward contract. By selling $(1 + i_£)/E$ pounds to be received in a future period in the forward market today, the investor has guaranteed a certain dollar value of the pound investment opportunity. The *covered return* is equal to $(1 + i_£)F/E$ dollars. The U.S. investor can earn either $1 + i_\$$ dollars by investing \$1 at home or $(1 + i_£)F/E$ dollars by investing the dollar in the United Kingdom. Arbitrage between the two investment opportunities results in

$$1 + i_\$ = (1 + i_£)\frac{F}{E}$$

which may be rewritten as

$$\frac{1 + i_\$}{1 + i_£} = \frac{F}{E} \tag{5.1}$$

Equation (5.1) can be put in a more useful form by subtracting 1 from both sides, giving us the *interest rate parity* equation:

$$\frac{i_\$ - i_£}{1 + i_£} = \frac{F - E}{E} \tag{5.2}$$

which is sometimes approximated as

$$i_\$ - i_£ = \frac{F - E}{E} \tag{5.3}$$

The smaller $i_£$, the better the approximation of Equation (5.3) to (5.2). Equation (5.3) indicates that the interest differential between a comparable U.S. and U.K. investment is equal to the forward premium or discount on the pound. (We must remember that since interest rates are quoted at annual rates or percent per annum, the forward premiums or discounts must also be quoted at annual rates.)

Now let's consider an example. Ignoring bid-ask spreads, we observe the following interest rates:

Euro \$: 15%

Euro £: 10%

The exchange rate is quoted as the dollar price of pounds and is currently $E = 2.00$. Given the previous information, what do you expect the 12-month forward rate to be?

Using Equation (5.3), we can plug in the known values for the interest rates and spot exchange rate and then solve for the forward rate:

$$0.15 - 0.10 = \frac{F - 2.00}{2.00} \rightarrow$$

$$0.05 = \frac{F - 2.00}{2.00} \rightarrow$$

$$0.10 = F - 2.00 \rightarrow F = 2.10$$

Thus, we would expect a 12-month forward rate of \$2.10 to give a 12-month forward premium equal to the 0.05 interest differential.

Suppose the actual 12-month forward rate is not \$2.10, but is instead \$2.15. What would profit-seeking arbitragers do? They could buy pounds at the spot rate and then invest and sell the pounds forward for dollars, because the future price of pounds is higher than that implied by the interest parity relation. These actions would tend to increase the spot rate and lower the forward rate, thereby bringing the forward premium back in line with the interest differential. The interest rates could also move, because the movement of funds into pound investments would tend to depress the pound interest rate, whereas the shift out of dollar investments would tend to raise the dollar rate.

The interest parity relationship can also be used to illustrate the concept of the *effective return* on a foreign investment. Equation (5.3) can be rewritten so that the dollar interest rate is equal to the pound rate plus the forward premium. Thus

$$i_{\$} = i_{£} + \frac{F - E}{E} \tag{5.4}$$

Interest parity ensures that Equation (5.4) will hold. But suppose we do not use the forward market, yet we are U.S. residents who buy U.K. bonds. The interest rate on the bond $i_£$ is not the relevant return measure, since this is the return in terms of a U.K. investment. The effective return on the bond is given by the interest rate plus the expected change in the exchange rate. In other words, the return on a U.K. investment, plus the expected change in the value of U.K. currency, is our expected return on a pound investment. If the forward exchange rate is equal to the expected future spot rate, then the forward premium is also the expected change in the exchange rate. (The next chapter introduces a reason why this might not hold—foreign exchange risk.)

Even though foreign exchange traders quote forward rates based on interest differentials and current spot rates, so that the forward rate will yield a forward premium equal to the interest differential, we may ask: How well does interest rate parity hold in the real world? Since deviations from interest rate parity would seem to present profitable arbitrage opportunities, we would expect profit-seeking arbitragers to eliminate any deviations. Still, careful studies of the data indicate that small deviations from interest rate parity do occur. Do these deviations indicate unexploited profit opportunities for the astute investor? It appears the answer is no. There are several reasons why interest rate parity may not hold exactly, and yet we can earn no arbitrage profits from the situation. The most obvious reason is the cost of transacting in the markets. Because buying and selling foreign exchange and international securities involves a cost for each transaction, there may exist deviations from interest rate parity that are equal to, or smaller than, these transaction costs. In this case, speculators cannot profit from the deviations, since the price of buying and selling in the market would wipe out any apparent gain. Studies indicate that for comparable financial assets that differ only in terms of currency of denomination (like dollar- and pound-denominated deposits in a London bank), 100 percent of the deviations from interest rate parity can be accounted for by transaction costs.

Besides transaction costs, there are other reasons why interest rate parity may not hold perfectly. These include differential taxation, government controls, political risk, and time lags between observing a profit opportunity and actually trading to realize the profit. If taxes differ according to the investor's residence, then the same investment opportunity may yield a different return to residents of different countries. Thus, it may be misleading to simply consider pretax effective returns to decide if profitable arbitrage is possible.

If government controls on financial capital flows exist, then an effective barrier between national markets is in place. If an individual cannot freely buy or sell the currency or securities of a country, then the free market forces that work in response to effective return differentials will not function. Indeed, even the serious threat of controls, or more generally any national emergency impinging on international trade in financial assets could make the political risk of investing in a country prohibitive. Political risk is often mentioned as a reason why interest rate parity does not hold. We should note, however, that the external or Eurocurrency market often serves as a means of avoiding political risk, since an individual can borrow and lend foreign currencies outside the home country of each currency. For instance, the Eurodollar market provides a market for U.S. dollar loans and deposits in major financial centers outside the United States. We will investigate in detail the Eurocurrency markets in Chapter 13.

Interest Rates and Inflation

To better understand the relationship between interest rates and exchange rates, we now consider how inflation can be related to both. To link exchange rates, interest rates, and inflation, we must first understand the role of inflation in interest rate determination. Economists distinguish between real and nominal rates of interest. The *nominal interest rate* is the rate actually observed in the market. The *real rate* is a concept that measures the return after adjusting for inflation. If you loan someone money and charge that person 5 percent interest on the loan, the real return on your loan is negative if the inflation rate exceeds 5 percent. For instance, if the rate of inflation is 10 percent, then the debtor is repaying the loan with dollars that are worth less, so much less that the loan is going to wind up providing you, the creditor, with less purchasing power after you are repaid the principal and interest than you had when you initially made the loan.

This all means that the nominal rate of interest will tend to incorporate inflation expectations in order to provide lenders with a real return for the use of their money. The expected effect of inflation on the nominal interest rate is often called the *Fisher effect* (after Irving Fisher, a pioneer of the determinants of interest rates), and the relationship between inflation and interest rates is given by the *Fisher equation:*

$$i = r + \pi \tag{5.5}$$

Table 5.1 Interest Rates and Inflation Rates for Selected Countries, 2001

Country	Inflation Rate (%)	Interest Rate (%)
Hong Kong	−3.5	0.5
United States	1.6	1.8
Mexico	4.4	2.9
Ivory Coast	4.8	3.5
Turkey	68.5	61.2

Note: The inflation rate is equal to the annual rate of change in the consumer price index. Interest rate is equal to the annual average of bank deposit rates.

where i is the nominal interest rate, r the real rate, and π the expected rate of inflation. Thus, an increase in π will tend to increase i. The fact that interest rates in the 1970s and 1980s were much higher than in the 1960s and 1990s is the result of higher inflation rates in the 1970s and 1980s. Across countries, at a specific time, we should expect interest rates to vary with inflation. Table 5.1 shows that nominal interest rates tend to be higher in countries with higher rates of inflation.

Exchange Rates, Interest Rates, and Inflation

If we combine the Fisher equation (5.5) and the interest parity equation (5.3), we can determine how interest rates, inflation, and exchange rates are all linked. First, consider the Fisher equation for the United States and the United Kingdom:

$$i_\$ = r_\$ + \pi_\$ \qquad\qquad i_£ = r_£ + \pi_£$$

If the real rate of interest is the same internationally, then $r_\$ = r_£$. In this case, the nominal interest rates, $i_\$$ and $i_£$, differ solely by expected inflation, so we can write

$$i_\$ - i_£ = \pi_\$ - \pi_£ \tag{5.6}$$

The interest parity condition of Equation (5.3) indicates that the interest differential is also equal to the forward premium, or

$$i_\$ - i_£ = \pi_\$ - \pi_£ = \frac{F - E}{E} \tag{5.7}$$

Equation (5.7) summarizes the link among interest, inflation, and exchange rates.

In the real world, the interrelationships summarized by Equation (5.7) are determined simultaneously, because interest rates, inflation expectations, and exchange rates are jointly affected by new events and information. For instance, suppose we begin from a situation of equilibrium, where interest parity holds. Suddenly, there is a change in U.S. policy that leads to expectations of a higher U.S. inflation rate. The increase in expected inflation will cause dollar interest rates to rise. At the same time, exchange rates will adjust to maintain interest parity. If the expected future spot rate is changed, we would expect F to carry much of the adjustment burden. If the expected future spot rate is unchanged, the current spot rate would tend to carry the bulk of the adjustment burden. Finally, if central bank intervention is pegging exchange rates at fixed levels by buying and selling to maintain the fixed rate, the domestic and foreign currency interest rates will have to adjust to parity levels. The fundamental point is that the initial U.S. policy change led to changes in inflationary expectations, interest rates, and exchange rates simultaneously, since they all adjust to new equilibrium levels.

Expected Exchange Rates and the Term Structure of Interest Rates

There is no such thing as *the* interest rate for a country. Interest rates within a country vary for different investment opportunities and for different maturity dates on similar investment opportunities. The structure of interest rates existing on investment opportunities over time is known as the *term structure of interest rates.* For instance, in the bond market we observe three-month, six-month, one-year, three-year, and even longer-term bonds. If the interest rates rise with the term to maturity, then we observe a rising term structure. If the interest rates were the same regardless of term, then the term structure would be flat. We describe the term structure of interest rates by describing the slope of a line connecting the various points in time at which we observe interest rates.

There are several competing theories that explain the term structure of interest rates. We will discuss three:

1. *Expectations.* This theory suggests that the long-term interest rate tends to be equal to an average of short-term rates expected over the long-term holding period. In other words, an investor could buy a long-term bond or a series of short-term bonds, so the expected

return from the long-term bond will tend to be equal to the return generated from holding the series of short-term bonds.

2. *Liquidity premium.* Underlying this theory is the idea that long-term bonds incorporate a risk premium since risk-averse investors would prefer to lend short term. The premium on long-term bonds would tend to result in interest rates rising with the holding period of the bond.
3. *Preferred habitat.* This approach contends that the bond markets are segmented by maturities. In other words, there is a separate market for short- and long-term bonds, and the interest rates are determined by supply and demand in each market.

Although we could use these theories to explain the term structure of interest rates in any one currency, in international finance we use the term structures for different currencies to infer expected exchange rate changes. For instance, if we compared Eurodollar and Euroeuro deposit rates for different maturities, like one-month and three-month deposits, the difference between the two term structures should reflect expected exchange rate changes. Of course, if there are capital controls, then the various national markets become isolated and there would not be any particular relationship between international interest rates.

Figure 5.1 plots the Eurocurrency deposit rates at a particular time for 1- to 12-month terms. We know from our previous discussion that when one country has higher interest rates than another, the high-interest-rate currency is expected to depreciate relative to the low-interest-rate currency. Since effective returns will tend to be equal everywhere, the only way an interest rate can be above another one is if the high-interest-rate currency is expected to depreciate; thus, the effective rate, $i + (F - E)/E$ [as shown in Equation (5.4), with the forward rate used as a predictor of the future spot rate], is lower than the observed rate, i, because of the expected depreciation of the currency ($F < E$).

If the distance between two of the term structure lines is the same at each point, then the expected change in the exchange rate is constant. To see this more clearly, let us once again consider the interest parity relation given by Equation (5.3):

$$i_{\$} - i_{£} = \frac{F - E}{E}$$

This expression indicates that the difference between the interest rate in two countries will be equal to the forward premium or discount when the inter-

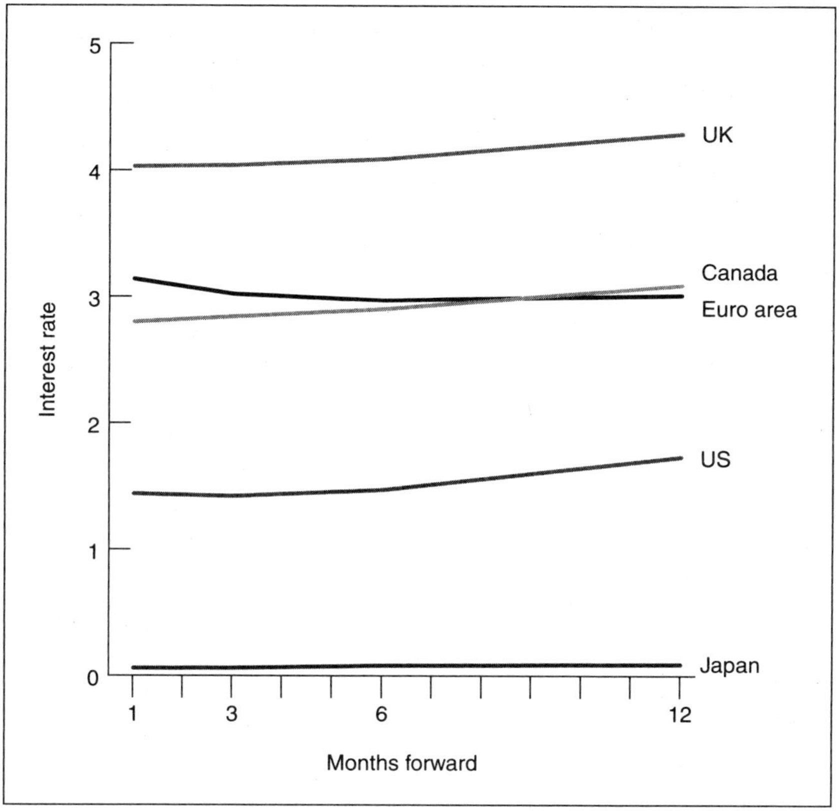

Figure 5.1 Eurocurrency interest rates for December 2, 2002.

est rates and the forward rate reflect the same term to maturity. If the forward rate is considered a market forecast of the future spot rate, which it often is, then we can say that the interest differential is also approximately equal to the expected change in the spot rate. This means that at each point in the term structure, the difference between the national interest rates should reflect the expected change in the exchange rate for the two currencies being compared. By examining the different points in the term structure, we can determine how the exchange rate expectations are changing through time. One implication of this is that even if we did not have a forward exchange market in a currency, the interest differential between that currency and other currencies would allow us to infer expected future exchange rates.

Now we can understand why a constant differential between two interest rates implies that future changes in the exchange rate are expected to occur at some constant rate. Thus, if two of the term structure lines are parallel, then the exchange rate changes are expected to be constant (the currencies will appreciate or depreciate against each other at a constant rate). On the other hand, if two term structure lines are diverging, or moving farther apart from one another, then the high-interest-rate currency is expected to depreciate at an increasing rate over time. For term structure lines that are converging, or moving closer together, the high-interest-rate currency is expected to depreciate at a declining rate relative to the low-interest-rate currency.

To illustrate the exchange rate–term structure relationship, let us look at Figure 5.1. In Figure 5.1 the term structure line for Japan lies below that of the United States. We should then expect the Japanese yen to appreciate against the U.S. dollar and the dollar should sell at a forward discount against the yen. The term structure line for the U.K. lies above that of the United States so we should expect the pound to depreciate in value against the dollar and sell at a forward discount against the dollar. With regard to the slopes of the curves, the term structure line for Japan is almost flat, while the U.S. term structure is rising from 6 to 12 months. The divergence of the U.S. line from the Japanese line suggests that the yen is expected to appreciate against the dollar at a faster rate over time. The fact that the term structure line for Canada is closest to that for the United States, while the line for the U.K. lies farther away from the United States curve, indicates that the Canadian dollar should have a smaller expected change in value against the U.S. dollar than the British pound. Thus, we can see from the figure that the term structure of interest rates roughly reflects expected exchange rate changes, and the forward discount on the pound should be greater than that for the Canadian dollar.

Summary

1. The interest parity relationship indicates that the interest differential between investments in two currencies will equal the forward premium or discount between the currencies.
2. Covered interest arbitrage ensures interest parity.
3. Deviations from interest rate parity could be the result of transaction costs, differential taxation, government controls, or political risk.
4. The real interest rate is equal to the nominal interest rate minus expected inflation.
5. If real interest rates are equal in two countries, then the interest differential on their currencies will equal the inflation differential, which will equal the forward premium or discount.

6. Differences between the term structure of interest rates in two countries will reflect expected exchange rate changes.

Exercises

1. Suppose you want to infer expected future exchange rates in a less-developed country that has free-market-determined interest rates but does not have a forward exchange market. Is there any other way of inferring expected future exchange rates? Under what assumptions?
2. a. Show that there is a direct relationship between the forward premium and the "real" interest rate differential between two currencies.
   b. Under what conditions will the forward premium equal the expected "inflation" differential between two currencies?
3. Give four reasons why, when interest parity does not hold exactly, we are unable to take advantage of arbitrage to earn profits.
4. Suppose the one-year interest rate on British pounds is 11 percent, the dollar interest rate is 6 percent, and the current $/£ spot rate is $1.80.
   a. What do you expect the spot rate to be in one year?
   b. Why can we not observe the expected future spot rate?
5. Expected inflation differentials cause interest rate changes, which in turn bring about exchange rate changes. Is this statement true? Explain very carefully.
6. The British pound is selling in the spot market for $1.76, while in the 180-day forward market it sells for $1.74.
   a. Is the dollar selling at a premium or discount?
   b. What is the forward premium (discount) on the pound at an annual rate?
7. If two countries had identical term structures of interest rates, what is the expected future exchange rate change between the two currencies?

References

"Capital Goes Global," *The Economist,* October 25, 1997.

Choudhry, Bhagwan, and Sheridan Titman, "Why Real Interest Rates, Cost of Capital and Price/Earnings Ratios Vary across Countires," *Journal of International Money and Finance,* April 2001, 165–190.

McKinnon, Ronald I., *Money in International Exchange,* New York: Oxford, 1979.

Pigott, Charles, "International Interest Rate Convergence: A Survey of the Issues and Evidence," *Quarterly Review,* Federal Reserve Bank of New York, Winter 1993–1994.

Solnik, Bruno, "International Parity Conditions and Exchange Risk," *Journal of Banking and Finance,* 2, 1978, 281–293.

Throop, Adrian W., "Linkages of National Interest Rates," *FRBSF Weekly Letter,* September 2, 1994.

APPENDIX: What Are Logarithms, and Why Are They Used in Financial Research?

Although this is not a course in mathematics, there are certain techniques that are so prevalent in modern financial research that not to use them would be a disservice to the student. Logarithms are a prime example. One major reason why financial researchers use logarithms is to make calculations easier.

What Are Logarithms?

Logarithms are a way of transforming numbers to simplify mathematical analysis of a problem. One way to view a logarithm is as the *power* to which some *base* must be raised to give a certain number. For example, we all know that the square of 10 is 100, or $10^2 = 100$. Therefore, if 10 is our base, we know that 10 must be raised to the second power to equal 100. We could then say that the logarithm of 100 to the base 10 is 2. This is written as

$$\log_{10} 100 = 2$$

What then is the $\log_{10}$ of 1000? Of course, $\log_{10} 1000 = 3$, because $10 \times 10 \times 10 = 10^3 = 1000$.

In general, any number greater than 1 could serve as the base by which we could write all positive numbers. Picking any arbitrary number designated as *a*, where *a* is greater than 1, we could write any positive number *b* as

$$\log_a b = c$$

where *c* is the power to which *a* must be raised to equal *b*.

Rather than pick any arbitrary number for our base *a*, there is a particular number that arises naturally in economic phenomena. This number is approximately 2.71828, and it is called *e*. The value of *e* arises in the continuous compounding of interest. Specifically, $e = \lim_{n\to\infty}(1 + 1/n)^n$, where *n* is the number of times interest is compounded per year. The value of some principal amount, *P*, in 1 year, compounded continuously at *r* percent interest, is $V = Pe^r$. If $r = 100$ percent, then the amount of principal and interest after 1 year is $V = Pe$. Since *e* comes *naturally* out of continuous compounding, we refer to *e* as the base of the *natural logarithms*. Financial researchers utilize logarithms to the base *e*. Rather than write the log of some number b as $\log_e b = c$, it is common to express $\log_e$ as ln, so that we write

$$\ln b = c$$

In all uses of logarithms in this text, we assume $\log b$ is actually $\ln b$ or the natural logarithm; it is for convenience that we drop the e subscript and simply write $\log b$ rather than $\log_e b$.

Why Use Logarithms in Financial Research?

If the lesson so far has seemed rather esoteric and unrelated to your interests, here is the payoff. There are three extremely helpful properties of logarithms that are used frequently in international finance:

1. The log of a product of two numbers is equal to the sum of the logs of the individual numbers:

$$\log(MN) = \log M + \log N$$

2. The log of a quotient is equal to the difference of the logs of the individual numbers:

$$\log(M/N) = \log M - \log N$$

3. The log of some number M raised to the N power is equal to N times the log of M:

$$\log(M^N) = N \log M$$

Since many relationships in financial research are products or ratios, by taking the logs of these relationships, we are able to analyze simple, linear, additive relationships rather than more complex phenomena involving products and quotients.

Another useful feature of logarithms is that the change in the logarithm of some variable is commonly used to measure the percentage change in the variable (the measure is precise for compound changes and approximate for simple rates of change). If we want to calculate the percentage change in the \$/£ exchange rate (E) between today (period t) and yesterday (period $t - 1$), we could calculate $(E_t - E_{t-1})/E_{t-1}$. Alternatively, we could calculate $\log E_t - \log E_{t-1}$. This is a very convenient feature of logarithms that will appear in later chapters.

This appendix serves as a brief introduction or review of logarithms. Rather than provide more illustrations of the specific use of logarithms in international finance, at this point it is preferable to study the examples that arise in the context of the problems, as analyzed in subsequent chapters. More general examples of the use of logarithms may be found in the text listed in the references.

References

Chiang, Alpha C., *Fundamental Methods of Mathematical Economics.* New York: McGraw-Hill, 1984.

6

Foreign Exchange Risk and Forecasting

International business involves foreign exchange risk since the value of transactions in different currencies will be sensitive to exchange rate changes. Although it is possible to manage a firm's foreign-currency-denominated assets and liabilities to avoid exposure to exchange rate changes, the benefit involved is not always worth the effort.

The appropriate strategy for the corporate treasurer and the individual speculator will be at least partly determined by expectations of the future path of the exchange rate. As a result, exchange rate forecasts are an important part of the decision-making process of international investors.

In this chapter we first consider the issue of foreign exchange risk, which is the presence of risk that arises from uncertainty regarding the future exchange rate; this uncertainty makes forecasting necessary. If future exchange rates were known with certainty, there would be no foreign exchange risk.

Types of Foreign Exchange Risk

One problem we encounter when trying to evaluate the effect of exchange rate changes on a business firm arises in determining the appropriate concept of exposure to foreign exchange risk.

We can identify three principal concepts of *exchange risk* exposure:

1. *Translation exposure.* This is also known as accounting exposure and is the difference between foreign-currency-denominated assets and foreign-currency-denominated liabilities.
2. *Transaction exposure.* This is exposure resulting from the uncertain domestic currency value of a foreign-currency-denominated transaction to be completed at some future date.
3. *Economic exposure.* This is exposure of the firm's value to changes in exchange rates. If the value of the firm is measured as the present value of future after-tax cash flows, then economic exposure is concerned with the sensitivity of the real domestic currency value of long-term cash flows to exchange rate changes.

Economic exposure is the most important to the firm. Rather than worry about how accountants will report the value of our international operations (translation exposure), it is far more important to the firm (and to rational investors) to focus on the purchasing power of long-run cash flows insofar as these determine the real value of the firm.

Let us consider an example of a hypothetical firm's situation to illustrate the differences among the alternative exposure concepts. Suppose we have the balance sheet of XYZ-France, a foreign subsidiary of the parent U.S. firm XYZ, Inc. The balance sheet in Table 6.1 initially shows the position of XYZ-France in terms of euros. A balance sheet is simply a recording of the firm's assets (listed on the left side) and liabilities (listed on the right side). A balance sheet must balance. In other words, the value of assets must equal the value of liabilities so that the sums of the two columns are equal. Equity is the owners' claims on the firm and is a sort of residual value in that equity will change to keep liabilities equal to assets.

Although the balance sheet at the top of Table 6.1 is stated in terms of euros, the parent company, XYZ, Inc., consolidates the financial statements of all foreign subsidiaries into its own statements. Thus, the euro-denominated balance sheet items must be translated into dollars to be included in the parent company's balance sheet. *Translation* is the process of expressing financial statements measured in one unit of currency in terms of another unit of currency.

Assume that initially the exchange rate equals €1 = \$1. The balance sheet in the middle of Table 6.1 uses this exchange rate to translate the balance sheet items into dollars. Current U.S. accounting standards, introduced in 1981, require all foreign-denominated assets and liabilities to be

Table 6.1 Balance Sheet of XYZ-France, May 31

Cash	€1,000,000	Debt	€5,000,000
Accounts receivable	3,000,000	Equity	6,000,000
Plant & equipment	5,000,000		
Inventory	2,000,000		
	€11,000,000		€11,000,000
	Dollar translation on May 31 $1 = €1		
Cash	$1,000,000	Debt	$5,000,000
Accounts receivable	3,000,000	Equity	6,000,000
Plant & equipment	5,000,000		
Inventory	2,000,000		
	$11,000,000		$11,000,000
	Dollar translation on June 1 $0.90 = €1		
Cash	$ 900,000	Debt	$4,500,000
Accounts receivable	2,700,000	Equity	5,400,000
Plant & equipment	4,500,000		
Inventory	1,800,000		
	$9,900,000		$9,900,000

translated at current exchange rates. In the United States, accounting standards are set by the Financial Accounting Standards Board (FASB). On December 7, 1981, the FASB issued Financial Accounting Standard No. 52, commonly referred to as FAS 52. FAS 52 essentially requires that balance sheet accounts be translated at the exchange rate prevailing at the date of the balance sheet. The issue in translation exposure is the sensitivity of the equity account of the balance sheet to exchange rate changes. The equity account equals assets minus liabilities and measures the accounting or book value of the firm. As the domestic currency value of the foreign-currency-denominated assets and liabilities of the foreign subsidiary changes, the domestic currency book value of the subsidiary will also change.

The top two balance sheets in Table 6.1 give us the euro and dollar position of the firm on May 31. However, suppose there is a devaluation of the euro on June 1 from $1 = €1 to $.90 = €1. The balance sheet in terms of dollars will change as illustrated by the new translation at the bottom of the table. Now the owners' claim on the firm in terms of dollars, or in terms of the book value measured by equity, has fallen from $6 million to $5.4 million. Given the current method of translating exchange rate changes, when the currency used to denominate the foreign subsidiaries' statements is depreciating relative to the dollar, then the owners' equity will fall. We must realize that this drop in equity does not necessarily represent any real loss to the firm or real drop in the value of the firm. The euro position of the firm is unchanged; only the dollar value to the U.S. parent is altered by the exchange rate change.

Since the balance sheet translation of foreign assets and liabilities does not by itself indicate anything about the real economic exposure of the firm, we must look beyond the balance sheet and the translation exposure. Transaction exposure can be viewed as a kind of economic exposure, since the profitability of future transactions is susceptible to exchange rate change, and these changes can have a big effect on future cash flows—as well as on the value of the firm. Suppose XYZ-France has contracted to deliver goods to a Japanese firm and allows 30 days' credit before payment is received. Furthermore, suppose that at the time the contract was made, the exchange rate was 100 yen per euro (¥100 = €1). Suppose also that the contract called for payment in yen of exactly ¥100,000 in 30 days. At the current exchange rate the value of ¥100,000 is €1,000. But if the exchange rate changes in the next 30 days, the value of ¥100,000 would also change. Should the yen depreciate unexpectedly, then in 30 days XYZ-France will receive ¥100,000; however, this will be worth less than €1,000, so that the transaction is not as profitable as originally planned. This is transaction exposure. XYZ has committed itself to this future transaction, thereby exposing itself to exchange risk. Had the contract been written to specify payment in euros, then the transaction exposure to XYZ-France would have been eliminated; the Japanese importer would now have the transaction exposure. Firms can, of course, hedge against future exchange rate uncertainty in the forward-looking markets discussed in Chapter 4. The Japanese firm could buy yen in the forward market to be delivered in 30 days and thus eliminate the transaction exposure.

The example of transaction exposure just analyzed illustrates how exchange rate uncertainty can affect the future profitability of the firm. The possibility that exchange rate changes can affect future profitability, and therefore the current value of the firm, is indicative of economic exposure. Managing foreign exchange risks involves the sorts of operations considered in Chapter 4. There we covered the use of forward markets, swaps, options, futures, and borrowing and lending in international currencies, and so will not review that information here. Note, however, that firms should manage cash flows carefully, with an eye toward expected exchange rate changes, and should not always try to avoid all risks since risk taking can be profitable. Firms practice risk minimization subject to cost constraints and eliminate foreign exchange risk only when the expected benefits from it exceed the costs.

Although forward exchange contracts may be an important part of any corporate hedging strategy, there exist other alternatives that are frequently used. For example, suppose a firm has assets and liabilities denominated both in a weak currency *X*, which is expected to depreciate, and in a strong currency *Y*, which is expected to appreciate. The firm's treasurer would try to minimize the value of accounts receivable denominated in *X*, which could mean tougher credit terms for customers paying in currency *X*. The firm may also delay the payment of any accounts payable denominated in *X*, because it expects to be able to buy *X* for repayment at a cheaper rate in the future. Insofar as is possible, the firm will try to reinforce these practices on payables and receivables by invoicing its sales in currency *Y* and its purchases in *X*. Although institutional constraints may exist on the ability of the firm to specify the invoicing currency, it would certainly be desirable to implement such policies.

We see, then, that corporate hedging strategies involve more than simply minimizing holdings of currency *X* and currency-*X*-denominated bank deposits. Managing cash flows, receivables, and payables will be the daily activity of the financial officers of a multinational firm. In instances when it is not possible for the firm successfully to hedge a foreign currency position internally, there is always the forward or futures market. If the firm has a currency-*Y*-denominated debt and it wishes to avoid the foreign exchange risk associated with the debt, it can always buy *Y* currency in the forward market and thereby eliminate the risk.

In summary, foreign exchange risk may be hedged or eliminated by the following strategies:

1. Trading in forward, futures, or options markets
2. Invoicing in the domestic currency
3. Speeding (slowing) payments of currencies expected to appreciate (depreciate)
4. Speeding (slowing) collection of currencies expected to depreciate (appreciate)

Foreign Exchange Risk Premium

Let us now consider the effects of foreign exchange risk on the determination of forward exchange rates. As mentioned previously, the forward exchange rate may serve as a predictor of future spot exchange rates. We may question whether the forward rate should be equal to the expected future spot rate, or whether there is a *risk premium* incorporated in the forward rate that serves as an insurance premium inducing others to take the risk, in which case the forward rate would differ from the expected future spot rate by this premium. The empirical work in this area has dealt with the issue of whether the forward rate is an unbiased predictor of future spot rates. An *unbiased* predictor is one that is correct on average, so that over the long run the forward rate is just as likely to overpredict the future spot rate as it is to underpredict. The property of unbiasedness does not imply that the forward rate is a good predictor. For example, there is the story of an old lawyer who says, "When I was a young man I lost many cases that I should have won; when I was older I won many that I should have lost. Therefore, on average, justice was done." Is it comforting to know that on average the correct verdict is reached when we are concerned with the verdict in a particular case? Likewise, the forward rate could be unbiased and "on average" correctly predict the spot rate without ever actually predicting the future realized spot rate. All we need for unbiasedness is that the forward rate is just as likely to guess too high as it is to guess too low.

The effective return differential between two countries' assets should be dependent on the perceived risk of each asset and the risk aversion of the investors. Now let us clarify what we mean by *risk* and *risk aversion.* The risk associated with an asset is the contribution of that asset to the overall portfolio risk of the investor. Modern financial theory has commonly associated the riskiness of a portfolio with the variability of the returns from that portfolio. This is reasonable in that investors are concerned with the future value of any investment, and the more variable the return from an investment is, the less certain we can be about its value at any particular future date. Thus, we are concerned with the variability of any individual asset insofar as it contributes to the variability of our portfolio return (our portfolio return is simply the total return from all our investments).

Risk aversion is the real-world phenomenon of preferring less risk to more risk. In terms of investments, two individuals may agree on the degree of risk associated with two assets, but the more risk-averse individual would require a higher interest rate on the riskier asset to induce him or her to hold it than would the less risk-averse individual. Risk aversion implies that people must be paid to take risk—individuals and corporations with bad credit must pay a higher interest rate than those with good credit. The interest differential is required to induce creditors to make loans to the bad credit risks.

It was already stated that the effective return differential between assets of two countries is a function of risk and risk aversion. The effective return differential between a U.S. security and a security in the United Kingdom is

$$i_{\mathrm{US}} - \frac{E^*_{t+1} - E_t}{E_t} - i_{\mathrm{UK}} = f\,(\text{risk aversion, risk})\cdot \tag{6.1}$$

The left-hand side of the equation is the effective return differential measured as the difference between the domestic U.S. return, i_{US}, and the foreign asset return, $[E^*_{t+1} - E_t)/E_t] + i_{\mathrm{UK}}$. We must remember that the effective return on the foreign asset is equal to the interest rate in terms of foreign currency plus the expected change in the exchange rate, where E^*_{t+1} is the expected dollar currency price of pounds next period. The right-hand side of Equation (6.1) indicates that the return differential is a function of risk aversion and risk. In this case, to say that the return differential is a function of risk and risk aversion means that changes in risk and risk aversion will cause changes in the return differential.

We can view the effective return differential shown in Equation (6.1) as a risk premium. Let us begin with the approximate interest parity relation:

$$i_{\mathrm{US}} - i_{\mathrm{UK}} = \frac{F - E_t}{E_t} \tag{6.2}$$

To convert the left-hand side to an effective return differential, we must subtract the expected change in the exchange rate (but since this is an equation, whatever is done to the left-hand side must also be done to the right-hand side):

$$i_{\mathrm{US}} - \frac{E^*_{t+1} - E_t}{E_t} - i_{\mathrm{UK}} = \frac{F - E_t}{E_t} - \frac{E^*_{t+1} - E_t}{E_t} \tag{6.3}$$

or

$$i_{\mathrm{US}} - \frac{E^*_{t+1} - E_t}{E_t} - i_{\mathrm{UK}} = \frac{F - E^*_{t+1}}{E_t}$$

Thus, we find that the effective return differential is equal to the percentage difference between the forward and expected future spot exchange rate. The right-hand side of Equation (6.3) may be considered a measure of the risk premium in the forward exchange market. Therefore, if the effective return differential is zero, then there would appear to be no risk premium. If the effective return differential is positive, then there is a positive risk premium on the domestic currency, since the expected future spot price of pounds is less than the prevailing forward rate. In other words, traders offering to sell pounds for dollars in the future will receive a premium, in that pounds are expected to depreciate (relative to dollars) by an amount greater than the current forward rate. Conversely, traders wishing to buy pounds for delivery next period will pay a premium to the future sellers to ensure a set future price.

For example, suppose $E_t = \$2.10$, $E^*_{t+1} = \$2.00$, and $F = \$2.05$. The foreign exchange risk premium is

$$\frac{F - E^*_{t+1}}{E_t} = \frac{\$2.05 - \$2.00}{\$2.10} = 0.024$$

The expected change in the exchange rate is equal to

$$\frac{E^*_{t+1} - E_t}{E_t} = \frac{\$2.00 - \$2.10}{\$2.10} = -0.048$$

The forward discount on the pound is

$$\frac{F - E_t}{E_t} = \frac{\$2.05 - \$2.10}{\$2.10} = -0.024$$

Thus, the dollar is expected to appreciate against the pound by approximately 4.8 percent, but the forward premium indicates an appreciation of only 2.4 percent if we use the forward rate as a predictor of the future spot rate. The discrepancy results from the presence of a risk premium that makes the forward rate a biased predictor of the future spot rate. Specifically, the forward rate overpredicts the future dollar price of pounds in order to allow the risk premium.

Given the positive risk premium on the dollar, the expected effective return from holding a U.K. bond will be less than the domestic return to U.S. residents holding U.S. bonds. This nonzero effective return differential can be an equilibrium result consistent with rational investor behavior.

To continue the previous example, let us suppose that the U.K. interest rate is 0.124, whereas the U.S. rate is 0.100. Then the interest differential is

$$i_{US} - i_{UK} = -0.024$$

The expected return from holding a U.K. bond is

$$i_{\mathrm{UK}} + \frac{E^*_{t+1} - E_t}{E_t} = 0.124 - 0.048 = 0.076$$

The return from the U.S. bond is 0.10, which exceeds the expected effective return on the foreign bond; yet this can be an equilibrium solution given the risk premium. Investors are willing to hold U.K. investments yielding a lower expected return than comparable U.S. investments because there is a positive risk premium on the dollar. Thus, the higher dollar return is necessary to induce investors to hold the riskier dollar-denominated investments.

Market Efficiency

A market is said to be *efficient* if prices reflect all available information. In the foreign exchange market this means that spot and forward exchange rates will quickly adjust to any new information. For instance, an unexpected change in U.S. economic policy that informed observers feel will be inflationary (like an unexpected increase in money supply growth) will lead to an immediate depreciation of the dollar. If markets were inefficient, then prices would not adjust quickly to the new information, and it would be possible for a well-informed investor to make profits consistently from foreign exchange trading that would otherwise be excessive relative to the risk undertaken.

With efficient markets, the forward rate would differ from the expected future spot rate only by a risk premium. If this were not the case, and the forward rate exceeded the expected future spot rate plus a risk premium, an investor could realize certain profits by selling forward currency now, because she or he would be able to buy the currency at a lower price in the future than the forward rate at which the currency will be sold. Although profits can most certainly be earned from foreign exchange speculation in the real world, it is also true that there are no sure profits. The real world is characterized by uncertainty regarding the future spot rate, since the future cannot be foreseen. Yet forward exchange rates adjust to the changing economic picture according to revisions of what the future spot rate is likely to be (as well as to changes in the risk attached to the currencies involved). It is this ongoing process of price adjustments in response to new information in the efficient market that rules out any certain profits from speculation. Of course, the fact that the future will bring unexpected events ensures that profits and losses will result from foreign exchange speculation. If an astute investor possessed an ability to forecast exchange rates better than the rest of the market, the profits resulting would be enormous. Foreign exchange forecasting will be discussed in the next section.

Many studies have tested the efficiency of the foreign exchange market. The fact that they have often reached different conclusions regarding the efficiency of the market emphasizes the difficulty involved in using statistics in the social sciences. Such studies have usually investigated whether the forward rate contains all the relevant information regarding the expected future spot rate. They test whether the forward rate alone predicts the future spot rate well or whether additional data will aid in the prediction. If further information adds nothing beyond that already embodied in the forward rate, the market is said to be efficient. On the other hand, if some data are found that would permit a speculator consistently to predict the future spot rate better than can be done using the forward rate (including a risk premium), then this speculator would earn a consistent profit from foreign exchange speculation, and one could conclude that the market is not efficient.

It must be recognized that such tests have their weaknesses. Although a statistical analysis must make use of past data, speculators must actually predict the future. The fact that a researcher could find a forecasting rule that would beat the forward rate in predicting past spot rates is not particularly useful for current speculation and does not rule out market efficiency. The key point is that such a rule was not known during the time the data were actually being generated. So, if a researcher in 2004 claims to have found a way to predict the spot rates observed in 2002 better than the 2002 forward rates, this does not mean that the foreign exchange market in 2002 was necessarily inefficient. Speculators in 2002 did not have the forecasting rule developed in 2004, and thus could not have used such information to outguess the 2002 forward rates consistently.

Foreign Exchange Forecasting

Since future exchange rates are uncertain, participants in international financial markets can never know for sure what the spot rate will be one month or one year ahead. As a result, forecasts must be made. If we could forecast more accurately than the rest of the market, the potential profits would be enormous. An immediate question is: What makes a good forecast? In other words, how should we judge a forecast of the future spot rate?

We can certainly raise objections to rating forecasts on the basis of simple forecast errors. Even though, other things being equal, we should prefer a smaller forecast error to a larger one, in practice other things are not equal. To be successful, a forecast should be on the correct side of the forward rate. For instance, consider the following example:

Current spot rate: ¥120 = $1
Current 12-month forward rate: ¥115 = $1
Mr. A forecasts: ¥106 = $1
Ms. B forecasts: ¥116 = $1
Future spot rate realized in 12 months: ¥113 = $1

A Japanese firm has a $1 million receipt due in 12 months and uses the forecasts to help decide whether to cover the dollar receivable with a forward contract or wait and sell the dollars in the spot market in 12 months. In terms of forecast errors, Mr. A's prediction of ¥106 = $1 yields an error of 6.2 percent against a realized future spot rate of ¥113. Ms. B's prediction of ¥116 = $1 is much closer to the realized spot rate, with an error of only 2.6 percent. While Ms. B's forecast is closer to the rate eventually realized, this is not the important feature of a good forecast. Ms. B forecasts a future spot rate in excess of the forward rate, so if it followed her prediction, the Japanese firm would wait and sell the dollars in the spot market in 12 months (or would take a *long position* in dollars). Unfortunately, since the future spot rate ¥113 = $1 is less than the current forward rate at which the dollars could be sold (¥115 = $1), the firm would receive ¥113 million rather than ¥115 million for the $1 million.

Following Mr. A's forecast of a future spot rate below the forward rate, the Japanese firm would sell dollars in the forward market (or take a *short position* in dollars). The firm would then sell dollars at the current forward rate of ¥115 per dollar rather than wait and receive only ¥113 per dollar in the spot market in the future. The forward contract yields ¥2 million more than the uncovered position. The important lesson is that a forecast should be on the correct side of the forward rate; otherwise, a small forecasting error is not useful. Corporate treasurers or individual speculators want a forecast that will give them the direction the future spot rate will take relative to the forward rate.

If the foreign exchange market is efficient so that prices reflect all available information, then we may wonder why anyone would pay for forecasts. There is some evidence that advisory services have been able to "beat the forward rate" at certain times. If such services could consistently offer forecasts that are better than the forward rate, what can we conclude about market efficiency? Evidence that some advisory services can consistently beat the forward rate is not necessarily evidence of a lack of market efficiency. If the difference between the forward rate and the forecast represents transaction costs, then there is no abnormal return from using the forecast. Moreover, if the difference is the result of a risk premium, then any returns earned from the forecasts would be a normal compensation for risk bearing. Finally, we must realize that the services are rarely free. Although the economics departments of larger banks sometimes provide free forecasts to corporate customers, professional advisory services charge anywhere from several hundred to many thousands of dollars per year for advice. If the potential profits from speculation are reflected in the price of the service, then once again we cannot earn abnormal profits from the forecasts.

Exchange rate forecasters typically use two types of models: technical or fundamental. A *fundamental model* forecasts exchange rates based on variables that are believed to be important determinants of exchange rates. As we shall learn later in the text, fundamentals-based models of exchange rates view as important things like government monetary and fiscal policy, international trade flows, and political uncertainty. An expected change in some fundamental variable leads to a current change in the forecast. A *technical trading model* uses the past history of exchange rates to predict future movements. Technical traders are sometimes called *chartists* because they use charts or diagrams depicting the time path of an exchange rate to infer changing trends. Finance scholars typically have taken a dim view of technical analysis, since the ability to predict future price movements by looking only at the past would bring the concept of efficient markets into question. However, recent research has led to a more supportive view of technical analysis by some scholars and the method is widely popular among foreign exchange market participants. Surveys indicate that nearly 90 percent of foreign exchange dealers use some sort of technical analysis to form their expectations of exchange rates. However, the same surveys suggest that technical models are seen as particularly useful for short-term forecasting, while fundamentals are seen as more important for predicting long-run changes.

Although the returns to a superior forecaster would be considerable, there is no evidence to suggest that abnormally large profits have been produced by following the advice of professional advisory services. But then if you ever developed a method that consistently outperformed other speculators, would you tell anyone else?

Summary

1. Foreign exchange risk may be analyzed as translation exposure, transaction exposure, or economic exposure to exchange rate change.
2. Exchange risk hedges are accomplished by using the forward, futures, or options market; invoicing in domestic currency; speeding (slowing) payments of currencies expected to appreciate (depreciate); and speeding (slowing) collection of currencies expected to depreciate (appreciate).
3. The foreign exchange risk premium is equal to the difference between the forward rate and the expected future spot rate.
4. In an efficient market, prices reflect all available information.
5. A good spot rate forecast should be on the correct side of the forward rate.

Exercises

1. Distinguish among translation exposure, transaction exposure, and economic exposure. Define each concept and then indicate how they may be interrelated.
2. The six-month interest rate in the United States is 10 percent; in Mexico it is 12 percent. The current spot rate (dollars per peso) is $0.40.
   a. What do you expect the six-month forward rate to be?
   b. Is the peso selling at a premium or discount?
   c. If the expected spot rate in six months is $0.38, what is the risk premium?
3. We discussed risk aversion as being descriptive of investor behavior. Can you think of any real-world behavior that you might consider to be evidence of the existence of risk preferrers?
4. Does an efficient market rule out all opportunities for speculative profits? If so, why? If not, why not?
5. You are the treasurer of a U.S. firm that has a €1 million commitment due to a German firm in 90 days. The current spot rate is $1.00 per euro. Ali forecasts that the spot rate in 90 days will be $1.01. Jahangir forecasts that the spot rate will be $1.12 in 90 days. The 90-day forward rate is $1.11 and the actual spot rate in 90 days turns out to be $1.10. Who had the best forecast and why?
6. It was reported in the *Financial Times* that "Toyota suffers a ¥20 billion drop in operating profits for every ¥1 rise (in the exchange rate, yen per dollar) against the dollar." Does this statement have implications for transaction, translation, or economic exposure primarily?

References

Bekaert, Geert, and Robert J. Hodrick, "On Biases in the Measurement of Foreign Exchange Risk Premiums," *Journal of International Money and Finance,* April 1993.

Boothe, Paul, and David Longworth, "Foreign Exchange Market Efficiency Tests: Implications of Recent Empirical Findings," *Journal of International Money and Finance,* June 1986.

Elliott, Graham, and Takatoshi Ito, "Heterogeneous Expectations and Tests of Efficiency in the Yen/Dollar Forward Exchange Market," *Journal of Monetary Economics,* 1999.

Engel, Charles, "The Forward Discount Anomaly and the Risk Premium: A Survey of Recent Evidence," *Journal of Empirical Finance,* September 1996.

Lui, Yu-Hon, and David Mole, "The Use of Fundamental and Technical Analysis by Foreign Exchange Dealers: Hong Kong Evidence," *Journal of International Money and Finance,* June 1998.

Wang, Peijie, and Trefor Jones, "Testing for Efficiency and Rationality in Foreign Exchange Markets," *Journal of International Money and Finance,* April 2002.

7

International Investment and Capital Flows

In the early 1960s international investment was thought to be motivated by interest differentials among countries. If the interest rate in one country exceeded that of another, then financial capital was expected to flow between the countries until the rates were equal. Modern capital market theory provided a new basis for analysis. There were obvious problems with the old theory, since interest differentials can explain one-way flows of capital, from the low- to the high-interest-rate country; yet, realistically, capital flows both ways between most pairs of countries.

In this chapter we apply some basic ideas of modern finance to understand and analyze the incentives for international investment.

Portfolio Diversification

No doubt the differences in the returns on various countries' assets provide an incentive for capital flows. However, we would not expect interest rates to be equalized throughout the world, since risk differs from one asset to another. Furthermore, we would anticipate a certain random component in international capital flows because money flows to new investment opportunities as they open up in various countries. Given the short time needed to shift funds around the world, the expected profit (adjusted for risk differences) from investing in different assets should be equal. If this were not the case, then money would flow internationally until it was true.

Yet even with constant interest rates internationally, there would still be an incentive for international capital flows. This additional incentive is provided by the desire to hold diversified portfolios. It is this diversification motive that leads to the two-way flows of capital between countries. Besides the return on an investment, investors are concerned with the risk attached to the investment. It is very unlikely that an individual who has \$100,000 to invest will invest the entire amount in one asset. By choosing several investment alternatives and holding a *diversified portfolio,* the investor can reduce the risk associated with his or her investments. Modern financial literature has emphasized the concept of variability of return as a measure of risk. This is reasonable in that investors are interested in the future value of their portfolios, and the more variable the value of the portfolios, the less certain they can be of the future value.

By diversifying and selecting different assets (including assets of different countries) for a portfolio, we can reduce the variability of the portfolio. To see the effects of diversification, let us consider a simple example of an investor facing a world with two investment opportunities: asset A and asset B. The investor will hold a portfolio of A and B, with the share of the portfolio devoted to A denoted by a and the share devoted to B denoted by b. Thus, if the investor holds only A, then $a = 1$ and $b = 0$. If only B is held, then $a = 0$ and $b = 1$. Most likely the investor will choose some amount of diversification by holding both A and B.

The return on the portfolio (R_p) can be written as a weighted average of the returns on the individual assets (R_{A} and R_{B}):

$$R_p = aR_{\mathrm{A}} + bR_{\mathrm{B}} \tag{7.1}$$

The expected future return on the portfolio will then be determined by the expected future return on the individual assets:

$$R_p^* = aR_{\mathrm{A}} + bR_{\mathrm{B}}^* \tag{7.2}$$

where R_p^*, R_{A}^*, and R_{B}^* are the expected values of the portfolio and individual asset returns, respectively. We said earlier that the idea of portfolio risk was associated with the variability of the return on the portfolio. The measure of the degree to which a variable deviates from its mean or average value is known as the *variance.* The variance of the portfolio will depend on the share of the portfolio held by each asset and the variance of the individual assets, as well as their covariance. Specifically,

$$\mathrm{var}(R_p) = a^2\,\mathrm{var}(R_{\mathrm{A}}) + b^2\,\mathrm{var}(R_{\mathrm{B}}) + 2ab\,\mathrm{cov}(R_{\mathrm{A}}, R_{\mathrm{B}}) \tag{7.3}$$

where *var* stands for variance and *cov* stands for covariance. The *covariance* is a measure of the degree to which the two assets move together. If, when one return is higher than average, the return on the other asset is lower than average, the covariance is negative. Looking at Equation (7.3), we see that a negative covariance could contribute greatly to reducing the overall portfolio variance and, therefore, risk.

To see the effects of diversification more clearly, let us use a simple example:

Probability	R_A (%)	R_B (%)
.25	−2	16
.25	9	9
.25	19	−4
.25	14	11

Note: $R_A{}^* = 10\%$; $R_B{}^* = 8\%$; $\text{var}(R_A) = 0.00605$; $\text{var}(R_B) = 0.00545$; $\text{cov}(R_A, R_B) = -0.004825$.

This table is a hypothetical assessment of the investment opportunity that is available. If we hold only asset A, our expected return is 10 percent, with a variance of 0.00605. If we hold only asset B, our expected return is 8 percent with a variance of 0.00545. By holding 50 percent of our portfolio in A and 50 percent in B, our expected return is $R_p = 0.5(10 \text{ percent}) + 0.5(8 \text{ percent}) = 9$ percent with a variance [using Equation (7.3)] of

$$\begin{aligned} \text{var}(R_p) &= .25(0.00605) + .25(0.00545) + 2(.25)(-0.004825) \\ &= 0.0004625 \end{aligned}$$

We need not be concerned with the statistical theory underlying the example. The important result for our use is the large reduction in variability of return achieved by diversification. By investing half of our wealth in A and half in B, we expect to receive a return on our portfolio that is halfway between what we would expect from just holding A or B alone. However, the variance of our return is much less than half the variance of either R_A or R_B. The substantially lower risk achieved by diversification will lead investors to hold many different assets, including assets from different countries.

As the size of the investor's portfolio grows, the investor will want to buy more assets in the proportions that are already held in order to maintain the desired degree of diversification. This means that as wealth increases, we could anticipate international capital flows between countries, as investors maintain these optimal portfolios. Thus, even with constant international interest rates, we should expect to observe two-way flows of capital as international wealth increases.

We should recognize that diversification will not eliminate all risk to the investor, since there will still exist *systematic risk*—the risk present in all investment opportunities. For instance, in the domestic context we know that different industries have different time patterns of performance. While one industry is enjoying increasing sales and profits, another industry might be languishing in the doldrums. Then, at some later period, the reverse might be true, and the once-thriving industry is now the stagnant one. This is similar to the example of opportunities A and B previously presented. The negative covariance between them indicates that when one is enjoying better-than-average times, the other is suffering, and vice versa. Yet there is still a positive portfolio variance, even when we diversify and hold both assets. The variance that can be eliminated through diversification is called *nonsystematic risk;* this is the risk that is unique to a particular firm or industry. Systematic risk is common to all firms and remains even in diversified portfolios. Systematic risk results from events that are experienced jointly by all firms, like the overall business cycle of recurrent periods of prosperity and recession that occur at the national level.

By extending our investment alternatives internationally, we can gain by international diversification. There appears to be nonsystematic risk at the national level that can be reduced with international portfolio diversification. Moreover, business cycles do not happen uniformly across countries, so when one country is experiencing rapid growth, another may be in a recession. By investing across countries, we eliminate part of the cyclical fluctuation in our portfolio that would arise from the domestic business cycle. Therefore, some of what would be considered systematic risk, in terms of strictly domestic investment opportunities, becomes nonsystematic risk when we broaden our opportunities to include foreign as well as domestic investment. Thus, we can say that not only will investors tend to diversify their portfolio holdings across industries, but they can also realize additional gains by diversifying across countries.

One might wonder whether the gains from international diversification could be realized by investing in domestic multinational firms. If we consider a multinational firm—a firm doing business in many countries—to be affected significantly by foreign factors, then we may view multinational stock as similar to an international portfolio. Since multinational firms have operations in many countries, we may hypothesize that multinational stock prices behave more like an internationally diversified portfolio than like just another domestic stock. The evidence indicates that domestic multinational firms are poor substitutes for international diversification. While the variability of returns from a portfolio of U.S. multinational stock tends to be somewhat lower than the variability of a portfolio of purely domestic-oriented stocks, a portfolio invested across different national stock markets can reduce portfolio return variance by substantially more.

Home Bias in International Investment

Many studies have demonstrated the gain from international diversification. However, recent research has indicated that investors seem to greatly favor domestic assets and invest much less in foreign assets than one would expect given the expected gains from diversification. Linda Tesar and Ingrid Werner examined the foreign investment positions of major industrial countries and found that international investment as a fraction of the total domestic market for stocks and bonds equaled about 3 percent for the United States, 4 percent for Canada, 10 percent for Germany, 11 percent for Japan, and 32 percent for the United Kingdom. Calculations of an "optimal" investment portfolio would have much higher fractions devoted to international assets.

Why do investors seem to have this bias in favor of securities of their home country? There are several possible reasons: taxes, transaction costs, or something else that is missing from the standard model of international investment. Let's consider the alternatives in turn:

1. *Taxes.* If home bias is due to taxes, then the tax on foreign securities would have to be high enough to offset the higher return (or lower risk) expected from these securities. However, taxes paid to foreign governments can usually be credited against domestic taxes. Even if there is some net increase in the tax paid on foreign investment, it is unlikely that this increase could be high enough to discourage foreign investment to the extent observed.

2. *Transaction costs.* The cost associated with buying and selling foreign securities includes explicit monetary costs, like fees, commissions, and bid-ask spreads, and implicit costs such as differences in regulations protecting investors, language differences, and costs of obtaining information about foreign investment opportunities. Familiarity with domestic assets and lower explicit costs of trading at home may lead to home bias.

3. *What else?* One possibility is that the gains from international diversification have been overstated. If countries tend to specialize in the production of certain goods and services and trade with the rest of the world for other goods and services, it is possible to imagine a situation where incomes fluctuate less than one might think based on fluctuations in domestic production. As output fluctuates for certain industries, relative prices change and this relative price change helps to smooth out income fluctuations. For instance, if the Philippines specializes in pineapple production and bad weather reduces the harvest, pineapple prices rise due to the reduction in supply. This price increase helps to cushion the fall in income related to the poor harvest. In this manner, relative price changes may serve as a natural hedge against output fluctuations, so that there is less income variability to be reduced through diversification.

The puzzle of home bias has not been answered adequately. It may be that there is no answer that can be related easily to financial models of investment. The surprisingly low level of international securities in investment portfolios may reflect investors' decisions to hold undiversified portfolios, both internationally as well as domestically. Further research is needed to understand these issues better.

Although the investor risk considered so far has focused on the variability of portfolio return, it should be realized that in international investment there is always the potential for political risk, which may involve the confiscation of foreigners' assets. Chapter 13 explicitly considers the analysis of such risk and includes a recent ranking of countries in terms of the perceived political risk attached to investments made in that country.

International Investment Opportunities

As with domestic markets, there are international investment opportunities in stocks, bonds, and mutual funds. The United States is the largest market, with financial investment opportunities well in excess of the next-largest market, Japan. The differences in size of the various national markets can (and does at times) prove problematic for investors seeking to trade quickly in the smaller markets.

A good example of the problems that can arise in turbulent times is provided by the stock market collapse of October 1987. In mid-October, prices collapsed dramatically in all stock markets around the world. The price fall brought huge orders to sell stocks as investors liquidated their positions and mutual funds raised cash to pay off customers' redemption requests. Stock exchanges in the United States are relatively *deep*—meaning that there are enough potential buyers and sellers and a large number of securities traded so that the market permits trading at all times. Other markets are relatively *thin*—with a much smaller number of potential buyers and sellers and a smaller volume of securities traded.

During the stock market collapse in 1987, the New York Stock Exchange was able to trade 600 million shares, while markets in Hong Kong, Singapore, Italy, Spain, France, and Germany weren't nearly as liquid. In fact, at the peak of the trading frenzy, the Hong Kong market closed for a week. Can you imagine the frustration of a U.S. portfolio manager wanting to sell shares in Hong Kong while trading has stopped?

It is not always necessary to transfer funds abroad to buy foreign securities. Many foreign stocks are traded in the United States in the form of *American depositary receipts,* or *ADRs.* ADRs are negotiable instruments certifying that shares of a foreign stock are being held by a foreign custodian. ADRs have become increasingly popular because they offer an easy way for U.S. investors to diversify internationally and allow non-U.S. firms access to raising money in the United States. Even though these stocks are bought and sold on the U.S. market, they are still subject to foreign exchange risk because the dollar price of the ADR shares reflects the dollar value of the foreign currency price of the stock in the foreign country of origin. Furthermore, foreign government policy will have an impact on the value of ADRs. For instance, in April 1987, the British government imposed a 5 percent tax on conversion of British stocks into ADRs. Trading in these ADRs dropped dramatically until the British government reduced the tax.

Firms that list their stocks as ADRs have some choice as to what type of listing they desire. The available types of ADR programs include the following:

Level I ADR

- No requirement to file financial statements that conform to U.S. accounting standards.
- Traded in the so-called over the counter (OTC) market and are not traded on an exchange like NASDAQ or the New York Stock Exchange.
- Created from existing shares in foreign market; no new capital can be raised.

Level II ADR

- Must file financial statements conforming to U.S. accounting standards.
- Traded on organized exchanges like NASDAQ or the New York Stock Exchange.
- Created from existing shares in foreign market; no new capital can be raised.

Level III ADR

- Must file financial statements conforming to U.S. accounting standards.
- Traded on organized exchanges like NASDAQ or the New York Stock Exchange.
- New issues of stock in order to raise new capital for firm.

Rule 144A ADR

- No requirement to file financial statements conforming to U.S. accounting standards.
- Not traded on OTC or exchanges; strictly for private trades among qualified institutional buyers.
- New issues of stock in order to raise new capital for firm.

In addition to ADRs, there are also *global depositary receipts,* or *GDRs,* which are traded in more than one market location. For instance, a firm may have a GDR that is traded in the United States, London, and Tokyo.

Why do non-U.S. firms list their shares in the United States? The U.S. listing provides the following benefits: an enlarged investor base, the ability to raise new capital in the world's largest financial market, and lower transaction costs than in the home market. In addition, a firm generally finds that the price of its home market shares rises with a U.S. listing. This is likely due to the greater liquidity of trade in the firm's stock, meaning that there are more counterparties with which to trade and the ease of buying or selling at a good price is enhanced. In addition, a firm that is located in a country with weak accounting standards sends a signal to investors of its quality when it lists in the United States and files financial statements conforming to U.S. accounting standards. In addition, non-U.S. firms may list on a U.S. exchange to use the ADR as a means to take over a U.S. firm.

For instance, when Daimler Benz bought Chrysler Corporation, Daimler exchanged ADRs for shares of Chrysler stock.

The Globalization of Equity Markets

If we go back to just a couple of decades ago, many countries had equity (stock) markets that were segmented. A *segmented market* is one in which foreign investors are not allowed to buy domestic stocks and domestic investors are not allowed to buy foreign stocks. Part of the process of the globalization of world economies is the liberalization of stock market restrictions to open markets to the world. Table 7.1 provides dates of first stock market liberalizations for several countries. What happens when a country moves from a segmented market, cut off from foreign investors and foreign markets, to a globalized market in which the domestic restrictions are lifted, the domestic stock market is now freely open to the world, and domestic investors can hold stocks of both domestic and foreign firms?

Table 7.1 Date of First Stock Market Liberalization

Argentina	November 1989
Brazil	March 1988
Chile	May 1987
Colombia	December 1991
Greece	December 1987
India	June 1986
Indonesia	September 1989
Jordan	December 1995
South Korea	June 1987
Malaysia	May 1987
Mexico	May 1989
Nigeria	August 1995
Pakistan	February 1991
Philippines	May 1986
Portugal	July 1986
Taiwan	May 1986
Thailand	January 1988
Turkey	August 1989
Venezuela	January 1990
Zimbabwe	June 1993

Source: Peter Blair Henry, "Stock Market Liberalization, Economic Reform, and Emerging Market Equity Prices," *Journal of Finance,* 55, 529–564, April 2000; and Geert Beckaert and Campbell R. Harvey, "Foreign Speculators and Emerging Equity Markets," *Journal of Finance,* 55, 565–614, April 2000.

To answer this question, we shall assume that risk is represented by the variance of the return on a portfolio of assets as discussed earlier in the chapter. Now, we can think about a risk premium that must be paid to compensate investors for taking risk. Let us denote the return on the risk-free asset (like a U.S. government security) as R_f. Then we can consider the risk premium on small country C's assets as being equal to the return on C's assets minus the risk-free rate of return, or: Risk Premium $= R_C - R_f$. The size of this risk premium should depend upon the variance of the return on the market portfolio and the price of risk.

In a segmented market, the variance of returns is just the variance of the domestic market return, so the risk premium before globalization is:

$$\text{Risk Premium in segmented market} = P\text{var}(R_C) \tag{7.4}$$

where P is the price of risk. So, the risk premium required on domestic stocks in segmented financial market C will just depend upon the variance of stock prices in country C multiplied by the price of risk P. P is determined by the risk aversion of investors. If all investors are the same everywhere, then P is a constant across countries. In a world of segmented markets, a country with a variance of returns twice as high as another country would have twice the risk premium on its stocks. This risk premium is what investors require in order to willingly hold shares of the stocks.

In the globalized equity market we can think of the portfolio return volatility for the residents of small country C as the variance of a portfolio comprised of the stocks of country C and the stocks of the rest of the world. Using the formula for portfolio variance introduced earlier in the chapter, this would be:

$$\text{var}(R_p) = w^2\,\text{var}(R_W) + c^2\,\text{var}(R_C) + 2wc\,\text{cov}(R_W, R_C) \tag{7.5}$$

where w and c are the fraction of the portfolio devoted to stocks from the rest-of-the-world and the small country, respectively; R_W and R_C are the returns on the stocks of the rest-of-the world and small country C, respectively. Equation (7.5) shows that the variance of the portfolio is determined by the amount invested in each area, the variance of returns on the stocks of the two areas, and the covariance between the returns on the two kinds of stocks.

If country C is a segmented market, then the portfolio return variance would just be equal to the variance of the return on country C stocks as in Equation (7.4) as w would equal zero and c would equal one. Now, think what would happen if the government of country C would open up or liberalize its financial markets and become globalized. The risk premium on C's stock should depend upon the contribution of C's stock to the variance of the world portfolio, which is given by the covariance of the return on stock in country C with the returns in the rest-of-the-world, or

$$\text{Risk Premium in globalized market} = P\text{cov}(R_W, R_C) \qquad (7.6)$$

Should we expect the risk premium on country C stock to rise or fall with globalization? To answer that question, compare Equations (7.4) and (7.6). For globalization to reduce the risk premium on country C, we need var(R_C) > cov(R_W, R_C). This can be converted into a more useful statement if we know that the square root of the variance is known as the *standard deviation.* So $SD(R_C) = \sqrt{\text{var}(R_C)}$. The standard deviation is just another measure of how a variable deviates from its mean or average value. What is useful for our purposes is that the covariance is equal to the *correlation coefficient* between two variables multiplied by the product of their standard deviations, or cov(R_W, R_C) = $\rho SD(R_W)SD(R_C)$ where ρ is the correlation coefficient. The correlation coefficient is a number between 1 and −1 that indicates how these two variables change together. If $\rho = 1$, then the two variables are perfectly correlated and move together about their respective means. If $\rho = -1$, then the two variables are perfectly negatively correlated and move exactly opposite to each other so that when one is above its mean value, the other is below its mean value. If $\rho = 0$, then the two variables are independent and have no relationship.

Now we can find the conditions under which globalizing a financial market will reduce the risk premium on a country's stock. Comparing Equations (7.4) and (7.6) again, we need var(R_C) > cov(R_W, R_C), which may be written as:

$$\text{var}(R_C) > \rho SD(R_W)SD(R_C) \qquad (7.7)$$

If we divide both sides of this inequality by $SD(R_W)SD(R_C)$†, we have:

$$\frac{SD(R_C)}{SD(R_W)} > \rho \qquad (7.8)$$

†Note that var(R_C) = $(SD(R_C))^2$ so that var(R_C)/($SD(R_W)SD(R_C)$) = $SD(R_C)/SD(R_W)$.

So the risk premium on country C stock will fall with globalization if the ratio of the standard deviation of the stock returns in C to the stock returns in the rest-of-the-world is greater than the correlation coefficient between the two. Since standard deviations are always positive, if the correlation coefficient is negative, then this must always be true. In this case, country C stock prices would tend to rise when the rest-of-the-world stock prices tend to fall, and the risk premium on C's stock will always fall with globalization. In general, we need a relatively small ρ and a large $SD(R_C)$ relative to $SD(R_W)$. This is, in fact, what one usually observes in the world. Small countries with segmented stock markets typically have relatively small correlations of their stock prices with the rest-of-the-world. In addition, the volatility of their stock prices tends to be high relative to rest-of-the-world volatility. So, in general, we expect that when a government liberalizes its financial markets to become globalized, or integrated with the rest of the world, the risk premium on its stock falls.

This, then, points out a major benefit of globalized financial markets: a lower risk premium on domestic financial assets allows domestic firms to lower their *cost of capital*. The cost of capital is what firms have to pay investors to raise new funds. If a domestic firm sells new shares of stock, then the lower the risk premium, the smaller dividends or cash flows the firm must pay stockholders. This allows firms to raise money more cheaply and will allow greater investment spending and expansion than otherwise.

Direct Foreign Investment

So far we have considered international investment in the form of portfolio investment, like the purchase of a stock or bond issued in a foreign currency. There is, however, another type of international investment activity called direct foreign investment. *Direct foreign investment* is the money spent by a domestic firm to establish foreign operating units. In the U.S. balance of payments, direct investment is distinguished from portfolio investment solely on the basis of percentage of ownership. Capital flows are designated as direct investment when a foreign entity owns 10 percent or more of a firm, regardless of whether the capital flows are used to purchase new plant and equipment or to buy an ownership position in an existing firm. The growth of direct foreign investment spending corresponds to the growth of the multinational firm. Although direct investment is properly emphasized in international trade discussions of the international movement of factors of production, students should be able to distinguish portfolio investment from direct investment.

The motives for portfolio investment are easily seen in terms of the risk and return concepts already examined. In a general sense, the concern with a firm's return, subject to risk considerations, may be thought of as motivating all firm decisions, including those of direct investment. However, a literature has developed to offer more specific motives for desiring domestic ownership of foreign production facilities. Theories of direct foreign investment typically explain the incentive for such investment in terms of some imperfection in free-market conditions. If markets were perfectly competitive, the domestic firm could just as well buy foreign securities to transfer capital abroad rather than actually establishing a foreign operating unit. One line of theorizing on direct foreign investment is that individual firms may not attempt to maximize profits, which would be in the interest of the firm's stockholders; instead, they would attempt to maximize growth in terms of firm size. This is a concept that relies on an oligopolistic form of industry that would allow a firm to survive without maximizing profits. In this case direct foreign investment is preferred since domestic firms cannot depend on foreign-managed firms to operate in the domestic firm's best interests.

Other theories of direct foreign investment are based on the domestic firm possessing superior skills, knowledge, or information as compared to foreign firms. Such advantages would allow the foreign subsidiary of the domestic firm to earn a higher return than is possible by a foreign-managed firm.

Direct investment has become an increasingly important source of finance for developing countries. Prior to the rapid growth of bank lending following the oil price shocks of 1973 and 1974, direct investment exceeded bank lending as a source of funds in developing countries. However, through the late 1970s, bank lending grew in size and came to dominate direct investment by the early 1980s. In more recent years that trend has been reversed. Table 7.2 illustrates how sources of funds to developing countries have changed recently. In 1970 direct investment in developing countries accounted for 19 percent of money inflows. By 1980 this figure had fallen to 12 percent. In recent years, direct investment has accounted for more than 100 percent of net capital flows to developing countries. Other kinds of capital flows, like bank loans, deposits, and trade credit, have been negative, indicating more money flowing out of developing countries than in. In part,

Table 7.2 Net Capital Flows to Developing Countries (fraction of total)

	1990	1992	1994	1996	1998	2000
Direct investment	38%	30%	57%	54%	330%	450%
Portfolio investment	36	45	78	38	53	180
Other	25	25	−35	8	−281	−530

Source: The World Bank, *World Development Report,* various issues.

the net outflow of "Other" funds is a result of financial crises that increased perceptions of bank lending risk to developing countries.

Direct foreign investment is often politically unpopular in developing countries because it is associated with an element of foreign control over domestic resources. Nationalist sentiment, combined with a fear of exploitation, has often resulted in laws restricting direct investment.

It may be that direct foreign investment contributes more to economic development than do bank loans, since more of the funds go to actual investment in productive resources. Bank loans to sovereign governments were (and are) often used for consumption spending rather than investment. In addition, direct foreign investment may involve new technologies and productive expertise not available in the domestic economy. If foreign firms make a bad decision regarding a direct investment expenditure, the loss is sustained by the foreign firm. If the domestic government uses bank loans inefficiently, the country still faces a repayment obligation to the banks.

Capital Flight

In the discussion of portfolio investment, we emphasized expected risk and return as determinants of foreign investment. When the risk of doing business in a country rises sharply or the expected return falls, we sometimes observe large outflows of investment funds so that the country experiences massive capital account deficits. Such outflows of funds are often descriptively referred to as *capital flight.* The change in the risk-return relationship that gives rise to capital flight may be the result of political or financial crisis, tightening capital controls, tax increases, or fear of a domestic currency devaluation.

One of the issues arising from the developing-country debt crisis of the 1980s was an assertion by bankers that some of the borrowed money was not put to use in the debtor nations but, instead, was misappropriated by individuals and deposited back in the developed countries. In addition to allegedly misappropriated funds, wealthy individuals and business firms often shipped capital out of the debtor nations at the same time that these nations were pleading for additional funds from developed-country banks.

It is estimated that over the period from 1977 to 1987, $20 billion of flight capital left Argentina. This $20 billion is almost half of the debt, totaling $46 billion, that was incurred through 1984. The data suggest a crude interpretation that for every $1 borrowed by Argentina, about 50 cents came out of the country as flight capital. Similar statements might be made for other countries. An important aspect of the capital outflows is that fewer resources are available at home to service the debt, and more borrowing is required. In addition, capital flight may be associated with a loss of international reserves and greater pressure for devaluation of the domestic currency.

The discussion of capital flight highlights the importance of economic and political stability for encouraging domestic investment. Business firms and individuals respond to lower risk and higher return. The stable and growing developing country faces little, if any, capital flight and attracts foreign capital to aid in expanding the productive capacity of the economy.

Capital Inflow Issues

The early 1990s were characterized by a surge of capital inflows to developing countries. Interest in countries with emerging financial markets stimulated both direct and portfolio investment in these countries. The inflows were welcome in that they helped poor countries finance domestic infrastructure to aid in development, and they provided additional opportunities for international diversification for investors. However, some countries that experienced particularly large capital inflows exhibited problems that could reduce the positive effects of the capital flows.

A large capital inflow in a short period of time can lead to an appreciation of the recipient country's currency. This appreciation may reduce the competitiveness of the nation's export industries and cause a fall in output and rise in unemployment in these industries. We learned in Chapter 2 that a large rise in the capital account surplus will be accompanied by a large rise in the current account deficit. The capital inflow may also be associated with a rapid increase in the country's money supply, which would create inflationary conditions. As a result of potential problems associated with capital inflows, some countries have imposed policies aimed at limiting the effects of these inflows.

Fiscal restraint is a policy of cutting government expenditures, or raising taxes, so that the expansionary effect of the capital flows is partially offset by the contractionary fiscal policy. Chile, Malaysia, and Thailand followed such policies. Many countries have used some sort of exchange rate policy measures. Generally, these involved an appreciation of the currency in countries where the exchange rate has maintained little flexibility. Allowing the currency to appreciate may hurt export industries, but it allows the money supply to be insulated from the capital flow so that inflationary monetary policy does not occur. Some countries also permitted greater exchange rate flexibility as a way to insulate the domestic money supply from the capital flows. Some countries imposed capital controls to limit the inflow of capital. Such measures include taxes and quantity quotas on capital flows, increased reserve requirements on bank borrowing in foreign currency, or limits on foreign exchange transactions.

Overall, the experience of the 1990s has created an awareness that capital inflows can be both a blessing and a curse. The attempts to manage the risks associated with such inflows have met with varied degrees of success, and further studies of the experiences of countries that followed different policies will yield suggestions for appropriate government policy measures.

Summary

1. Even with constant interest rates, portfolio diversification provides an incentive for international capital flows.
2. The less variable the return on a portfolio, the more certain the return.
3. Portfolio diversification eliminates the nonsystematic risk that is unique to an individual asset. The systematic risk, common to all assets, will remain.
4. American depositary receipts (ADRs) are negotiable instruments sold in the United States that represent ownership of shares in a foreign firm.
5. Direct foreign investment is spending to establish foreign operating units.
6. Capital flight arises when there is increased risk of doing business in a country.
7. High capital inflows can have negative effects on some industries and can create inflationary conditions.

Exercises

1. How can investment flows be motivated by interest differentials and still allow two-way capital flows to be observed between countries?
2. How does diversification reduce risk? Give an example.
3. Why might we expect the stock of a domestic multinational firm to have different risk characteristics than the stock of a firm with purely domestic operations? If the difference does not exist, why might that be?
4. Why might U.S. investors prefer to invest in U.S. assets rather than in foreign assets?
5. What is the difference between direct foreign investment and financial portfolio investment? In what ways are the motives for direct foreign investment similar to the motives for portfolio investment? In what ways are they different?
6. What policy would you recommend to a country facing substantial capital flight? In other words, knowing nothing about the details of the country, what do you suppose is the most important policy change it should make?
7. How can capital inflows be viewed as both beneficial and harmful?

References

Errunza, Vihang, Kedreth Hogan, and Mao-Wei Hung, "Can the Gains from International Diversification Be Achieved without Trading Abroad?" *Journal of Finance,* December 1999.

Foerster, Stephen R., and G. Andrew Karolyi, "The Effects of Market Segmentation and Investor Recognition on Asset Prices: Evidence from Foreign Stocks Listing in the United States," *Journal of Finance,* June 1999.

Hasan, Iftekhar, and Yusif Simaan, "A Rational Explanation for Home Country Bias," *Journal of International Money and Finance,* June 2000.

International Monetary Fund, "Developing Countries Get More Private Investment, Less Aid," *Finance and Development,* June 1997.

Kasa, Kenneth, "Measuring the Gains from International Portfolio Diversification," *FRBSF Weekly Letter,* 94–14, April 1994.

Kim, Yoonbai, "Causes of Capital Flows in Developing Countries," *Journal of International Money and Finance,* April 2000.

Stulz, René M., "Globalization of Equity Markets and the Cost of Capital," Ohio State University Working Paper, available at www.cob.ohio-state.edu/fin/stulz.

Tesar, Linda L., and Ingrid M. Werner, "Home Bias and High Turnover," *Journal of International Money and Finance,* 4, August 1995, 467–492.

8

Prices and Exchange Rates: Purchasing Power Parity

Chapter 1 discussed the role of foreign exchange market arbitrage in keeping foreign exchange rates the same in different locations. If the dollar price of a yen is higher at Bank of America in San Francisco than at Citibank in New York, we would expect traders to buy yen from Citibank and simultaneously sell yen to Bank of America. This activity would raise the dollar/yen exchange rate quoted by Citibank and lower the rate at Bank of America until the exchange rate quotations are transaction costs close. Such arbitrage activity is not limited to the foreign exchange market. We would expect arbitrage to be present in any market where similar goods are traded in different locations. For instance, the price of gold is roughly the same worldwide at any point in time. If gold sold at a higher price in one location than in another, arbitragers would buy gold where it is cheap and sell where it is high until the prices are equal (allowing for transaction costs). Similarly, we would expect the price of tractors or automobiles or sheet steel to be related across geographically disparate markets. However, there are good economic reasons why prices for some goods are more similar across countries than others.

This tendency for similar goods to sell for similar prices globally provides a link between prices and exchange rates. If we wanted to know why exchange rates change over time, one obvious answer is that, as prices change internationally, exchange rates must also change to keep the prices measured in a common currency equal across countries. In other words, exchange rates should adjust to offset differing inflation rates between countries. This relationship between the prices of goods and services and exchange rates is known as *purchasing power parity.* Although we are hesitant to refer to purchasing power parity as a theory of the exchange rate, for reasons that will be made apparent shortly, it is important to study the relationship between price levels and exchange rates in order to understand the role of goods markets (as distinct from financial asset markets) in international finance.

Absolute Purchasing Power Parity

Our first view of purchasing power parity (PPP) is absolute purchasing power parity. Here we consider the exchange rate to be given by the ratio of price levels between countries. If E is the spot exchange rate (domestic currency units per foreign unit), P the domestic price index, and P^F the foreign price index, the absolute PPP relation is written as

$$P/P^F = E \tag{8.1}$$

For those readers who are not familiar with price indexes, P and P^F may be thought of as consumer price indexes or producer price indexes. A price index is supposed to measure average prices in an economy and therefore is subject to the criticism that, in fact, it measures the actual prices faced by no one. To construct such an index, we must first determine which prices to include—that is, which goods and services are to be monitored. Then these various items need to be assigned weights reflecting their importance in total spending. Thus, the consumer price index would weight housing prices very heavily, but bread prices would have only a very small weight. The final index is a weighted average of the prices of the goods and services surveyed.

Phrased in terms of price indexes, absolute PPP, as given in Equation (8.1), indicates that the exchange rate between any two currencies is equal to the ratio of their price indexes. Therefore, the exchange rate is a *nominal* magnitude, dependent on prices. We should be careful when using real-world price index data that the various national price indexes are comparable in terms of goods and services covered as well as base year (the reference year used for comparisons over time). If changes in the world were only nominal, the results of price level change, then we would expect PPP to hold if we had true price indexes. The significance of this last sentence will be illustrated soon.

Equation (8.1) can be rewritten as

$$P = EP^F \tag{8.2}$$

so that the domestic price level is equal to the product of the domestic currency price of foreign currency and the foreign price level. Equation (8.2) is called the *law of one price* and indicates that goods sell for the same price worldwide. For instance, we might observe a shirt selling for $10 in the United States and £4 in the United Kingdom. If the $/£ exchange rate is $2.50 per pound, then $P = EP^F = (2.50)(4) = 10$. Thus, the price of the shirt in the United Kingdom is the same as the U.S. price once we use the exchange rate to convert the pound price into dollars and compare prices in a common currency.

Unfortunately for this analysis, the world is more complex than the simple shirt example. The real world is characterized by differentiated products, costly information, and all sorts of impediments to the equalization of goods prices worldwide. Certainly, the more homogeneous goods are, the more we expect the law of one price to hold. Some commodities, which retain essentially the same form worldwide, provide the best examples of the law of one price. Gold, for instance, is quoted in dollar prices internationally, and so we would be correct in stating that the law of one price holds quite closely for gold. However, shirts come in different styles, brand names, and prices, and we do not expect the law of one price to hold domestically for shirts, let alone internationally.

Figure 8.1 illustrates some international price differences of comparable goods and services across countries. We might be able to quarrel with the international comparability of the goods and services chosen, but any international traveler is aware that wide discrepancies exist between prices of similar products and services across countries.

One might wonder why we would ever expect PPP to hold, since we know that international trade involves freight charges and tariffs. Given the costs associated with shipping goods, we would not expect PPP to hold for any particular good—so why would we anticipate the relationship phrased in terms of price indexes to hold as in Equation (8.1)? Furthermore, not all goods are traded internationally, yet the prices of these goods are captured in the national price indexes. As the prices of nontraded goods change, the

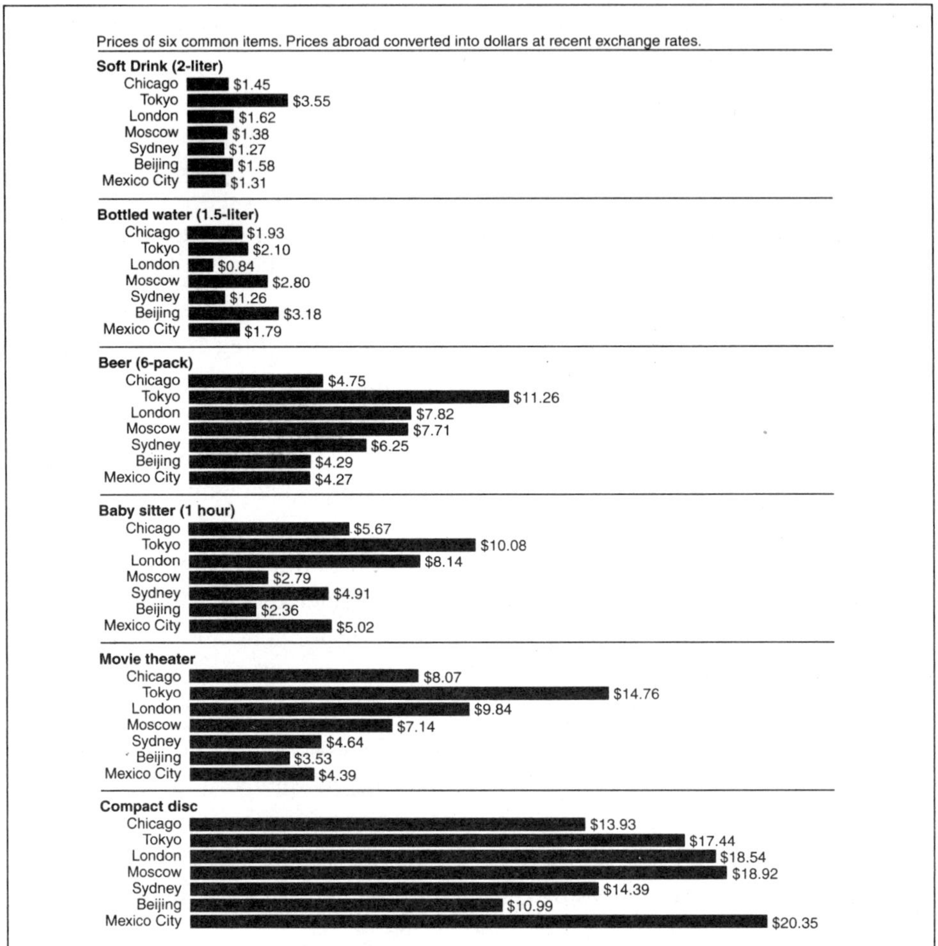

Figure 8.1 Dollar prices around the world (all foreign prices converted to U.S. dollar equivalents); prices and exchange rates as of early 2002.
(*Source:* Figure is constructed from data reported by Runzheimer International.)

price indexes change. But this does not affect exchange rates since the changing prices of nontraded goods does not give rise to international trade flows, and so no change in the supply and demand for currencies need result. Recently, economists have added many refinements to the analysis of PPP that we need not consider here. The important lesson to be learned is the potential problem associated with using price indexes to explain exchange rate changes.

So far we have emphasized variations in the exchange rate brought about by changing price indexes or nominal changes. However, it is reasonable to assume that much of the week-to-week change in exchange rates is the result of real rather than nominal events. Besides variations in the price level due to general inflation, we can also identify *relative price changes.* Inflation results in an increase in all prices, but relative price changes indicate that not all prices move together. Some prices increase faster than others, and some rise while others fall. An old analogy that students often find useful is to think of inflation as an elevator carrying a load of tennis balls, which represent the prices of individual goods. As the inflation continues, the balls are carried higher by the elevator, which means that all prices are rising. But as the inflation continues and the elevator rises, the balls, or individual prices, are bouncing up and down. So while the elevator raises all the balls inside, the balls do not bounce up and down together. The balls bouncing up have their prices rising relative to the balls going down.

If we think of different elevators as representing different countries, then if the balls were still while the elevators rose at the same rate, the exchange rate would be constant, as suggested by purchasing power parity. Moreover, if we looked at sufficiently long intervals, we could ignore the bouncing balls, since the large movements of the elevators would dominate the exchange rate movements. If, however, we observed very short intervals during which the elevators move only slightly, we would find that the bouncing balls, or relative price changes of individual goods, would largely determine the exchange rate.

Arbitrage in goods markets makes it easy to understand why price level changes affect exchange rates, but the effect of relative price changes is more subtle. The following example will illustrate how exchange rates can change because of relative price change even though there is no change in the overall price level (no inflation). Table 8.1 summarizes the argument. Let us suppose there are two countries, France and Japan, and each consumes wine and sake. Initially, in period 0, wine and sake each sell for 1 euro in France and 1 yen in Japan. In a simple world of no transport costs or other barriers to the law of one price, the exchange rate, E = €/¥, must equal 1. Note that initially the relative price of one bottle of wine is equal to one bottle of sake (since sake and wine sell for the same price in each country). To determine the inflation rate in each country, we must calculate price indexes that indicate the value of the items consumed in each country for each period. Suppose that initially France consumes 9 units of wine and 1 unit of sake, whereas Japan consumes 1 wine and 9 sake. At the domestic

Table 8.1 The Effect of a Relative Price Change on the Exchange Rate

France

	Period 0		Period 1	
	Price in Euros	**Quantity Consumed**	**Price in Euros**	**Quantity Consumed**
Wine	1	9	1.111	8
Sake	1	1	0.741	1.5
Value of consumption	10		10	

Japan

	Period 0		Period 1	
	Price in Yen	**Quantity Consumed**	**Price in Yen**	**Quantity Consumed**
Wine	1	1	1.5	0.333
Sake	1	9	1	9.5
Value of consumption	10		10	

Note: Exchange rate, €/¥, in period 0 = 1; exchange rate, €/¥, in period 1 = 0.741.

Source: adapted from Bruno Solnik, "International Parity Conditions and Exchange Risk," *Journal of Banking and Finance,* 2, October 1978, 289.

prices of 1 unit of domestic currency per unit of wine or sake, we can see that the total value of the basket of goods consumed in France is 10 euros, whereas the total value of the goods consumed in Japan is 10 yen.

Now let us suppose that there is a bad grape harvest, so that in the next period wine is more expensive. In terms of relative prices, we know that the bad harvest will make wine rise in price relative to sake. Suppose now that instead of the original relative price of 1 sake = 1 wine, we now have 1.5 sake = 1 wine. Consumers will recognize this change in relative prices and tend to decrease their consumption of wine and increase consumption of sake. Suppose in period 1 the French consume 8 wine and 1.5 sake, whereas the Japanese consume 0.333 wine and 9.5 sake. Let us further assume that the central banks of Japan and France follow a policy of zero inflation, where inflation is measured by the change in the cost of current consumption. With no inflation, the value of the consumption basket will be unchanged from period 0 and will equal 10 in each country. Thus, although average prices have not changed, we know that individual prices must change because of the rising price of wine relative to sake.

The determination of the individual prices is a simple exercise in algebra, but is not needed to understand the central message of the example; therefore, students could skip this paragraph and still retain the benefit of the lesson. Since we know that France consumes 8 wine and 1.5 sake with a total value of 10 francs and that the relative price is 1.5 sake = 1 wine, we can solve for the individual prices by letting $1.5P_s = P_w$, and we can then substitute this into our total spending equation ($8P_w + 1.5P_s = 10$) to determine the prices. In other words, we have a system with two equations and two unknowns that is solvable:

$$8P_w + 1.5P_s = 10 \tag{8.3}$$

$$1.5P_s = P_w \tag{8.4}$$

Substituting Equation (8.4) into the previous equation, we obtain

$$8P_w + 1P_w = 10 \rightarrow P_w = {}^{10}\!/_{9} = 1.111 \tag{8.5}$$

Since $P_w = 1.111$, we can use this to determine P_s:

$$1.5P_s = 1.111 \rightarrow P_s = {}^{1.111}\!/_{1.5} = 0.741 \tag{8.6}$$

Thus, we have our prices in France in period 1. For Japan it is even easier:

$$\tfrac{1}{3}P_w + 9.5P_s = 10 \tag{8.7}$$

$$1.5P_s = P_w \tag{8.8}$$

Substituting Equation (8.8) into the preceding equation, we obtain

$$\tfrac{1}{3}P_w + 6\tfrac{1}{3}P_w = 10 \rightarrow P_w = 1.5 \tag{8.9}$$

Thus,

$$1.5P_s = 1.5 \rightarrow P_s = 1 \tag{8.10}$$

Given the new prices in period 1, we can now determine the exchange rate implied by the law of one price. Since sake sells for 0.741 euros in France and 1 yen in Japan, the euro price of yen must be €/¥ = 0.741.

In summary, this example has shown how exchange rates can change because of real economic events, even when average price levels are constant. Since PPP is usually discussed in terms of price indexes, we find that real events, such as the relative price changes brought about by a poor harvest, will cause deviations from absolute PPP as the exchange rate changes, even though the price indexes are constant. Note also that the relative price effect leads to an appreciation of the currency in the country where consumption of the good that is increasing in price is heaviest. In our example the euro appreciates as a result of the increased relative price of wine.

The previous discussion has illustrated why absolute PPP probably fails to hold at most points in time. Stating that the level of the exchange rate is equal to the ratio of price indexes is quite a strong statement to make. In the next section, a less restrictive relationship between prices and exchange rates is discussed.

Relative Purchasing Power Parity

There is an alternative view of PPP besides the absolute PPP just discussed. Relative PPP is said to hold when

$$\hat{E} = \hat{P} - \hat{P}^F \tag{8.11}$$

where a hat (^) over a variable denotes percentage change. So Equation (8.11) says that the percentage change in the exchange rate ($\hat{E}$) is equal to the percentage change in the domestic price level ($\hat{P}$), minus the percentage change in the foreign price level ($\hat{P}^F$)Therefore, although absolute PPP states that the exchange rate is equal to the ratio of the price indexes, relative PPP deals with percentage changes in these variables.

We usually refer to the percentage change in the price level as the rate of inflation. So another way of stating the relative PPP relationship is by saying that the percentage change in the exchange rate is equal to the inflation differential between the domestic and foreign country. If we say that the percentage change in the exchange rate is equal to the inflation differential, then we can ignore the actual levels of E, P, and P^F and consider the changes, which is not so strong an assumption as absolute PPP. It should be noted that, if absolute PPP holds, then relative PPP will also hold. But if absolute PPP does not hold, relative PPP still may. This is so because the level of E may not equal P/P^F, but the change in E could still equal the inflation differential.

Having observed in the preceding section how relative prices can determine exchange rates, we can, with reason, believe that over time these relative price changes will decrease in importance compared to inflation rates, so that in the long run inflation differentials will dominate exchange rate movements. The idea is that the real events that cause relative price movements are often random and short run in nature. By *random,* we mean they are unexpected and equally likely to raise or lower the exchange rate. Given this characterization, it follows that these random relative price movements will tend to cancel out over time (otherwise, we would not consider them equally likely to raise or lower E).

Time, Inflation, and PPP

Several researchers have found that PPP holds better for high-inflation countries. When we say "holds better," we mean that the equalities stated in Equations (8.1) and (8.11) are more closely met by actual exchange rate and price level data observed over time in high-inflation countries compared to low-inflation countries. In high-inflation countries, changes in exchange rates are highly correlated with inflation differentials because the sheer magnitude of inflation overwhelms the relative price effects, whereas in low- or moderate-inflation countries the relative price effects dominate exchange rate movements and lead to discrepancies from PPP. In terms of our earlier example, when the elevator is moving faster (high inflation), the movement of the balls inside (relative prices) is less important; however, when the elevator is moving slowly (low inflation), the movement of the bouncing balls is quite important.

Besides the rate of inflation, the period of time analyzed has an effect on how well PPP holds. We expect PPP to hold better for annual data than for monthly data, since the longer time frame allows for more inflation. Thus, random relative price effects are less important, and we find exchange rate changes closely related to inflation differentials. Using the elevator analogy, the longer the time frame analyzed, the farther the elevator moves, and the more the elevator moves, the less important will be the balls inside. This suggests that studies of PPP covering many years are more likely to yield evidence of PPP than studies based on a few years' data.

The literature on PPP is voluminous and tends to confirm the conclusions we have made. Researchers have presented evidence that real relative price shifts can have an important role in the short run, but over time the random nature of the relative price changes minimizes the importance of these unrelated events. Investigations over long periods of time (100 years, for instance) have concluded that PPP holds better in the long run.

Deviations from PPP

So far the discussion has included several reasons why deviations from PPP occur. When discussing the role of arbitrage in goods markets, it was said that the law of one price would not apply to differentiated products or products that are not traded internationally. Furthermore, since international trade involves shipping goods across national borders, prices may differ because of shipping costs or tariffs. Relative price changes have been emphasized as a reason why PPP would hold better in the long run than the short run. Such relative price changes result from real economic events, like changing tastes, bad weather, or government policy. As illustrated in Table 8.1, relative price changes cause deviations from PPP in terms of national price indexes. The law of one price could hold for individual goods, yet PPP could be violated for a price index. This, of course, just points out a problem in using price indexes rather than individual goods prices to measure PPP. Since consumers in different countries consume different goods, price indexes are not directly comparable internationally. We know that evaluating PPP between the United States and Japan using the U.S. and Japanese consumer price indexes is weakened by the fact that the typical Japanese consumer buys a different basket of goods than the typical U.S. consumer. In this case, the law of one price could hold perfectly for individual goods, yet we would observe deviations from PPP using the consumer price index for Japan and the United States.

Recognizing that there are problems in using national price indexes to measure PPP might lead us to believe that PPP, or the law of one price, should hold well for individual goods. There is, however, evidence that PPP does not hold well for many individual goods traded internationally. There are several reasons why this may be true. First, it is important to realize that PPP is not a theory of exchange rate determination. In other words, inflation differentials do not *cause* exchange rate change. PPP is an equilibrium relationship between two *endogenous* variables. When we say that prices and exchange rates are endogenous, we mean that they are simultaneously determined by other factors. The other factors are called *exogenous* variables. Exogenous variables may change independently, as with bad weather or government policy. Given a change in an exogenous variable, as with poor weather and a consequent poor harvest, both prices and exchange rates will change. Deviations in measured PPP will occur if prices and exchange rates change at different speeds. Evidence suggests that following some exogenous *shock,* changes in exchange rates precede changes in prices.

Such a finding can be explained by theorizing that the price indexes used for PPP calculations move slowly because commodity prices are not as flexible as financial asset prices (the exchange rate is the price of monies). We know that exchange rates vary throughout the day as the demand and supply for foreign exchange vary. But how often does the department store change the price of furniture, or how often does the auto parts store change the price of tires? Since the prices that enter into published price indexes are slower to adjust than are exchange rates, it is not surprising that exchange rate changes seem to lead price changes. Yet if exchange rates change faster than goods prices, then we have another reason why PPP should hold better in the long run than in the short run. When economic *news* is received, both exchange rates and prices may change. For instance, suppose the Federal Reserve announces today that it will promote a 100 percent increase in the U.S. money supply over the next 12 months. Such a change would cause greater inflation because more money in circulation leads to higher prices. The dollar would also fall in value relative to other currencies because the supply of dollars rises relative to the demand.

Following the Fed's announcement, would you expect goods prices in the United States to rise before the dollar depreciates on the foreign exchange market? While there are some important issues in exchange rate determination that must wait until later chapters, we generally can say here that the dollar would depreciate immediately following the announcement. If traders believe that the dollar will be worth less in the future, they will attempt to sell dollars now, and this selling activity drives down the dollar's value today. There should be some similar forces at work in the goods market as traders expecting higher prices in the future buy more goods today. But for most goods, the immediate short-run result will be a depletion of inventories at constant prices. Only over time will most goods prices rise. Figure 8.2 illustrates how the exchange rate will shift with news. The figure illustrates the quantity of dollars bought and sold on the horizontal axis and the yen price of the dollar on the vertical axis. Initially, the foreign exchange market equilibrium occurs where the demand curve, D_0, intersects the supply curve, S_0, at an exchange rate of 120 yen per dollar with quantity $\$_0$ of dollars being bought and sold. Suppose the Federal Reserve now issues a

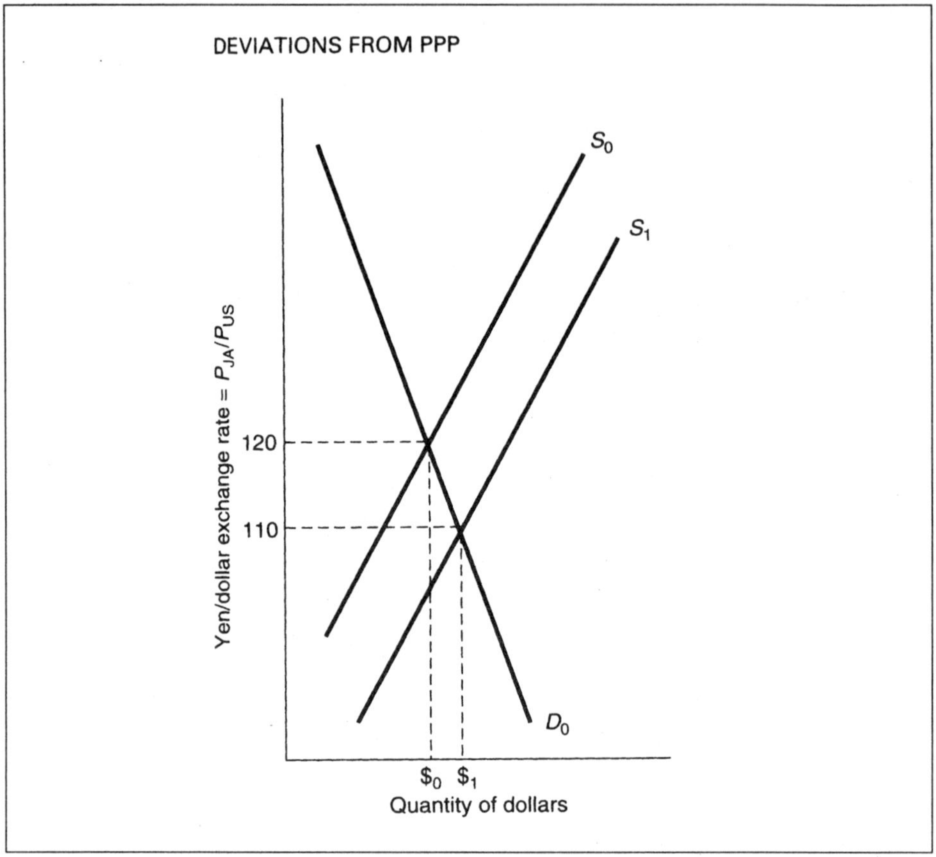

Figure 8.2 Shifts in the foreign exchange market and deviations from PPP.

statement causing people to expect the U.S. money supply to grow more rapidly in the future. This causes foreign exchange traders to expect the dollar to depreciate in the future. As a result, they attempt to sell more dollars now, shifting the supply curve out to S_1 in Figure 8.2. This shift in supply, with constant demand, causes the dollar to depreciate down to 110 yen per dollar. At this new exchange rate, a quantity $\$_1$ is traded.

Suppose initially PPP holds, so that $E = 120 = P_{JA}/P_{US}$. The announced change in monetary policy has an immediate effect on the exchange rate because currencies are traded continuously throughout the day. Prices of goods and services will change much more slowly. In the short run the ratio of the price level in Japan to the price level in the United States may remain unchanged at 120. So while E falls today to 110 in Figure 8.2, the ratio of the national price levels is still equal to the initial exchange rate of 120, and there is an apparent deviation from PPP.

Therefore, periods with important economic news will be periods where PPP deviations are large—the exchange rate adjusts while prices lag behind. In addition to the differential speed of adjustment between exchange rates and prices, periods dominated by news are likely to be periods involving much relative price change, so that PPP deviations would tend to appear even without exchange rates and prices changing at different speeds.

Deviations from PPP are also likely because international trade involves lags between order and delivery. Prices are often set by contract today for goods that are to be delivered several months later. If we compare goods prices and exchange rates today to evaluate PPP, we are using the exchange rate applicable to goods delivered today with prices that were set some time in the past. Ideally, we should compare contract prices in each country at the time contracts are signed with the exchange rate that is expected to prevail in the future period when goods are actually delivered and payment is made. If the exchange rate actually realized in the future period is the same as that expected when the goods prices were agreed upon, then there would be no problem in using today's exchange rate and today's delivered goods prices. The problem is that, realistically, exchange rates are very difficult to forecast, so that seldom would today's realized exchange rate be equal to the trader's forecast at some past period.

Let's consider a simple example. Suppose that on September 1, Mr. U.S. agrees to buy books from Ms. U.K. for £1 per book. At the time the contract is signed, books in the United States sell for \$2, and the current exchange rate of $E_{\$/£} = 2$ ensures that the law of one price holds—a £1 book from the United Kingdom is selling for the dollar equivalent of \$2 (the pound book price of 1 times the dollar price of the pound of \$2). If the contract calls for delivery and payment on December 1 of £1 per book and Mr. U.S. expects the exchange rate and prices to be unchanged until December 1, he *expects* PPP to hold at the time the payment is due. Suppose that on December 1, the actual exchange rate is £1 = \$1.50. An economist researching the law of one price for books would compare book prices of £1 and \$2 with the exchange rate of $E_{\$/£} = 1.50$, and examine if $E_{\$/£} = P_{US}/P_{UK}$. Since $\$1.50 \neq 2/1$, he would conclude that there are important deviations from PPP. Yet these deviations are *spurious*. At the time the prices were set, PPP was expected to hold. We generate the appearance of PPP deviations by comparing exchange rates today with prices that were set in the past.

The possible explanations for deviations from PPP include factors that would suggest permanent deviations (shipping costs and tariffs), factors that would produce temporary deviations (differential speed of adjustment between financial asset markets and goods markets, or real relative price changes), and factors that cause the appearance of deviations where none may actually exist (comparing current exchange rates with prices set in the past or using national price indexes when countries consume different baskets of goods). Since PPP measurements convey information regarding the relative purchasing power of currencies, such measurements have served as a basis for economic policy discussions. The next section will provide an example of policy-related information contained in PPP measurement.

Overvalued and Undervalued Currencies

If we observe E, P, and P^F over time, we find that the absolute PPP relationship does not hold very well for any pair of countries. If, over time, P^F rises faster than P, then we would expect E, the domestic currency price of the foreign currency, to fall. If E does not fall by the amount suggested by the lower P/P^F, then we could say that the domestic currency is undervalued or (the same thing) that the foreign currency is overvalued.

In the early 1980s, there was much talk of an *overvalued* dollar. The foreign exchange value of the dollar appeared to be too high relative to the inflation differentials between the United States and the other developed countries. The term overvalued suggests that the exchange rate is not where it should be, yet if the free-market supply and demand factors are determining the exchange rate, then the overvalued exchange rate is actually the free-market equilibrium rate. In this case, the term overvalued might suggest that this equilibrium is but a temporary deviation from PPP, and over time the exchange rate will fall in line with the inflation differential.

In the early 1980s, the foreign exchange price of the dollar grew at a faster rate than the inflation differential between the other industrial nations and the United States. It appears, then, that for more than four years, a dollar overvaluation developed. Not until 1985 did the exchange rate begin to return to a level consistent with PPP. Figure 8.3 illustrates what this pattern of percentage changes in exchange rates and price levels meant for the

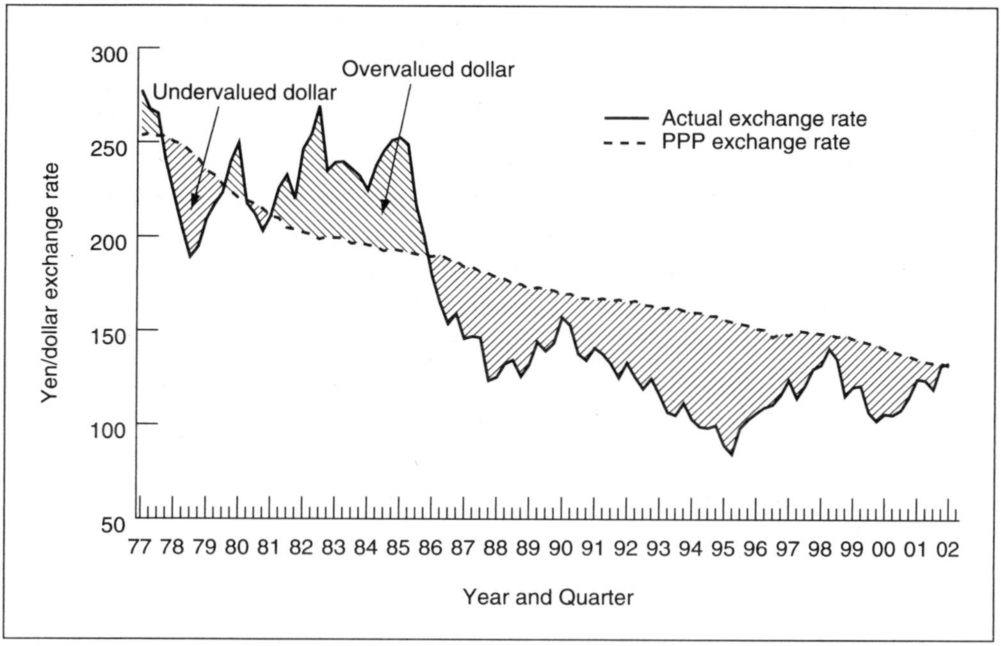

Figure 8.3 The actual yen/dollar exchange rate and the PPP implied exchange rate.

actual level of the yen/dollar exchange rate. Prior to 1981, the dollar appears to be undervalued in that the actual exchange rate is below that implied by PPP as measured by inflation differentials. In other words, the line labeled "PPP exchange rate" measures the values the exchange rate would take if the percentage change in the exchange rate equalled the inflation differential between Japan and the United States. Figure 8.3 indicates that the actual exchange rate was below the PPP level—thus, the undervalued dollar. After 1981, the dollar appreciated against the yen at a rate faster than the inflation differential, so the dollar becomes overvalued. By 1985, the dollar begins to depreciate against the yen and move toward the PPP value of the exchange rate.

Since we know that PPP does not hold well for any pair of countries with moderate inflation in the short run, we must always have currencies that appear overvalued or undervalued in a PPP sense. The issue becomes important when the apparent over- or undervaluation persists for some time and has significant macroeconomic consequences. In the early 1980s, the U.S. political issue at the forefront of this apparent dilemma was that the overvalued dollar was hurting export-oriented industries. U.S. goods were rising in price to foreign buyers as the dollar appreciated. The problem was made visible by a large balance of trade deficit that became a major political issue. In 1985, intervention in the foreign exchange market by major central banks contributed to a dollar depreciation that reduced the PPP-implied dollar overvaluation.

Besides the dollar overvaluation relative to the other developed countries' currencies, from time to time many developing countries have complained that their currencies are overvalued against the developed countries' currencies, and thus their balance of trade sustains a larger deficit than would otherwise occur. If PPP applied only to internationally traded goods, then we could show how lower labor productivity in developing countries could contribute to apparently overvalued currencies. For nontraded goods we assume that production methods are similar worldwide. It may make more sense to think of the nontraded goods sector as being largely services. In this case, more-productive countries tend to have higher wages and thus higher prices in the service sector than less-productive, low-wage countries. We now have a situation in which the price indexes used to calculate PPP vary with productivity and hence with wages in each country. If we assume that exchange rates are determined only by traded goods prices (the idea being that if a good does not enter into international trade, there is no reason for its price to be equalized internationally and thus no reason for changes in its price to affect the exchange rate), then we can find how price indexes vary with service prices while exchange rates are unaffected. For instance, the price of a haircut in Paris should not be affected by an increase in haircut prices in Los Angeles. So if the price of haircuts should rise in Los Angeles, other things being equal, the average price level in the United States increases. But this U.S. price increase should not have any impact on the dollar per euro exchange rate. If, instead, the price of an automobile rises in the United States relative to French auto prices, we would expect the dollar to depreciate relative to the euro because demand for French autos, and thus euros, increases while demand for U.S. autos, and thus dollars, decreases.

If the world operates in the way just described, then we would expect that the greater are the traded goods productivity differentials between countries, the greater will be the wage differentials reflected in service prices, and thus the greater will be the deviations from absolute PPP over time. Suppose that developing countries, starting from lower absolute levels of productivity, have higher productivity growth rates. If per capita income differences between countries give a reasonable measure of the productivity differences, then we would anticipate that as developing country per capita income increases relative to developed country per capita income, the developing country price index will grow faster than that of the developed country. But at the same time, the depreciation of the developing country's currency lags behind the inflation differentials, as measured by the average price levels in each country that include traded and nontraded goods prices. Thus, over time, the currency of the developing country will tend to appear overvalued (the foreign exchange value of the developing country's money has not depreciated as much as called for by the movements in the average price levels), whereas the developed country's currency will appear undervalued (the exchange value of the developed country's money has not appreciated as much as the price level changes would indicate).

Does the preceding discussion describe the real world? Do you believe that labor-intensive services (domestic servants, haircuts, etc.) are cheaper in poorer countries than in wealthy countries? Researchers have provided evidence suggesting that the deviations from PPP as previously mentioned do indeed occur systematically with changes in per capita income.

What is the bottom line of the foregoing consideration? National price indexes are not particularly good indicators of the need for exchange rate adjustments. In this respect it is not surprising to find that many studies have shown that absolute PPP does not hold. The idea that currencies are undervalued or overvalued can be misleading if exchange rates are free to change with changing market conditions. Only if central bank or government intervention interrupts the free adjustment of the exchange rate to market clearing levels can we really talk about a currency as being overvalued or undervalued (and in many such instances black markets develop where the currency is traded at free-market prices). The fact that changes in PPP over time present the appearance of an undervalued currency in terms of the price indexes of two countries is perhaps more an indicator of the limitations of price indexes than of any real market phenomena.

Real Exchange Rates

All discussions of exchange rates so far have been with respect to the *nominal exchange rate.* This is the exchange rate that is actually observed in the foreign exchange market. However, economists sometimes utilize the concept of the *real exchange rate* to represent changes in the competitiveness of a currency. The real exchange rate is an alternative way to think about currencies being over- and undervalued. The real exchange rate is measured as

$$E_{\text{real}} = E/(P/P^F) \tag{8.12}$$

or the nominal exchange rate adjusted for the ratio of the home price level relative to the price level abroad. In Figure 8.3, one sees that the dollar appeared to be significantly overvalued against the yen in the early 1980s and then significantly undervalued in the mid-1990s. In terms of real exchange rate changes, this would mean that the real exchange rate in terms of yen per dollar would have risen in the early 1980s as the nominal exchange rate (yen per dollar) rose relative to the ratio of Japanese prices to U.S. prices. Then, in the 1990s, the real yen/dollar exchange rate fell as the nominal exchange rate decreased relative to the ratio of Japanese prices to U.S. prices.

If absolute PPP always held, the real exchange rate would equal 1. In such a world, nominal exchange rates would always change to mirror the change in the ratio of home prices to foreign prices. Since the real world has deviations from PPP, we also observe real exchange rates rising and falling. When the real exchange rate rises beyond some point, concern is expressed about an exchange rate overvaluation. When the real exchange rate falls beyond some point, concern is expressed about exchange rate undervaluation. As stated in the preceding section, terms like *overvaluation* and *undervaluation* must be used carefully. Such terms may sometimes reflect shortcomings of price indexes as inputs into measures of currency values.

Summary

1. If the exchange rate is equal to the ratio of the price indexes, absolute PPP holds.
2. If the percentage change in the exchange rate is equal to the inflation differential between two countries, relative PPP holds.
3. PPP holds better for high-inflation countries, or for long time periods when the movement of price levels overwhelms any relative price change.
4. Deviations from PPP may arise from the presence of nontraded goods prices in price indexes, differentiated goods, shipping costs, tariffs, relative price changes, different consumption bundles across countries (and thus different goods included in national price indexes), prices fixed by contract, or differential speeds of adjustment of exchange rates and goods prices.

5. Currencies are said to be overvalued (undervalued) if they have appreciated more (less) than the difference between the domestic and foreign inflation rate.

Exercises

1. Assume that the cost of a particular basket of goods is equal to $108 in the United States and ¥14,000 in Japan.
   a. What should the ¥/$ exchange rate be according to absolute purchasing power parity?
   b. If the actual exchange rate were equal to 120, would the dollar be considered undervalued or overvalued?
   c. Is purchasing power parity a good measure of what exchange rates should be?
2. Under what conditions is purchasing power parity most likely to hold best?
3. If nontradable goods prices rise faster in country A than in country B, and tradable goods prices remain unchanged, determine whether currency A will appear to be overvalued or undervalued.
4. Explain why relative purchasing power parity may hold when absolute purchasing power parity does not.
5. List four reasons why deviations from PPP might occur; then carefully explain how each causes such deviations.
6. What is the "real exchange rate"? What does the real exchange rate equal if absolute PPP holds? How do changes in the real exchange rate indicate whether currencies are changing in ways to make a country's goods more or less competitive?

References

"Big Mac Currencies," *The Economist,* April 25, 2002.

Lothian, J. R., and M. P. Taylor, "Real Exchange Rate Behavior: The Recent Float from the Perspective of the Past Two Centuries," *Journal of Political Economy,* 104, 1996.

Officer, L. H., *Purchasing Power Parity and Exchange Rates: Theory, Evidence, and Relevance.* Greenwich, Conn.: JAI Press, 1982.

Sarno, L., and M. P. Taylor, *New Developments in Exchange Rate Economics, Vol. II.* Cheltenham, U.K.: Elgar, 2002, part III.

9

Determinants of the Balance of Trade and Payments

Earlier chapters are full of discussions involving foreign exchange rates and the balance of payments. We now know the definitions and uses of these two important international finance terms, but have yet to consider what determines their values at any particular point in time. Why do some countries run a balance of payments surplus while others run deficits? It is worth noting that financial institutions, central banks, and governments invest many resources in trying to predict exchange rates and international trade and payments. The kinds of theories to be introduced in this chapter have shaped the way economists, investors, and politicians approach such problems. Exchange rate determination will be discussed in the next chapter.

Elasticities Approach to the Balance of Trade

Economic behavior involves satisfying unlimited wants with limited resources. One implication of this fact of budget constraints is that consumers and business firms will substitute among goods as prices change to stretch their budgets as far as possible. For instance, if Italian-made shoes and U.S.-made shoes are good substitutes, then as the price of U.S. shoes rises relative to Italian shoes, buyers will substitute the lower-priced Italian shoes for the higher-priced U.S. shoes. The crucial concept for determining consumption patterns is relative price—the price of one good relative to another.

Relative prices change as relative demand and supply for individual goods change. Such changes may result from changes in tastes, or production technology, or government taxes or subsidies, or many other possible sources. If the changes involve prices of goods at home changing relative to foreign goods, then international trade patterns may be altered. The elasticities approach to the balance of trade is concerned with how changing relative prices of domestic and foreign goods will change the balance of trade.

A change in the exchange rate will change the domestic currency price of foreign goods. Suppose initially that a pair of shoes sells for $50 in the United States and €50 in Italy. At an exchange rate of €1 = $1, the shoes sell for the same price in each country when expressed in a common currency. If the euro is devalued to €1.2 = $1, and shoe prices remain constant in the domestic currency of the producer, then shoes selling for €50 in Italy will now cost the U.S. buyer $41.67. After the devaluation, €1 = $0.8333, so €50 = $41.67, and the price of Italian shoes has fallen for U.S. buyers. Conversely, the price of $50 U.S. shoes to Italian buyers has risen from €50 to €60. The relative price effect of the lira devaluation should increase U.S. demand for Italian goods and decrease Italian demand for U.S. goods. How much quantity demanded changes in response to the relative price change is determined by the elasticity of demand.

In beginning economics courses, students learn that *elasticity* measures the responsiveness of quantity to changes in price. The *elasticities approach to the balance of trade* provides an analysis of how devaluations will affect the balance of trade depending on the elasticities of supply and demand for foreign exchange and foreign goods.

When demand or supply is elastic, it means that quantity demanded or supplied will be relatively responsive to the change in price. An inelastic demand or supply indicates that quantity is relatively unresponsive to price changes. We can make things more precise by using coefficients of elasticity. For instance, letting ϵ_d represent the coefficient of elasticity of demand, we can write ϵ_d as

$$\epsilon_d = \% \Delta Q / \% \Delta P \tag{9.1}$$

This implies that the coefficient of elasticity of demand is equal to the percentage change in the quantity demanded, divided by the percentage change in price. If the price increases by 5 percent and the quantity demanded falls by more than 5 percent, then ϵ_d exceeds 1 (in absolute value), and we say that demand is elastic. If the price increases by 5 percent, but quantity demanded falls by less than 5 percent, we would say that demand is inelastic and ϵ_d would be less than 1.

Just as we can compute a coefficient of elasticity of demand ϵ_d, so too can we compute a coefficient of elasticity of supply, ϵ_s, as the percentage change in the quantity supplied, divided by the percentage change in price. If ϵ_s exceeds 1, the quantity supplied is relatively responsive to price, and we say that supply is elastic. For ϵ_s less than 1, the quantity supplied is relatively unresponsive to price, so that the supply is inelastic.

Elasticity will determine what happens to total revenue (price times quantity) following a price change. With an elastic demand, quantity changes by a greater percentage amount than price, and thus total revenue will move in the opposite direction from the price change. Suppose the demand for black velvet paintings from Mexico is elastic. If the peso price rises 10 percent, the quantity demanded falls by more than 10 percent, so that the revenue received from sales will fall following the price change. If the demand for Colombian coffee is inelastic, then a 10 percent increase in price will result in a fall in the quantity demanded of less than 10 percent. The higher coffee price more than makes up for the lost sales and, therefore, coffee sales revenues rise following the price change. Obviously, elasticity of demand will be of great importance in determining export and import revenues as international prices change.

Now let us consider an example of supply and demand in the foreign exchange market. Figure 9.1 provides an example of the supply and demand for U.K. pounds. The demand curve labeled *D* is the demand for pounds, arising from the demand for British exports. The familiar downward slope indicates that the higher the price of pounds, the fewer the amount of pounds demanded. The supply curve labeled *S* is the supply of pounds to the foreign exchange market. The upward slope indicates the positive relationship between the foreign exchange price of pounds and the quantity of pounds supplied. The point where the supply and demand curves intersect is the equilibrium point where the quantity of pounds demanded just equals the quantity supplied. Suppose initially we have an equilibrium at E_0 and $£_0$; that is, $£_0$ is the quantity of pounds bought and sold at the exchange rate E_0. Now suppose there is an increase in demand for pounds (say, because of an increase in demand for U.K. exports). There are several possible responses to this shift in demand:

1. With freely floating exchange rates, the pound will appreciate, so that the exchange rate rises to E_1, and $£_1$ are bought and sold.
2. Central banks can peg the exchange rate at the old rate E_0 by providing $£_1' - £_0$ from their reserves (and thereby artificially shifting the supply of pounds).

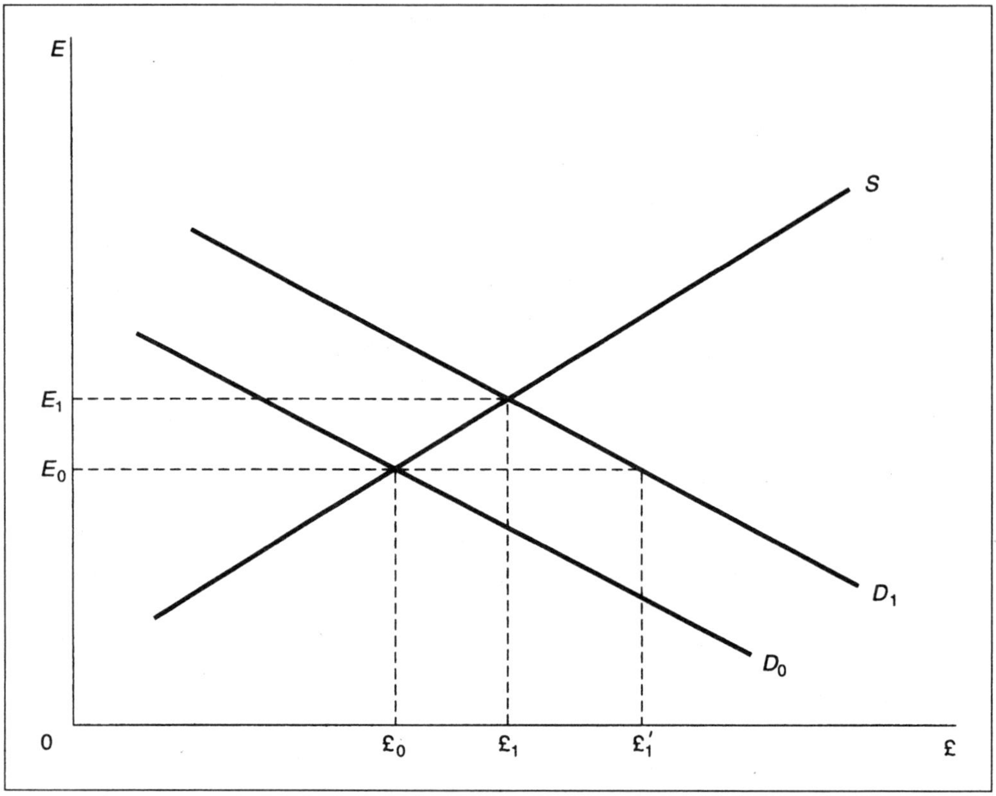

Figure 9.1 Supply and demand in the foreign exchange market.

3. The supply and demand curves can be artificially shifted by imposing controls or quotas on the supply of, or demand for, pounds.
4. Quotas or tariffs could be imposed on foreign trade to maintain the old supply and demand for pounds.

The elasticities approach recognizes that the effect of an exchange rate change on the equilibrium quantity of currency being traded will depend on the elasticities of the supply and demand curves involved. It is important to remember that the elasticities approach is a theory of the balance of trade and can only be a theory of the balance of payments in a world without capital flows.

Suppose that in Figure 9.1, E is the dollar price of pounds and the U.S. central bank decides to meet the increase in demand for pounds by supplying pounds to the market from U.S. reserves. Now the old exchange rate E_0 is maintained because of the central bank's addition of $£_1' - £_0$ to the market supply. If it becomes apparent that the increase in demand is a permanent change, then the Federal Reserve will devalue the dollar, driving up the dollar price of pounds. This, of course, means that U.K. goods will be more expensive to the United States, whereas U.S. goods will be cheaper to the United Kingdom. Will this improve the U.S. trade balance? It all depends on the elasticities of supply and demand. With inelastic demands, it is possible to get what is called *J-curve effects,* where the price of imports to the United States increases, but quantity of imports demanded changes little, so that total payments to the United Kingdom actually increase. Likewise, with an inelastic demand for U.S. exports in the United Kingdom, even though the price of imports from the United States falls, few more are demanded. In this case, the U.S. balance of trade deficit and the excess demand for pounds could actually increase following a devaluation. The J-curve effect refers to the pattern of the balance of trade following a devaluation. If the balance of trade is viewed over time, the initial decrease in the trade balance is followed by a growing trade balance, because of inelastic demand, and results in the time pattern of the trade balance shown in Figure 9.2. Note in the figure that the trade balance is initially negative, falling over time. The devaluation occurs at point t_0. Following the devaluation, the

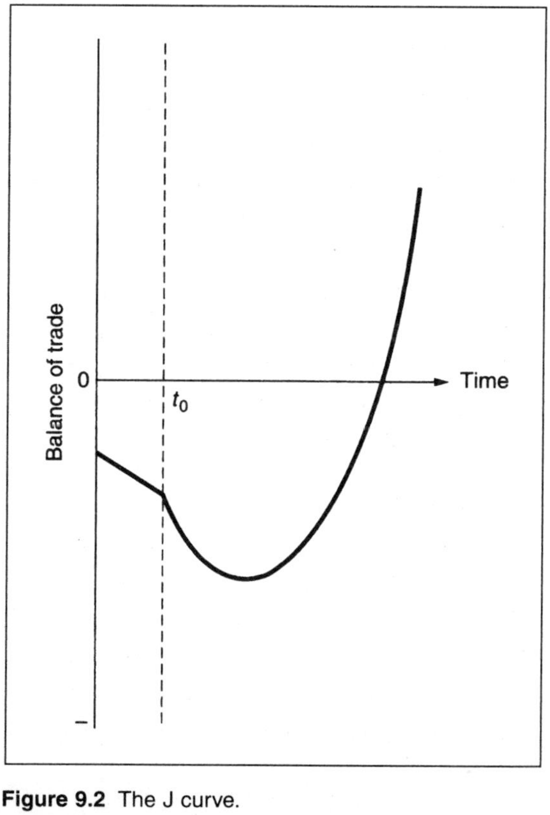

Figure 9.2 The J curve.

balance of trade continues to fall for a while before finally turning upward. The initial fall results from low elasticities in the short run. Over time, elasticities increase so that the balance of trade improves. This general pattern of the balance of trade falling before it increases traces a pattern that resembles the letter *J*.

Elasticities and J Curves

Devaluation is conventionally believed to be a tool for increasing a country's balance of trade. Yet the J-curve effect indicates that when devaluation increases the price of foreign goods to the home country and decreases the price of domestic goods to foreign buyers, there is a short-run period during which the balance of trade falls. We now consider why there may be low elasticities in the short run, to see what the possible underlying reasons are for a J curve.

We can identify different periods following a devaluation during which the ability of traders to respond to the new set of prices is at first limited, but over time becomes complete.

Currency Contract Period

Immediately following a devaluation, contracts negotiated prior to the exchange rate change become due. Let us refer to this as the *currency contract period.* Figure 9.3 illustrates the timing of events. Contracts are signed at time t_1. After the contracts are established, there is a currency devaluation at time t_2. Then the payments specified in the contracts are due at a later period t_3. The effects of such existing contracts on the balance of trade depend on the currency in which the contract is denominated. For instance, let us suppose that the United States devalues the dollar. Before the devaluation the exchange rate is \$1 per unit of foreign currency (to simplify matters, we will assume only one foreign currency); afterward the rate jumps to \$1.25. If a U.S. exporter has contracted to sell \$1 worth of goods to a foreign firm payable in dollars, the exporter will still earn \$1. However, if the export contract was written in terms of foreign currency (let FC stand for foreign currency), then the exporter expected to receive FC1, which would be equal to \$1. Instead, the devaluation leads to FC1 = \$1.25, so the U.S. exporter receives an unexpected gain from the dollar devaluation. On the other hand, consider an import contract where a U.S. importer contracts to buy from a foreign firm. If the contract calls for payment of \$1, then the

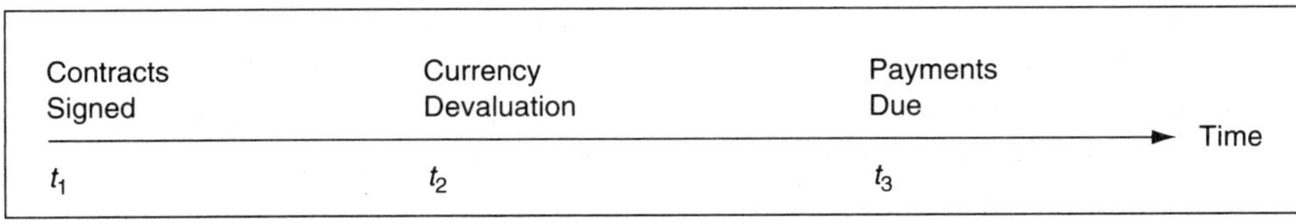

Figure 9.3 The currency contract period.

U.S. importer is unaffected by the devaluation. If the contract had been written in terms of foreign currency so that the U.S. importer owes FC1, then the importer would have to pay $1.25 to buy the FC1 that the exporter receives. In this case the importer faces a loss because of the devaluation.

In the simple world under consideration here we would expect sellers to prefer a contract in the currency expected to appreciate, whereas buyers would prefer contracts written in terms of the currency expected to depreciate. Table 9.1 summarizes the possible trade balance effects during the currency contract period.

Table 9.1 divides the effects into four cells. Cell I represents the case in which U.S. export contracts are written in terms of foreign currency, although import contracts are denominated in dollars. In this case the dollar

Table 9.1 U.S. Trade Balance Effects during Currency Contract Period Following a Devaluation

U.S. Export Contracts Written in	**U.S. Import Contracts Written in**	
	Dollars	**Foreign Currency**
Foreign currency	I. Exports increase Imports constant Balance of trade increases	II. Exports increase Imports increase Initial surplus: balance of trade increases Initial deficit: balance of trade decreases
Dollars	III. Exports constant Imports constant Balance of trade unchanged	IV. Exports constant Imports increase Balance of trade decreases

value of exports will increase since the foreign buyer must pay in foreign currency, which is worth more after the devaluation. Because imports are paid for with dollars, the devaluation will have no effect on the dollar value of U.S. imports. As a result, the balance of trade must increase.

Cell II indicates the trade balance effects when U.S. exports and imports are paid for with foreign currency. Since the dollar devaluation increases the value of foreign currency, the dollar values of both exports and imports will increase. The net effect on the U.S. trade balance depends on the magnitude of U.S. exports relative to imports. If exports exceed imports, so that there is an initial trade surplus, then the increase in export values will exceed the increase in imports and the balance of trade will increase. Conversely, if there is an initial trade deficit, so that imports exceed exports, then the increase in imports will exceed the increase in exports and the balance of trade will decrease.

If both exports and imports are payable in dollars, then the balance of trade is unaffected by a devaluation, as indicated in Cell III. But if exports are payable in dollars and imports require payment in foreign currency, the dollar value of exports will be unaffected by the devaluation and import values will increase; in this case the trade balance decreases as in Cell IV. Note that only in the case of Cell IV is there a decline in the trade balance during the currency contract period following a devaluation. A decline could also occur in Cell II, although only if there is an initial trade deficit. The key feature of Table 9.1 is that foreign-currency-denominated imports provide a necessary condition for the U.S. trade balance to take the plunge observed in the J-curve phenomenon during the currency contract period.

Pass-Through Analysis

The currency contract period refers to the period following a devaluation when contracts negotiated prior to the devaluation come due. During this time it is assumed that goods prices do not adjust instantaneously to the change in currency values. Eventually, of course, as new trade contracts are negotiated, goods prices will tend toward the new equilibrium. *Pass-through* analysis considers the ability of prices to adjust in the short run. The kind of adjustment expected is an increase in the price of import goods in the devaluing country and a decrease in the price of this country's exports to the rest of the world. If goods prices do not adjust in this manner, then spending patterns will not be altered, so that the desirable balance of trade effects of devaluation do not appear.

Devaluation is normally a response to a persistent and growing balance of trade deficit. As import prices rise in the devaluing country, fewer imports should be demanded. At the same time, the lower price of domestic exports to foreigners should increase the demand for exports. The combination of a higher demand for domestic exports and a lower domestic demand for imports should bring about an improvement in the trade balance. In the short run, however, if the response to the new prices is so slow that the quantities traded don't change much, then the new prices could contribute to the J curve. For instance, if the demand for imports is inelastic, then buyers will be relatively unresponsive to the higher price of imports, and thus the total import bill could rise rather than fall after the devaluation. Such behavior is not unreasonable since it takes time to find good substitutes for the now higher-priced import goods. Eventually, such substitutions will occur, but in the short run buyers may continue to buy imports in large enough quantities so that the now higher price results in a greater rather than a smaller value of domestic imports after the devaluation. The same explanation could hold on the other side of the market if foreign demand for domestic exports is inelastic. In this case, foreign buyers will not buy much more in the short run even though the price of domestic exports has fallen.

Table 9.2 summarizes the possible effects following a U.S. devaluation during the brief pass-through period before quantities adjust. The worst case is presented in Cell IV. With an inelastic demand for U.S. imports and an inelastic demand for U.S. exports, there will be a full pass-through of prices. To understand this effect fully, we should realize that the inelastic demands are in this case holding quantity fixed. Figure 9.4*a* illustrates the case of perfectly inelastic demand for U.S. imports. Who demands U.S. imports?—U.S. buyers, so the relevant price in Figure 9.4*a* is the dollar price of imports. Note that the U.S. demand for imports is fixed at Q_0. This means that in the short run, U.S. importers will buy Q_0 at any relevant price. After the devaluation, the supply curve shifts to the left, representing the fact that foreign exporters now want to charge a higher dollar price for their exports to the United States because the dollar is worth less. The vertical distance between the old and new supply curves indicates how much more sellers wish to charge for any given quantity. Since the demand curve is a vertical line, fixed at Q_0, sellers will be able to pass through the full amount of the desired price increase to importers; thus importers will be buying Q_0 at a higher price than before, and the total dollar value of imports will increase. This is the situation in Cell IV of Table 9.2, where the U.S. balance of trade decreases because of the full pass-through. Figure 9.4*b* shows why exports remain constant in Cell IV. Because foreign buyers purchase U.S. exports, the relevant price is the foreign currency price in Figure 9.4*b*. Foreign buyers want to purchase Q_F amount of U.S. exports regardless of the price in the short run. Note that now the relevant price to foreign buyers is the foreign currency price. After the devaluation, the supply curve shifts to the right to reflect the fact that U.S. exporters are willing to sell goods for less foreign currency because foreign currency is now worth more. However, with the perfectly inelastic demand curve, there is a full pass-through, lowering the foreign currency price by the full amount of the devaluation. In other words, if the devaluation increased the value of foreign currency by 10 percent, the foreign currency price of U.S. exports falls by 10 percent and the total dollar value of U.S. exports remains constant.

Note that Cell III of Table 9.2 pairs the inelastic demand for U.S. exports, as just discussed, with an inelastic supply of U.S. imports. Figure 9.4*c* illustrates the effect of the inelastic supply. Since imports into the United States are supplied by foreign sellers, the relevant price is the foreign currency price in Figure 9.4*c*. In this case, foreign sellers will sell Q_F imports to the United States independent of price. After the devaluation, the U.S.

Table 9.2 U.S. Trade Balance Effects during Pass-Through Period following a Devaluation

	U.S. Imports	
U.S. Exports	**Inelastic Supply**	**Inelastic Demand**
Inelastic supply	I. Exports increase Imports constant Balance of trade increases	II. Exports increase Imports increase Initial surplus: balance of trade increases Initial deficit: balance of trade decreases
Inelastic demand	III. Exports constant Imports constant Balance of trade constant	IV. Exports constant Imports increase Balance of trade decreases

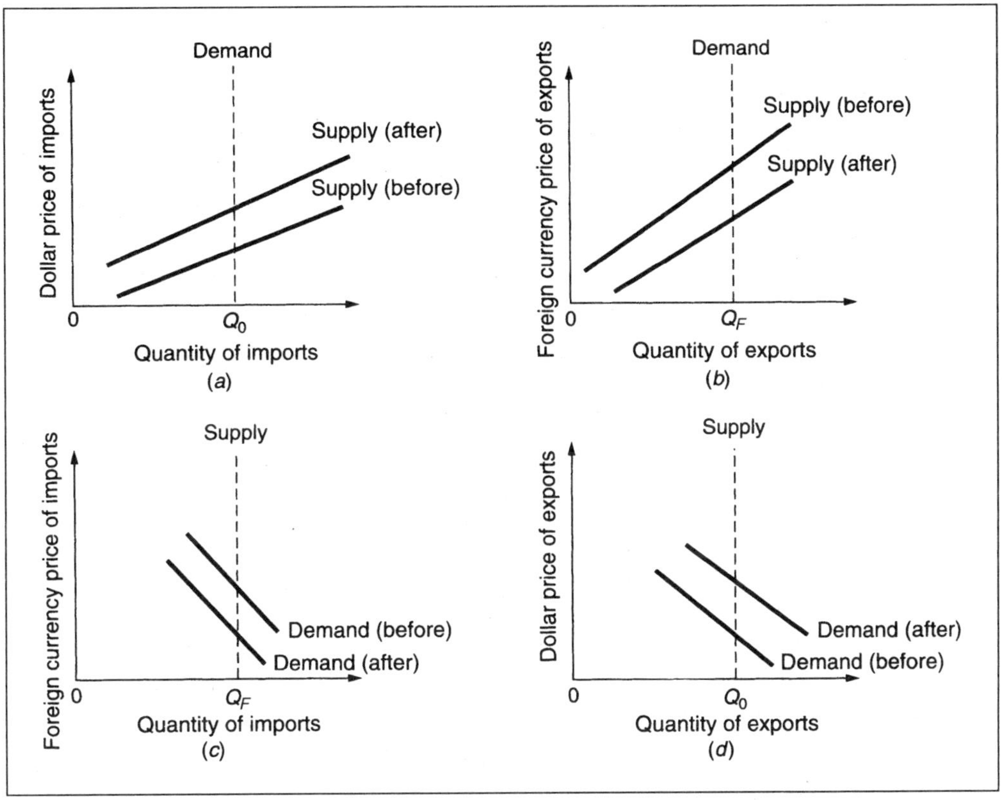

Figure 9.4 (*a*) Perfectly inelastic U.S. import demand; (*b*) perfectly inelastic demand for U.S. exports; (*c*) perfectly inelastic supply of U.S. imports; (*d*) perfectly inelastic supply of U.S. exports.

demand for imports in terms of foreign currency shifts to the left, indicating that buyers are willing to pay fewer units of foreign currency than before for a given quantity of imports. Because the supply curve is perfectly inelastic, the foreign currency price of imports falls by the amount of the devaluation, and thus there is no pass-through. After a dollar devaluation we expect imports to become more expensive to the United States; yet with a perfectly inelastic import supply curve, as in Figure 9.4*c,* U.S. dollar import prices are unchanged so that the dollar value of imports is also unchanged.

Cell II of Table 9.2 couples the inelastic U.S. import demand, as previously discussed and illustrated in Figure 9.4*a,* with an inelastic supply of U.S. exports. Figure 9.4*d* shows the supply effect. Because U.S. exports are supplied by U.S. sellers, the dollar price is the relevant price in Figure 9.4*d.* After the devaluation, foreigners are willing to pay a higher dollar price for U.S. exports because dollars are cheaper. With the perfectly inelastic supply curve, the dollar price of exports rises by the full amount of the devaluation. Thus, rather than having a devaluation pass-through lower U.S. export prices to foreigners, the increase in dollar prices has foreign buyers paying the same price as before (because the foreign currency price is unchanged). But the higher dollar price results in an increase in the dollar value of U.S. exports. Since the inelastic demand for U.S. imports also causes the dollar value of imports to increase, the net result for the balance of trade depends on whether initially exports exceeded imports, in which case the increase in exports after the devaluation will be larger than the import increase. If imports initially exceeded exports, then the devaluation will lower the trade balance.

Finally, we have the case of Cell I, where the balance of trade clearly increases during the pass-through period when quantities are fixed. The inelastic supply of U.S. exports leads to an increase in the dollar value of U.S. exports, whereas the inelastic supply of imports results in the value of imports holding constant.

The portrayal of perfectly inelastic supply and demand curves is made for illustrative purposes. We cannot argue that in the real world there is absolutely no quantity response to changing prices in the short run. The important contribution of the pass-through analysis is to indicate how changing goods prices in the short run, when the quantity response is likely to be quite small, can affect the balance of trade. If it is more reasonable to expect producers to be less able to alter quantities supplied than buyers can alter quantity demanded, then Cell I of Table 9.2 is the most likely real-world case. In this instance, the supplies of U.S. imports and exports are inelastic, so the U.S. trade balance should improve during the pass-through period.

The Evidence from Devaluations

The preceding discussion has shown the possible short-run effects of a devaluation on the trade balance through the currency contract and pass-through periods. What does the evidence of past devaluations have to offer regarding the *actual* effects? Unfortunately, the available evidence suggests that the effects of devaluation appear to differ across countries and time so that no strong generalizations are possible.

Some authors show that devaluation improves the trade account in the short run, while others disagree. The reasons for such disagreement come from the fact that different researchers use different sample periods and different statistical methodology.

Several researchers have focused on the manner in which producers in different countries adjust the profit margins on exports to partially offset the effect of exchange rate changes. This appears to be an important factor in explaining differences in the pass-through effect across countries. For instance, if the Japanese yen appreciates against the U.S. dollar, the yen appreciation would tend to be passed through to U.S. importers as a higher dollar price of Japanese exports. Japanese exporters could limit this pass through of higher prices by reducing the profit margins on their products and lowering the yen price to counter the effect of the yen appreciation. This *pricing to market* behavior has been found to be especially prevalent among Japanese and German exporters but is much less common among U.S. exporters. For example, Joseph Gagnon and Michael Knetter analyzed automobile trade and estimated that a 10 percent depreciation of the dollar against the yen would result in Japanese auto firms reducing their prices so that the dollar price to U.S. importers would rise by only 2.2 percent. There was no similar evidence of U.S. auto firms reducing prices for exported autos in response to dollar appreciation. Thomas Klitgaard found that Japanese exporters tend to lower their profit margins on exports by 4 percent (relative to margins on domestic sales) for every 10 percent appreciation of the yen. He also showed that in addition to cutting profit margins, in the 1990s Japanese exporters responded to yen appreciation by shifting production to high-valued products that are less sensitive to price increases. The Japanese resistance to allowing pass-through effects is another reason why the Japanese balance of trade may be less responsive to exchange rate changes than the U.S. trade balance.

There is some evidence that the impact of devaluations may differ over the short run and long run depending upon what happens to labor costs relative to the cost of capital. Kristin Forbes has found that in the short run following a devaluation, firm output and exports tend to rise as the cost of labor in the devaluing country falls and firms take advantage of this to expand production and increase their export sales. However, over time, capital becomes more expensive to firms in the devaluing country if the risk associated with that country rises or interest rates rise. So the net effect of devaluation depends upon the mix of capital and labor utilized in a nation's export industries. The evidence from a cross section of countries suggests that in countries where the ratio of capital to labor employed is low, devaluations are much more likely to result in export expansion and faster economic growth. But in countries where the capital/labor ratio is high, devaluations will tend to have little if any expansionary influence on exports and economic growth.

Absorption Approach to the Balance of Trade

The elasticities approach showed that it is possible for a country to improve its balance of trade through devaluation. Once the exchange rate effects pass through to import and export prices, imports should fall while exports increase, stimulating production of goods and services and income at home. If a country is at the full employment level of output prior to the devaluation, then it is already producing all it can so that no further output can be forthcoming. What happens in this case following a devaluation? We now turn to the absorption approach to the balance of trade to answer this question.

The *absorption approach to the balance of trade* is a theory that emphasizes how domestic spending on domestic goods changes relative to domestic output. In other words, the balance of trade is viewed as the difference between what the economy produces and what it takes, or absorbs, for domestic use. As commonly treated in introductory economics classes, we can write total output, Y, as being equal to total expenditures, or

$$Y = C + I + G + (X - M) \tag{9.2}$$

where C is consumption; I, investment; G, government spending; X, exports; and M, imports. We can define absorption, A, as being equal to $C + I + G$, and net exports as $(X - M)$. Thus we can write

$$Y = A + X - M$$

or

$$Y - A = X - M \tag{9.3}$$

Absorption, A, is supposed to represent total domestic spending. Thus, if total domestic production, Y, exceeds absorption (the amount of the output consumed at home), then the nation will export the rest of its output and run a balance of trade surplus. On the other hand, if absorption exceeds domestic production, then $Y - A$ is negative; thus by Equation (9.3), we note that $X - M$ will also be negative, which has the common-sense interpretation that the excess of domestic demand over domestic production will be met through imports.

The analysis of the absorption approach is really broken down into two categories, depending upon whether the economy is at full employment or has unemployed resources. If we have full employment, then all resources are being used so that the only way for net exports to increase is to have absorption fall. On the other hand, with unemployment, *Y* is not at its maximum possible value, and thus *A* could remain fixed and *Y* could increase because of increases in domestic sales to foreigners, *X*.

The absorption approach is generally concerned with the effects of a devaluation on the trade balance. If we begin from the case of unemployed resources, we know that domestic output, *Y*, could increase, so that a devaluation would tend to increase net exports (if the elasticity conditions discussed in the previous section are satisfied) and bring about an increase in output (given a constant absorption). If we start from full employment, then output, *Y*, is at the full employment level, and therefore it is not possible to produce more goods and services. If we devalue, then net exports will tend to increase and the result is strictly inflation. When foreigners try to spend more on our domestic production, and yet there is no increase in output forthcoming, the only result will be a bidding-up of the prices of the goods and services currently being produced.

Of course, we must realize that the absorption approach is providing a theory of the balance of trade, as did the elasticities approach. The absorption approach can be viewed as a theory of the balance of payments only in a world without capital flows.

Monetary Approach to the Balance of Payments

The elasticities approach and the absorption approach are theories of the balance of trade that have been popular for over 50 years. As we have seen, these are theories that emphasize trade in real goods and have little to say about the capital account. For some purposes, these theories can still provide useful intuition. However, the world today is characterized by well-developed financial markets and large-scale international capital flows. To fully understand international economic linkages, we must look beyond merchandise trade and incorporate the important role of financial assets. It was in this spirit that the *monetary approach to the balance of payments* (MABP) came to popularity in the 1970s; it emphasizes the monetary aspects of the balance of payments.

We may draw the line in the international accounts (see Chapter 2 for a review of balance of payments concepts) so that the current and capital accounts are above the line and only those items that directly affect the money supply are below the line [specifically, official holdings of gold, foreign exchange, special drawing rights (SDRs), and changes in reserves at the

International Monetary Fund (IMF)—but do not worry about these terms now]. This allows us to concentrate on the monetary aspects of the balance of payments.

The basic premise of the MABP is that any balance of payments disequilibrium is based on a monetary disequilibrium—that is, differences existing between the amount of money people wish to hold and the amount supplied by the monetary authorities. In very simple terms, if people demand more money than is being supplied by the central bank, then the excess demand for money would be satisfied by inflows of money from abroad. On the other hand, if the central bank (the Federal Reserve in the United States) is supplying more money than is demanded, the excess supply of money is eliminated by outflows of money to other countries. Thus the MABP analysis emphasizes the determinants of money demand and money supply, since these will also determine the balance of payments.

The monetary approach has a long and distinguished history, so the recent popularity of the approach can be viewed as a rediscovery rather than a modern innovation. In fact, the recent literature often makes use of a quote from *Of the Balance of Trade,* written by David Hume in 1752, to indicate the early understanding of the problem. Hume wrote:

> Suppose four-fifths of all the money in Great Britain to be annihilated in one night, and the nation reduced to the same condition, with regard to specie, as in the reigns of the Harrys and Edwards, what would be the consequence? Must not the price of all labour and commodities sink in proportion, and everything be sold as cheap as they were in these ages? What nation could then dispute with us in any foreign market, or pretend to navigate or to sell manufactures at the same price, which to us would afford sufficient profit? In how little time, therefore, must this bring back the money which we had lost, and raise us to the level of all the neighboring nations? Where after we have arrived, we immediately lose the advantage of the cheapness of labor and commodities; and the farther flowing in of money is stopped by our fullness and repletion.

Hume's analysis is a strict monetary approach to prices and the balance of payments. If England's money stock suddenly was reduced by four-fifths, we know from principles of economics that the price level would fall dramatically. The falling price level would give England a price advantage over its foreign competitors, so that its exports would rise and its imports fall. As the foreign money (gold in Hume's day) poured in, England's money supply would rise and its price level would follow. This process continues until England's prices reach the levels of its competitors, after which the system is back in equilibrium.

Thus far we have only discussed the monetary approach to the balance of payments, which is fine for a world with fixed exchange rates or a gold standard. For a world with flexible exchange rates, we have the *monetary approach to the exchange rate* (MAER). The dichotomy between fixed and floating exchange rates is an important one. When exchange rates are fixed between countries, we will observe money flowing between countries to adjust to disequilibrium. With floating exchange rates, the exchange rates are allowed to fluctuate with the free-market forces of supply and demand for each currency. The free-market equilibrium exchange rate occurs at a point where the flow of exports just equals the flow of imports so that no net international money flows are required. International economists refer to this choice of money flows or exchange rate changes as the choice of an international *adjustment mechanism.* With fixed exchange rates the adjustment to changes in international monetary conditions comes through international money flows, whereas with floating rates the adjustment comes through exchange rate changes. To organize our thoughts and provide a convenient framework for distinguishing the analysis between MABP and MAER, we outline a simple economic model relating money demand, money supply, the balance of payments, and exchange rates.

Before turning to the model, we should consider some basic concepts and assumptions. In principles of macroeconomics we learn that the Federal Reserve controls the money supply by altering *base money* (currency plus commercial bank reserves held against deposits). As base money changes, the lending ability of commercial banks changes. Increases in base money tend to result in an expansion of the money supply, whereas decreases in base money tend to contract the money supply. For MABP purposes it is useful to divide base money into domestic and international components. We refer to the domestic component of base money as *domestic credit;* the remainder is made up of *international reserves* (money items that can be used to settle international debts, primarily foreign exchange). The international money flows that respond to excess demands or excess supplies at home affect base money and then the money supply. For instance, if a U.S. exporter receives payment in foreign currency, this payment will be presented to a U.S. commercial bank to be converted into dollars and deposited in the exporter's account. If the commercial bank has no use for the foreign currency, the bank will exchange the foreign currency for dollars at the Federal Reserve (or Fed). The Fed creates new money with which to buy the foreign currency by increasing the commercial bank's reserve deposit with the Fed. Thus, the Fed is accumulating international reserves, and this reserve accumulation brings about an expansion of base money. In the case of an excess supply of money at home, either domestic credit falls to reduce base money, or international reserves fall to lower base money to the desired level.

Now we are ready to construct a simple model of the MABP. The usual assumption is that we are analyzing the situation of a *small open economy.* It is small because we want to assume that this country cannot affect the international prices of goods or the interest rate it faces. Openness implies that this country is an active participant in international economic transactions. We could classify nations according to their degree of openness, or the degree to which they depend on international transactions. The United States would be relatively closed, considering the size of its GDP relative to the value of its international trade, whereas Belgium would be relatively open.

We can begin our model by writing the demand for money as

$$L = kPY \tag{9.4}$$

where L is the demand for money, P is the domestic price level, Y is real income or wealth, and k is a constant fraction indicating how money demand will change given a change in P or Y. Equation (9.4) is often stated as "money demand is a function of prices and income" or "money demand depends on prices and income." The usual story is that the higher the income, the more money people will hold in order to buy more goods. The higher the price level, the more money is desired to buy any given quantity of goods. So the demand for money should rise with an increase in either P or Y.

A strong assumption of the monetary approach is that there is a stable demand for money. This means that the relationship among money demand, income, and prices does not change significantly over time. Without a stable demand for money, the monetary approach will not provide a useful framework for analysis.

Letting M stand for money supply, R for international reserves, and D for domestic credit (we assume that base money equals the money supply to simplify matters), we can write the money supply relationship as

$$M = R + D \tag{9.5}$$

Letting P stand for the domestic price level, E for the domestic currency price of foreign currency, and P^F for the foreign price level, we can write the law of one price as

$$P = EP^F \tag{9.6}$$

Finally, we need the assumption that equilibrium in the money market holds so that money demand equals money supply, or

$$L = M \tag{9.7}$$

The adjustment mechanism that ensures equilibrium in Equation (9.7) will vary with the exchange rate regime. With fixed exchange rates, money supply adjusts to money demand through international flows of money via balance of payments imbalances. With flexible exchange rates, money demand will be adjusted to a money supply set by the central bank via exchange rate changes. In the case of a dirty or managed float, where theoretically we have floating exchange rates but the central banks intervene to keep exchange rates at desired levels, we have both international money flows and exchange rate changes. All three cases will be analyzed in the following pages.

Now we develop the model in a manner that will allow us to analyze the balance of payments and exchange rates in a monetary framework. We begin by substituting Equation (9.6) into Equation (9.4):

$$L = kEP^FY \tag{9.8}$$

Substituting Equations (9.8) and (9.5) into (9.7), we obtain

$$kEP^FY = R + D \tag{9.9}$$

Finally, we want to discuss Equation (9.9), money demand and money supply, in terms of percentage changes. Since k is a constant, the change is zero, and thus k drops out of the analysis and we are left with[†]

$$\hat{E} + \hat{P}^F + \hat{Y} = \hat{R} + \hat{D} \tag{9.10}$$

where the hat (^) over a variable indicates percentage change.

[†]If $a = bc$, the percentage change in a is equal to the sum of the percentage change in b plus the percentage change in c: $\hat{a} = \hat{b} + \hat{c}$. In Equation (9.10), $\hat{R} + \hat{D}$ is actually the change in $R + D$ as a fraction of the money supply, or the change in reserves plus the change in domestic credit divided by the money supply. So $\hat{R} = \Delta R/M$ and $\hat{D} = \Delta D/M$.

Since the goal of this analysis is to be able to explain changes in the exchange rate or reserves, we should have $\hat{R}$ and $\hat{E}$ on the left-hand side of the equation. Rearranging Equation (9.10) in this manner gives

$$\hat{R} - \hat{E} = \hat{P}^F + \hat{Y} - \hat{D} \tag{9.11}$$

This indicates that the change in reserves minus the percentage change in exchange rates is equal to the foreign inflation rate, plus the percentage growth of real income, minus the change in domestic credit. With fixed exchange rates, $\hat{E} = 0$ and we have the monetary approach to the balance of payments:

$$\hat{R} = \hat{P}^F + \hat{Y} - \hat{D} \tag{9.12}$$

Therefore, with fixed exchange rates, an increase in domestic credit with constant prices and income (and thus constant money demand) will lead to a decrease in international reserves. This means that if the central bank expands domestic credit, creating an excess supply of money, reserves will flow out or there will be a balance of payments deficit as people spend to lower the excess cash balances. Conversely, a decrease in domestic credit will lead to an excess demand for money, since money demand is unchanged for a given $\hat{P}^F$ and $\hat{Y}$; yet because D is falling, R will increase to bring money supply equal to money demand.

Given the framework just developed, we can now consider some of the implications and extensions of the monetary approach. First, the assumption of purchasing power parity implies that the central bank must make a policy choice between an exchange rate or a domestic price level. Since $P = EP^F$, under fixed exchange rates E is constant; therefore, maintaining the pegged value of E implies that the domestic price level will correspond to that of the rest of the world. This is the case in which people discuss imported inflation. If the foreign price level is increasing rapidly, then our price must follow if we are to maintain the fixed E. On the other hand, with flexible rates E is free to vary to whatever level is necessary to clear the foreign exchange market, and so we can choose our domestic rate of inflation independent of the rest of the world. If we select a lower rate of inflation than foreigners do, then PPP suggests that our currency will tend to appreciate. This issue of choosing between the domestic inflation rate or a preferred exchange rate has important economic as well as political implications, and is not made without much thought and consultation among central bankers.

We might mention at this point that there are two views of how PPP operates in the short run, and these two views imply a different mechanism of adjustment to a change in the world economy like a change in the foreign price level. One view is that PPP holds strictly, even in the short run. In this case, a change in the foreign price induces an immediate change in the domestic price and a corresponding change in money demand or money supply. The other view is along the lines of the Hume quote cited previously. The idea here is that prices adjust slowly through the balance of payments effects on the money supply. Thus, if foreign prices rise relative to domestic prices, we tend to sell more to foreigners and run a larger balance of trade surplus. Since we gain international reserves from these goods sales, over time our money supply rises and our prices increase until PPP is restored. We find that the two approaches differ primarily with regard to timing. The first case assumes that PPP holds in the short run because international reserves flow quickly in response to new events and prices adjust quickly to new equilibrium levels. This fast adjustment is supposedly due to an emphasis on the role of financial assets being bought and sold, resulting in international capital flows. Since financial assets are easily bought and sold, it is easy to understand why many believe that PPP should hold in the short run (ignoring any relative price effects, which we are not discussing in this section). The second case also assumes that PPP holds, but only in the long run. This approach emphasizes the role of goods markets in international adjustment. Since goods prices are supposedly slow to adjust, short-run deviations from PPP will occur that give rise to the balance of trade effects previously discussed. The truth most likely lies between these two extremes. It is reasonable to expect goods prices to adjust slowly over time to changing economic conditions, so it may be reasonable to doubt that PPP holds well in the short run. On the other hand, PPP is not strictly dependent on goods markets. To ignore international capital flows is to miss the potential for a faster adjustment than is possible strictly through goods markets.

We can summarize the policy implications of the monetary approach to the balance of payments as follows:

1. Balance of payments disequilibria are essentially monetary phenomena. Thus, countries would not run long-term (or structural, as they are called) deficits if they did not rely so heavily on inflationary money supply growth to finance government spending.

2. Balance of payments disequilibria must be transitory. If the exchange rate remains fixed, eventually the country must run out of reserves by trying to support a continuing deficit.

3. Balance of payments disequilibria can be handled with domestic monetary policy rather than with adjustments in the exchange rate. Devaluation of the currency exchange rate is a substitute for reducing the growth of domestic credit in that devaluation lowers the value of a country's money relative to the rest of the world (conversely, an appreciation of the currency is a substitute for increasing domestic credit growth). Following any devaluation, if the underlying monetary cause of the devaluation is not corrected, then future devaluations will be required to offset the continued excess supply of the country's money.

4. Domestic balance of payments will be improved by an increase in domestic income via an increase in money demand, if not offset by an increase in domestic credit.

Summary

1. Consumption decisions respond to changes in relative prices.
2. The elasticity of supply or demand measures the responsiveness of quantity to changes in price.
3. A devaluation of the domestic currency should raise the price of foreign goods relative to domestic goods.
4. The J curve describes the pattern of the balance of trade following a devaluation; this is a pattern in which the trade balance at first falls and then rises.
5. Immediately following a devaluation, the invoicing currency used for contracts written prior to the devaluation becomes an important determinant of the value of the trade account.
6. The pass-through of devaluation to domestic and foreign prices depends on the elasticities of supply and demand for international trade.
7. The evidence regarding the effects of devaluation on the balance of trade indicates no standard pattern.
8. The balance of trade can improve only if income increases relative to absorption.
9. The monetary approach analyzes the balance of payments and exchange rates in terms of money supply and money demand.

10. With fixed exchange rates, money supply adjusts to money demand through international reserve flows.

Exercises

1. What does a J curve refer to?
2. Explain the conditions necessary for a devaluation to improve the balance of trade for each of the following:
   a. Elasticities approach
   b. Absorption approach
   c. Contract period
   d. Pass-through period
3. According to the monetary approach to the balance of payments, what type of economic policies would help a country resolve a balance of payments deficit?
4. Using the monetary approach to the balance of payments model developed in the text, explain how the following events would affect the domestic balance of payments:
   a. The Japanese inflation rate falls
   b. The Federal Reserve implements a restrictive monetary policy
   c. The United States increases tariffs against Japan
   d. The German economy suffers a recession

References

Connolly, Michael, "The Monetary Approach to an Open Economy: The Fundamental Theory," *The Monetary Approach to International Adjustment,* ed. Bluford Putnam and D. Sykes Wilford, New York: Praeger, 1978.

Devereaux, M. B., "How Does a Devaluation Affect the Current Account?" *Journal of International Money and Finance,* December 2000.

Forbes, Kristin, "Cheap Labor Meets Costly Capital: The Impact of Devaluations on Commodity Firms," National Bureau of Economic Research Working Paper No. 9053, July 2002.

Gagnon, Joseph E., and Michael M. Knetter, "Markup Adjustment and Exchange Rate Fluctuations: Evidence from Panel Data on Automobile Exports," *Journal of International Money and Finance,* April 1995.

Hume, David, "Of the Balance of Trade," *Essays, Moral, Political and Literary,* 1752, reprinted in *International Finance,* ed. R. N. Cooper, Middlesex, England: Penguin 1969.

Koray, Faik, and W. Douglas McMillin, "Monetary Shocks, the Exchange Rate, and the Trade Balance," *Journal of International Money and Finance,* December 1999.

Klitgaard, Thomas, "Coping with the Rising Yen: Japan's Recent Export Experience," *Current Issues in Economics and Finance,* Federal Reserve Bank of New York, January 1996.

Klitgaard, Thomas, "Exchange Rates and Profit Margins: The Case of Japanese Exporters," *FRBNY Economic Policy Review,* April 1999.

Rose, Andrew, "Are All Devaluations Alike?" *Weekly Letter,* Federal Reserve Bank of San Francisco, February 9, 1996.

10

Exchange Rate Determination

An exchange rate is a financial asset price. It is the price of one money in terms of another. It would seem straightforward to analyze exchange rate determination by considering the supply and demand for each money. As we shall see, the monetary approach to the exchange rate is just such an analysis. Prior to the monetary approach, it was common to emphasize international trade flows as primary determinants of exchange rates. The traditional approach emphasized the role of exchange rate changes in eliminating international trade imbalances. In this context we should expect countries with current trade surpluses to have appreciating currencies, while countries with trade deficits should have depreciating currencies. Such exchange rate changes would lead to changes in international relative prices that would work to eliminate the trade imbalance.

It is clear that the world does not work in the simple way just considered. We have seen some instances when countries with trade surpluses have depreciating currencies, while countries with trade deficits have appreciating currencies. Economists have responded to the real-world events by devising several alternative views of exchange rate determination. This chapter considers some of the recent advances in exchange rate theory.

The Asset Approach

Modern exchange rate models emphasize financial asset markets. Rather than the traditional view of exchange rates adjusting to equilibrate international trade in goods, the exchange rate is viewed as adjusting to equilibrate international trade in financial assets. Since goods prices adjust slowly relative to financial asset prices, and financial assets are traded continuously each business day, the shift in emphasis from goods markets to asset markets has important implications. Exchange rates will change every day or even every minute as supply and demand for financial assets of different nations change.

An implication of the asset approach is that exchange rates should be much more variable than goods prices. This seems to be an empirical fact. Table 10.1 lists the standard deviation of the percentage changes in prices and exchange rates calculated for four countries. Over the period covered in the table, we observe that spot exchange rates for the four countries studied were much more volatile than prices. Comparing the prices with the exchange rates, we find that the volatility of exchange rates averaged from 4 to 7 times the volatility of prices. Such figures are consistent with the fact that exchange rates respond to changing conditions in financial asset markets and are not simply reacting to changes in international goods trade.

Exchange rate models emphasizing financial asset markets typically assume perfect capital mobility. *Perfect capital mobility* means that capital will flow freely between nations because there are no significant transactions costs or capital controls to serve as barriers to investment. In such a world, covered interest arbitrage will ensure covered interest rate parity:

$$\frac{i - i_f}{1 + i_f} = \frac{F - E}{E}$$

where i is the domestic interest rate, i_f is the foreign interest rate, and F and E are in units of domestic currency per 1 unit of foreign currency. Since this relationship will hold continuously, spot and forward exchange rates, as well as interest rates, will adjust instantaneously to changing financial market conditions.

Within the family of asset approach models, there are two basic groups: the monetary approach and the portfolio-balance approach. The monetary approach to the balance of payments was introduced in Chapter 9. As stated there, in the monetary approach the balance of payments or exchange rate

Table 10.1 Standard Deviations of Prices and Exchange Rates

Country	Price	Exchange Rate
Canada	.0015	.0063
Japan	.0017	.0152
Mexico	.0046	.0211
United Kingdom	.0020	.0120

Note: The table reports the standard deviation of the percentage changes in the consumer price index and the spot exchange rate of each country's currency against the U.S. dollar for the period January 1990 to October 2002.

for any two currencies is determined by relative money demand and money supply between the two countries. Relative supplies of domestic and foreign bonds are unimportant. The *portfolio-balance approach* allows relative bond supplies and demands as well as relative money market conditions to determine the exchange rate.

The essential difference is that monetary approach (MA) models assume domestic and foreign bonds to be perfect substitutes, while portfolio-balance (PB) models assume imperfect substitutability. If domestic and foreign bonds are perfect substitutes, then demanders are indifferent to the currencies of denomination of the bonds as long as the expected return is the same. In this case, bond holders do not require a premium to hold foreign bonds—they would just as soon hold foreign bonds as domestic bonds—so there is no risk premium and uncovered interest rate parity holds in MA models.

With imperfect substitutability, demanders have preferences for distributing their portfolio over different countries' assets. They have a desired portfolio share for any particular country's assets. If the supply of one country's assets increases, they will hold a greater proportion of that country's assets only if they are compensated. This requires a premium to be paid on these assets. In general, then, PB models have risk premiums that are a function of relative asset supplies. As the supply of country A's financial assets rises relative to B's, there will be a higher premium paid on A's assets. An implication of this premium is that uncovered interest rate parity will not hold, since risk premiums will exist in the forward market. This premium is missing in the MA model, because there it is assumed that investors don't care whether they hold country A or country B bonds, or in what mix they are held.

We might guess that the PB approach is more relevant if we doubt the MA assumption of perfect substitutability of assets internationally. In such cases we would view the exchange rate as being determined by relative supplies of domestic and foreign bonds as well as domestic and foreign money. We may then modify the monetary approach to the exchange rate equation to incorporate this additional effect.

The Monetary Approach

Since Chapter 9 focused on balance of payments determination, we repeat the derivation of the monetary approach here with a focus on exchange rate determination. For those who have studied Chapter 9, this will be a simple review. Otherwise, the material here will serve as a sufficient introduction to the monetary approach.

In Chapter 9, we discussed the monetary approach only with respect to the balance of payments, which is fine for a world with fixed exchange rates. For a world with flexible exchange rates, we have the monetary approach to the exchange rate (MAER). The dichotomy between fixed and floating exchange rates is an important one. When exchange rates are fixed between countries, we observe money flowing between countries to adjust to disequilibrium. With floating exchange rates, the exchange rates are allowed to fluctuate with the free-market forces of supply and demand for each currency. The free-market-equilibrium exchange rate often is assumed to occur at a point where the flow of exports just equals the flow of imports, so that no net international money flows are required. To provide a convenient framework for the analysis under the MAER, we outline a simple economic model relating money demand, money supply, the balance of payments, and exchange rates.

Before turning to the model, we should consider some basic concepts and assumptions. In principles of macroeconomics we learn that the Federal Reserve controls the money supply by altering *base money* (currency plus commercial bank reserves held against deposits). As base money changes, the lending ability of commercial banks changes. Increases in base money tend to result in an expansion of the money supply, whereas decreases in base money tend to contract the money supply. For our purposes, it is useful to divide base money into domestic and international components. The domestic component of base money is called *domestic credit,* whereas the remainder is made up of *international reserves* (money items that can be used to settle international debts, primarily foreign exchange). The international money flows that respond to excess demands or excess supplies of goods or financial assets at home affect base money and then the money supply. For instance, if a U.S. exporter receives payment in foreign currency, this payment will be presented to a U.S. commercial bank to be converted into dollars and deposited in the exporter's account. If the commercial bank has no use for the foreign currency, the bank will exchange the foreign currency for dollars with the Federal Reserve (the Fed). The Fed creates new base money to buy the foreign currency by increasing the commercial bank's reserve deposit with the Fed. Thus, the Fed is accumulating international reserves, and this reserve accumulation brings about an expansion of base money. In the case of an excess supply of money at home, either domestic credit falls to reduce base money, or international reserves will fall in order to lower base money to the desired level.

Now we are ready to construct a simple model of the monetary approach. The usual assumption is that we are analyzing the situation of a small, open economy. It is small because we want to assume that this country cannot affect the international price of goods or the interest rate it faces. Openness implies that this country is an active participant in international economic transactions. We could classify nations according to their degree of openness, or the degree to which they depend on international transactions. The United States would be relatively closed, considering the size of the U.S. GDP relative to the value of international trade, whereas Belgium would be relatively open.

We can being our model by writing the demand for money as

$$L = kPY \tag{10.1}$$

where L is the demand for money, P is the domestic price level, Y is real income or wealth, and k is a constant fraction indicating how money demand will change given a change in P or Y. Equation (10.1) is often stated as "money demand is a function of prices and income," or "money demand depends on prices and income." The usual story is that the higher the income, the more money people will hold to buy more goods. The higher the price level, the more money is desired to buy any given quantity of goods. So, the demand for money should rise with an increase in either P or Y.

A strong assumption of the monetary approach is that there is a stable demand for money. This means that the relationship among money demand, income, and prices does not change significantly over time. Without a stable demand for money, the monetary approach will not provide a useful framework for analysis.

Letting M stand for money supply, R for international reserves, and D for domestic credit, we can write the money supply relationship as†

$$M = R + D \tag{10.2}$$

Letting P stand for the domestic price level, E for the domestic currency price of foreign currency, and P^F for the foreign price level, we can write the law of one price as

$$P = EP^F \tag{10.3}$$

Finally, we need the assumption that equilibrium in the money market holds so that money demand equals money supply, or

$$L = M \tag{10.4}$$

The adjustment mechanism that ensures the Equation (10.4) equilibrium will vary with the exchange rate regime. With fixed exchange rates, money supply adjusts to money demand through international flows of money via balance of payments imbalances. With flexible exchange rates, money demand will be adjusted to a money supply set by the central bank via exchange rate changes. In the case of a managed float, where theoretically we have floating exchange rates but the central banks intervene to keep exchange rates at desired levels, we have both international money flows and exchange rate changes. All three cases will be analyzed subsequently.

Now, we develop the model in a manner that will allow us to analyze the balance of payments and exchange rates in a monetary framework. We begin by substituting Equation (10.3) into Equation (10.1).

$$L = kEP^FY \tag{10.5}$$

Substituting Equations (10.5) and (10.2) into (10.4) we obtain

$$kEP^FY = R + D \tag{10.6}$$

†We are assuming that base money and the money supply are equal. Realistically, the money supply is some multiple of base money. We assume that this multiple is 1 in order to simplify the analysis.

Finally, we want to discuss Equation (10.6), money demand and money supply, in terms of percentage changes. Since k is a constant, the change is zero, and thus k drops out of the analysis and we are left with[†]

$$\hat{E} + \hat{P}^F + \hat{Y} = \hat{R} + \hat{D} \tag{10.7}$$

where the hat (^) over a variable indicates percentage change.

Since the goal of this analysis is to be able to explain changes in the exchange rate or balance of payments, we should have $\hat{R}$ and $\hat{E}$ on the left-hand side of the equation. Rearranging Equation (10.7) in this manner gives

$$\hat{R} - \hat{E} = \hat{P}^F + \hat{Y} - \hat{D} \tag{10.8}$$

This indicates that the percentage change in reserves (the balance of payments) minus the percentage change in exchange rates is equal to the foreign inflation rate plus the percentage growth in real income minus the percentage change in domestic credit. With fixed exchange rates, $\hat{E} = 0$, and we have the monetary approach to the balance of payments, as was discussed in Chapter 9.

In the case of flexible exchange rates with no central bank intervention, we assume reserve flows $\hat{R}$ equal zero, whereas exchange rate changes are nonzero. The general Equation (10.8) is now written for the monetary approach to the exchange rate as $-\hat{E} = \hat{P}^F + \hat{Y} - \hat{D}$. However, since this chapter focuses solely on the exchange rate, we can simplify things by multiplying both sides of the equation by -1 so that the MAER equation is

$$\hat{E} = \hat{D} - \hat{P}^F - \hat{Y} \tag{10.9}$$

With the MAER, an increase in domestic credit, given a constant $\hat{P}^F$ and $\hat{Y}$ (so that money demand is constant), will result in $\hat{E}$ increasing and since $\hat{E}$ is domestic currency units per foreign currency unit, an increase in $\hat{E}$ means that domestic currency is either appreciating at a slower rate or depreciating at a faster rate. Under the MAER, domestic monetary policy will not cause flows of money internationally but will lead to exchange rate changes.

The fact that $\hat{P}^F$ and $\hat{Y}$ have signs opposite that of $\hat{E}$ in Equation (10.9) indicates that changes in inflation and income growth will cause changes in exchange rates in the opposite direction. For instance, if $\hat{P}^F$ and/or $\hat{Y}$ increase, we know that money demand increases. With constant domestic

[†]If $a = bc$, the percentage change in $\hat{a}$ is equal to the sum of the percentage change in b plus the percentage change in c: $\hat{a} = \hat{b} + \hat{c}$. In Equation (10.7), $\hat{R} + \hat{D}$ is actually the change in $R + D$ as a fraction of the money supply, or the change in reserves plus the change in domestic credit divided by the money supply, so $\hat{R} = \Delta R/M$ and $\hat{D} = \Delta D/M$.

credit, we have an excess demand for money. As individuals try to increase their money balances, we observe a decrease in $\hat{E}$ or faster appreciation (or slower depreciation) of the domestic currency.

So far, we have discussed the case of fixed or flexible exchange rates, but what is the framework for analysis of a managed float? Remember, a managed float means that although exchange rates are theoretically flexible and determined by the market forces of supply and demand, central banks intervene at times to peg the rates at some desired level. Thus, the managed float has the attributes of both a fixed and a floating exchange rate regime, because changing supply and demand will affect exchange rates, but the actions of the central bank will also allow international reserves to change. To allow for reserve changes, as well as for exchange rate changes, we can simply return to the initial Equation (10.8). Thus, we can see that given money demand or money supply changes, the central bank can choose to let $\hat{E}$ adjust to the free-market level; or, by holding E at some disequilibrium level, it will allow $\hat{R}$ to adjust.

The Portfolio-Balance Approach

If domestic and foreign bonds are perfect substitutes, then Equation (10.9) is a useful MA description of exchange rate determination. The PB approach assumes that assets are imperfect substitutes internationally because investors perceive foreign exchange risk to be attached to foreign-currency-denominated bonds. As the supply of domestic bonds rises relative to foreign bonds, there will be an increased risk premium on the domestic bonds that will cause the domestic currency to depreciate in the spot market. If the spot exchange rate depreciates today, and if the expected future spot rate is unchanged, the expected rate of appreciation over the future increases.

For instance, if the dollar/pound spot rate is initially $E_{\$/£} = 2.00$, and the expected spot rate in 1 year is $E_{\$/£} = 1.90$, then the expected rate of dollar appreciation is 5 percent [(1.90 − 2.00)/2.00]. Now suppose that an increase in the outstanding stock of dollar-denominated bonds results in a depreciation of the spot rate today to $E_{\$/£} = 2.05$. The expected rate of dollar appreciation is now approximately 7.3 percent [(1.90 − 2.05)/2.05].

If the spot exchange rate is a function of relative asset supplies, then the MA equation (10.9) should be modified to include the percentage change in the supply of domestic bonds ($\hat{B}$) and the percentage change in the supply of foreign bonds $\hat{B}^F$):

$$\hat{E} = \hat{D} + \hat{B} - \hat{B}^F - \hat{P}^F - \hat{Y} \tag{10.10}$$

This broader PB view might be expected to explain exchange rate changes better than the MA equation. However, the empirical evidence is not at all clear on this matter. One potential problem for analyzing the MA and PB models of exchange rate determination is central bank activities that are aimed at insulating the domestic money supply from international events. The next section discusses the importance of this issue.

Sterilization

Sterilization is the offsetting of international reserve flows by central banks that wish to follow an independent monetary policy. Under the monetary approach to the balance of payments (with fixed exchange rates), if a country has an excess supply of money, this country would tend to lose international reserves or run a deficit until money supply equals money demand. If for some reason the central bank desires a higher money supply and reacts to the deficit by further increasing the money supply, then the deficit will increase and persist as long as the central bank tries to maintain a money supply in excess of money demand. With an excess demand for money, the concept is reversed. The excess demand results in reserve inflows to equate money supply to money demand. If the central bank tries to decrease the money supply so that the excess demand still exists, its efforts will be thwarted by further reserve inflows, which will persist as long as the central bank tries to maintain the policy of a money supply less than money demand.

If sterilization is possible, then the monetary authorities may in fact be able to stabilize the money supply in the short run without having reserve flows offset their goals. This would be possible if the forces that lead to international arbitrage are slow to operate. For instance, if there are barriers to international capital mobility, then we might expect international asset return differentials to persist following a change in economic conditions. In this case, if the central bank wants to increase the growth of the money supply in the short run, it can do so regardless of money demand and reserve flows. In the long run, when complete adjustment of asset prices is possible, the money supply must grow at a rate consistent with money demand. In the short run, however, the central bank can exercise some discretion.

The actual use of the word *sterilization* derives from the fact that the central bank must be able to neutralize, or sterilize, any reserve flows induced by monetary policy if the policy is to achieve the central bank's money supply goals. For instance, if the central bank is following some money supply growth path, and then money demand increases, leading to reserve inflows, the central bank must be able to sterilize these reserve inflows to keep the money supply from rising to what it considers undesirable levels. This is done by decreasing domestic credit by an amount equal to the growth of international reserves, thus keeping base money and the money supply constant.

In Chapter 9 the fixed exchange rate monetary approach to the balance of payments equation was

$$\hat{R} = \hat{P}^F + \hat{Y} - \hat{D} \tag{10.11}$$

where $\hat{R}$ is the percentage change in international reserves. Given money demand, an increase in domestic credit would be reflected in a fall in $\hat{R}$ or lower growth of reserves. If sterilization occurs, then the causality implied in Equation (10.1) is no longer true.

Instead of the monetary approach equation previously written, where changes in domestic credit ($\hat{D}$, on the right-hand side of the equation) lead to changes in reserves ($\hat{R}$, on the left-hand side), with sterilization we also have changes in reserves inducing changes in domestic credit in order to offset the reserve flows. With sterilization, the causality implied in Equation (10.11), where domestic credit causes reserve changes, must be reconsidered. Sterilization means that there is also a causality flowing from reserve changes to domestic credit, as in

$$\hat{D} = \alpha - \beta\hat{R} \tag{10.12}$$

where β is the sterilization coefficient, ranging in value from 0 (when there is no sterilization) to 1 (complete sterilization). Equation (10.12) states that the percentage change in domestic credit will be equal to some constant amount (α) determined by the central bank's domestic policy goals, minus some number (β), times the percentage change in reserves. β will reflect the central bank's ability to use domestic credit to offset reserve flows. Of course, it is possible that the central bank cannot fully offset international reserve flows, and yet some sterilization is possible, in which case β will lie between 0 and 1. Evidence has in fact suggested both extremes as well as an intermediate value for β. It is reasonable to interpret the evidence regarding sterilization as indicating that central banks are able to sterilize a significant fraction of reserve flows in the short run. This means that the monetary authorities can likely choose the growth rate of the money supply in the short run, although long-run money growth must be consistent with money demand requirements.

Sterilized Intervention

We have, so far, discussed sterilization in the context of fixed exchange rates. Now let's consider how a sterilization operation might occur in a floating exchange rate system. Suppose the Japanese yen is appreciating against the dollar, and the Bank of Japan decides to intervene in the foreign exchange market to increase the value of the dollar and stop the yen appreciation. The Bank of Japan increases domestic credit in order to purchase U.S. dollar-denominated bonds. The increased demand for dollar bonds will mean an increase in the demand for dollars in the foreign exchange market. This results in the higher foreign exchange value of the dollar. Now suppose that the Bank of Japan has a target level of the Japanese money supply that requires the increase in domestic credit to be offset. The central bank will sell yen-denominated bonds in Japan to reduce the domestic money supply. The domestic Japanese money supply was originally increased by the growth in domestic credit used to buy dollar bonds. The money supply ultimately returns to its initial level because the Bank of Japan uses a domestic open-market operation (the formal term for central bank purchases and sales of domestic bonds) to reduce domestic credit. In this case of managed floating exchange rates, the Bank of Japan uses sterilized intervention to achieve its goal of slowing the appreciation of the yen while keeping the Japanese money supply unchanged. *Sterilized intervention* is ultimately an exchange of domestic bonds for foreign bonds. We may well ask how sterilized intervention could cause a change in the exchange rate if money supplies are unchanged. It is difficult to explain in terms of a monetary approach model but not in terms of a portfolio-balance approach. Equation (10.10) showed that the exchange rate will be a function of relative asset supplies. When the Bank of Japan buys dollar assets, this reduces the supply of dollar assets relative to yen assets available to private market participants. This should cause the yen to depreciate. This effect is reinforced by the open market sale of yen securities by the Bank of Japan.

Even in a monetary approach setting, it is possible for sterilized intervention with unchanged money supplies to have an effect on the spot exchange rate if money demand changes. The intervention activity could alter the private market view of what to expect in the future. If the intervention changes expectations in a manner that changes money demand (for instance, money demand in Japan falls because the intervention leads people to expect higher Japanese inflation), then the spot rate could change.

Exchange Rates and the Trade Balance

The introduction to this chapter discussed the modern shift in emphasis away from exchange rate models that rely on international trade in goods to exchange rate models based on financial assets. However, there is still a useful role for trade flows in asset approach models, since trade flows have implications for financial asset flows.

If balance of trade deficits are financed by depleting domestic stocks of foreign currency, and trade surpluses are associated with increases in domestic holdings of foreign money, we can see the role for the trade account. If the exchange rate adjusts so that the stocks of domestic and foreign money are willingly held, then the country with a trade surplus will be accumulating foreign currency. As holdings of foreign money increase relative to domestic, the relative value of foreign money will fall or the foreign currency will depreciate.

Although realized trade flows and the consequent changes in currency holdings will affect the current spot exchange rate, the expected future change in the spot rate will be affected by expectations regarding the future balance of trade and its implied currency holdings. An important aspect of this analysis is that changes in the future expected value of a currency can have an immediate impact on current spot rates. For instance, suppose there suddenly is a change in the world economy that leads to expectations of a larger trade deficit in the future, say, an international oil cartel develops and there is an expectation that the domestic economy will have to pay much more for oil imports. In this case forward-looking individuals will anticipate a decrease in domestic holdings of foreign money over time. This, in turn, will cause expectations of a higher rate of appreciation in the value of foreign currency, or a faster expected depreciation of the domestic currency. This higher expected rate of depreciation of the domestic currency leads to an immediate attempt by individuals and firms to shift from domestic into foreign money. Because, at this moment, the total stocks of foreign and domestic money are constant, the attempt to exchange domestic for foreign money will cause an immediate appreciation of the foreign currency to maintain equilibrium, and so the existing supplies of domestic and foreign money are willingly held.

We note that current spot exchange rates are affected by changes in expectations concerning future trade flows, as well as by current international trade flows. As is often the case in economic phenomena, the short-run effect of some new event determining the balance of trade can differ from the long-run result. Suppose the long-run equilibrium under floating exchange rates is balanced trade, where exports equal imports. If we are initially in equilibrium and then experience a disturbance like an oil cartel formation, in the short run we expect large balance of trade deficits, but in the long run, as all prices and quantities adjust to the situation, we return to the long-run equilibrium of balanced trade. The new long-run equilibrium exchange rate will be higher than the old rate, since, as a result of the period of the trade deficit, foreigners will have larger stocks of domestic currency while domestic residents hold less foreign currency. The exchange rate need not move to the new equilibrium immediately. In the short run during which trade deficits are experienced, the exchange rate will tend to be below the new equilibrium rate. Thus, as the outflow of money from the domestic economy proceeds with the deficits, there is a steady depreciation of the domestic currency to maintain the short-run equilibrium where quantities of monies demanded and supplied are equal. Figure 10.1 illustrates the effects just discussed. Some unexpected event occurs at time t_0 that causes a balance of trade deficit. The initial exchange rate is E_0. With the deficit, and the consequent outflow of money from home to abroad, the domestic currency will depreciate. Eventually, as prices and quantities adjust to the changes in the structure of trade, a new long-run equilibrium is reached at E_1, where the trade balance is restored. This move to the new long-run exchange rate, E_1, does not have to come instantaneously, because the deficit will persist for some time. However, the forward rate could jump to E_1 at time t_0 as the market now expects E_1 to be the long-run equilibrium exchange rate. The dashed line in Figure 10.1 represents the path taken by the spot exchange rate in the short run. At t_0 there is an instantaneous jump in the exchange rate even before any trade deficits are realized, because individuals try to exchange domestic money for foreign in anticipation of the domestic currency depreciation. Over time, as the trade deficits occur, there is a steady depreciation of the domestic currency, with the exchange rate approaching its new long-run steady-state value, E_1, as the trade deficit approaches zero.

The inclusion of the balance of trade as a determinant of exchange rates is particularly useful since the popular press often emphasizes the trade account in explanations of exchange rate behavior. As previously shown, it is possible to make sense of balance of trade flows in a model where the exchange rate is determined by desired and actual financial asset flows, so that the role of trade flows in exchange rate determination may be consistent with the modern asset approach to the exchange rate.

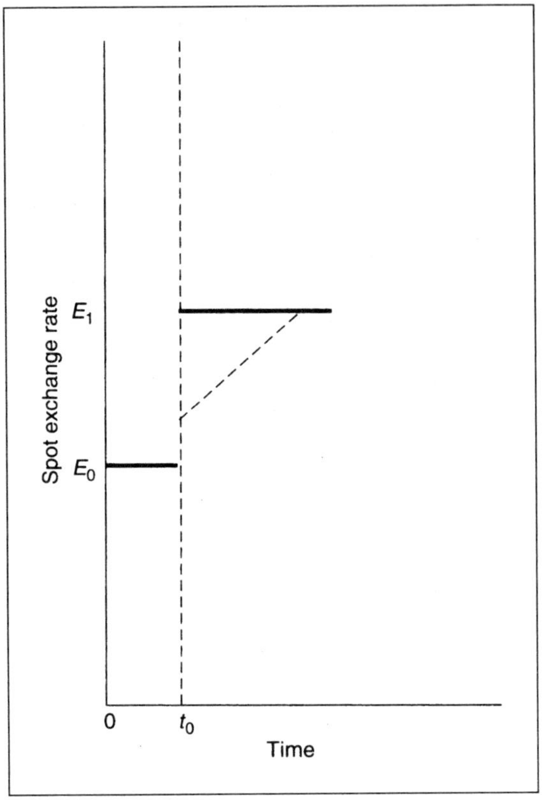

Figure 10.1 The path of the exchange rate following a new event that causes balance of trade deficits.

Overshooting Exchange Rates

Figure 10.1 indicates that with news regarding a higher trade deficit for the domestic country, the spot exchange rate will jump immediately above E_0 and will then rise steadily until the new long-run equilibrium, E_1, is reached. It is possible that the exchange rate may not always move in such an orderly fashion to the new long-run equilibrium following a disturbance.

We know that purchasing power parity does not hold well under flexible exchange rates. Exchange rates exhibit much more volatile behavior than do prices. We might expect that in the short run, following some disturbance to equilibrium, prices will adjust slowly to the new equilibrium level, whereas exchange rates and interest rates adjust quickly. This different speed of adjustment to equilibrium allows for some interesting behavior regarding exchange rates and prices.

At times it appears that spot exchange rates move too much, given some economic disturbance. Moreover, we have observed instances when country A has a higher inflation rate than country B, yet A's currency appreciates relative to B's. Such anomalies can be explained in the context of an "overshooting" exchange rate model. We assume that financial markets adjust instantaneously to an exogenous shock, whereas goods markets adjust slowly over time. With this setting, we analyze what happens when country A increases its money supply.

For equilibrium in the money market, money demand must equal money supply. Thus, if the money supply increases, something must happen to increase money demand. We assume money demand depends on income and the interest rate, so we can write a money demand function like

$$M^d = aY + bi \tag{10.13}$$

where M^d is the real stock of money demanded (the nominal stock of money divided by the price level), Y is income, and i is the interest rate. Money demand is positively related to income, so a exceeds zero. As Y increases, people tend to demand more of everything, including money. Since the interest rate is the opportunity cost of holding money, there is an inverse relationship between money demand and i, or b is negative. It is commonly believed that in the short run following an increase in the money supply, both income and the price level are relatively constant. As a result, interest rates must drop to equate money demand to money supply.

The interest rate parity relation for countries A and B may be written as

$$i_A = i_B + (F - E)/E \tag{10.14}$$

Thus, if i_A falls, given the foreign interest rate i_B, $(F - E)/E$, or the expected depreciation of currency A, must fall. When the money supply in country A increases, we expect that eventually prices there will rise, since we have more A currency chasing the limited quantity of goods available for purchase. This higher future price in A will imply a higher future exchange rate to achieve purchasing power parity:

$$E = P_A/P_B \tag{10.15}$$

Since P_A is expected to rise over time, given P_B, E will also rise. This higher expected future spot rate will be reflected in a higher forward rate now. But if F rises, while at the same time $F - E$ falls to maintain interest rate parity,

E will have to increase more than F. Then, once prices start rising, real money balances fall and the domestic interest rate rises. Over time, as the interest rate increases, E will fall to maintain interest rate parity. Therefore, the initial rise in E will be in excess of the long-run E, or E will overshoot its long-run value.

If the discussion seems overwhelming at this point, the reader will be relieved to know that a concise summary can be given graphically. Figure 10.2 summarizes the discussion thus far. The initial equilibrium is given by

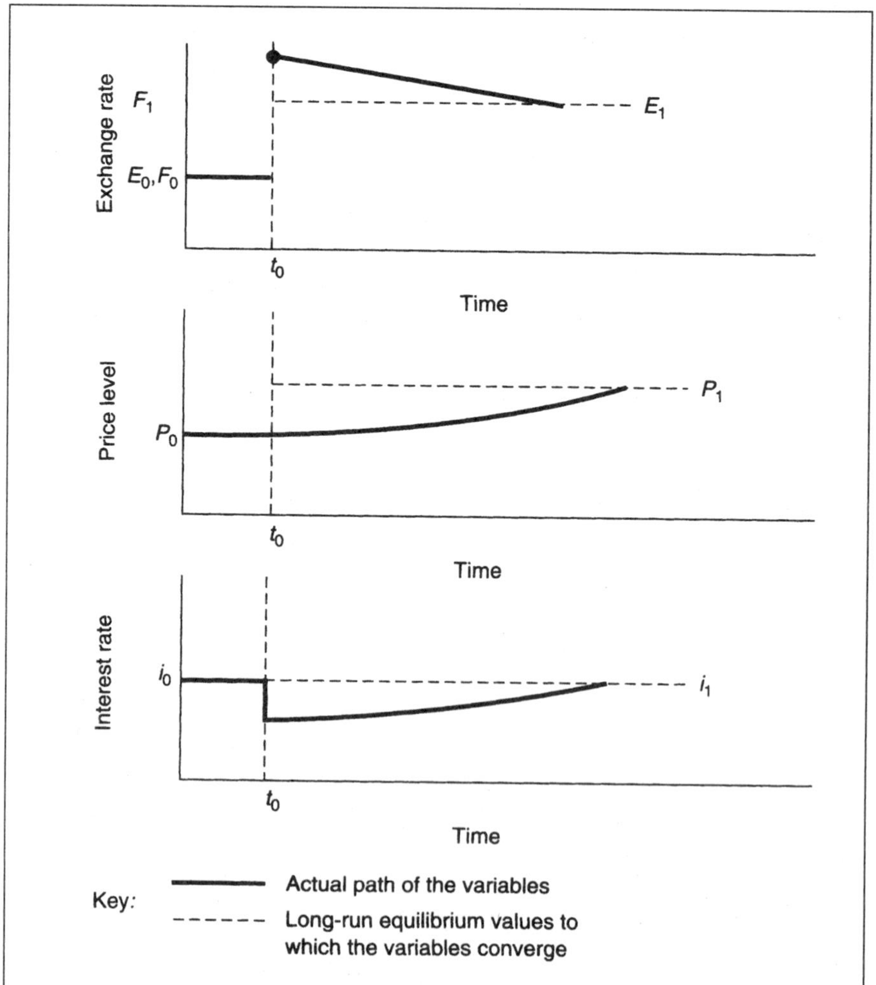

Figure 10.2 The time path of the forward and spot exchange rate, interest rate, and price level following an increase in the domestic money supply at time t_0.

E_0, F_0, P_0, and i_0. When the money supply increases at time t_0, the domestic interest rate falls, and the spot and forward exchange rates increase while the price level remains fixed. The eventual equilibrium price and exchange rate will rise in proportion to the increase in the money supply. Although the forward rate will move immediately to its new equilibrium, F_1, the spot rate will increase above the eventual equilibrium, E_1, because of the need to maintain interest parity (remember i has fallen in the short run). Over time, as prices start rising, the interest rate increases and the exchange rate converges to the new equilibrium, E_1.

As a result of the overshooting E, we observe a period where country A has rising prices relative to the fixed price of country B, yet A's currency appreciates along the solid line converging to E_1. We might explain this period as one in which prices increase, lowering real money balances and raising interest rates. Country A experiences capital inflows in response to the higher interest rates, so that A's currency appreciates steadily at the same rate as the interest rate increase in order to maintain interest rate parity.

Equilibrium Approach

Some economists do not believe in the slow adjustment of prices that underlies the overshooting model of exchange rates. The so-called *equilibrium approach* to exchange rates assumes that prices, interest rates, and exchange rates are always at their market clearing equilibrium levels. In this approach, changes in exchange rates occur because of changes in tastes or technology and are part of the adjustment to a shock to the world economy. For instance, suppose an improvement in technology in Switzerland increases Swiss output, and at the higher level of productivity the price of Swiss goods relative to other countries' goods falls through a depreciation of the franc. The lower relative price of Swiss output is associated with rising Swiss exports. In this scenario, the franc did not depreciate in order to make Swiss goods more competitive on world markets; instead it depreciated because the higher level of Swiss productivity made the relative price of Swiss goods fall.

According to the equilibrium approach, changes in exchange rates are caused by changes in tastes or technology, so the franc depreciation did not cause the increase in Swiss exports and output but instead was a result of these changes. Similarly, if tastes had changed so that Swiss goods were now more favored by consumers, this would increase the relative price of Swiss goods and would be associated with a franc appreciation. In this view of the world, exchange rate changes can never be viewed as good or bad—they simply occur in response to some other event and are part of the adjustment to a new equilibrium.

Currency Substitution

Economists have long argued that one of the advantages of flexible exchange rates is that countries become independent in terms of their ability to formulate domestic monetary policy. This is obviously not true when exchange rates are fixed. If country A must maintain a fixed exchange rate with country B, then A must follow a monetary policy similar to B's. Should A follow an inflationary policy in which prices are rising 20 percent per year while B follows a policy aimed at price stability, then a fixed rate of exchange between the money of A and B will prove very difficult to maintain. Yet with flexible exchange rates, A and B can each choose any monetary policy they like, and the exchange rate will simply change over time to adjust for the inflation differentials.

This independence of domestic policy under flexible exchange rates may be reduced if there is an international demand for monies. Suppose country B residents desire to hold currency A to use for future transactions or simply to hold as part of their investment portfolio. As demand for money shifts between currencies A and B, the exchange rate will shift as well. In a region with substitutable currencies, shifts in money demand between currencies will add an additional element of exchange rate variability.

With fixed exchange rates, central banks make currencies perfect substitutes on the supply side. They alter the supplies of currency to maintain the exchange rate peg. The issue of currency substitution deals with the substitutability among currencies on the demand side of the market. If currencies were perfect substitutes to money demanders, then all currencies would have to have the same inflation rates, or demand for the high-inflation currency would fall to zero (since the inflation rate determines the loss of purchasing power of a money). Perfectly substitutable monies indicate that demanders are indifferent between the use of one currency or another. If the cost of holding currency A rises relative to the cost of holding B, say because of a higher inflation rate for currency A, then demand will shift away from A to B if A and B are substitutes. This would cause the A currency to depreciate even more than was initially called for by the inflation differential between A and B.

For instance, suppose Canada has a 10 percent annual inflation rate while the United States has a 5 percent rate. With no currency substitution, we would expect the U.S. dollar to appreciate against the Canadian dollar on purchasing power parity grounds. Now suppose that Canadian citizens hold stocks of U.S. dollar currency, and these U.S. dollars are good substitutes for Canadian dollars. The higher inflation rate on the Canadian dollar means that stocks of Canadian dollars held will lose value more rapidly than U.S. dollars, so there is an increased demand for U.S. dollar currency. This attempt to exchange Canadian dollar currency for U.S. dollars results in a further depreciation of the Canadian dollar. Such shifts in demand between currencies can result in volatile exchange rates and can be very unsettling to central banks desiring exchange rate stability. Therefore, one implication of a high degree of currency substitution is a need for international coordination of monetary policy. If money demanders substitute between currencies to force each currency to follow a similar inflation rate, then the supposed independence of monetary policy under flexible exchange rates is largely illusory. Although central banks may attempt to follow independent monetary policies, money demanders will adjust their portfolio holdings away from high-inflation currencies to low-inflation currencies. This currency substitution leads to more volatile exchange rates, since not only does the exchange rate adjust to compensate for the original inflation differential, but it also adjusts as currency portfolios are altered.

We should expect currency substitution to be most important in a regional setting where there is a relatively high degree of mobility of resources between countries. For instance, the use of the euro by countries in Western Europe may be evidence of a high degree of currency substitution that once existed among the former European currencies. Alternatively, there is evidence of a high degree of currency substitution existing between the U.S. dollar and Latin American currencies. In many Latin American countries, dollars serve as an important substitute currency, both as a store of value (the dollar being more stable than the typical Latin American currency) and as a medium of exchange used for transactions. This latter effect is particularly pronounced in border areas. Aside from regional settings, it is not clear that currency substitution should be a potentially important source of exchange rate variability. At this point it is probably safe to treat currency substitution as a potentially important source of exchange rate variability, but one that may not be relevant to all country pairs.

The Role of News

Considering the theories of exchange rate determination discussed so far, we might believe that with all this knowledge, experts should be quite adept at forecasting future exchange rates. In fact, forecasting future spot exchange rates is very difficult. Although researchers have shown that the theories we have covered are relevant in terms of explaining systematic patterns of exchange rate behavior, the usefulness of these theories for predicting future exchange rates is limited by the propensity for the unexpected to occur. The real world is characterized by unpredictable shocks or surprises. When some unexpected event takes place, we refer to this as *news.* Since interest rates, prices, and incomes are often affected by news, it follows that exchange rates will also be affected by news. By definition, the exchange rate changes linked to news will be unexpected. Thus, we find great difficulty in predicting future spot rates, because we know the exchange rate will be determined in part by events that cannot be foreseen.

The fact that the predicted change in the spot rate, as measured by the forward premium, varies less over time than does the actual change indicates how much of the change in spot rates is unexpected. Periods dominated by unexpected announcements or realizations of economic policy changes will have great fluctuations in spot and forward exchange rates as expectations are revised subject to the news.

The news also has implications for purchasing power parity. Since exchange rates are financial asset prices that respond quickly to new information, news will have an immediate impact on exchange rates. Prices of goods and services, however, will not be affected by the news in such a rapid manner. One reason is that goods and services are often contracted for in advance, so that prices are inflexible for the duration of the contract. A more basic and general reason is that financial assets, like foreign exchange, have long lives relative to the goods and services that are incorporated in national price indexes. This is important, because longer-lived, or durable, goods prices are more sensitive to changes in expectations than are non-durable, or relatively short-lived, assets. For this reason, during periods dominated by news, we will observe exchange rates varying a great deal relative to prices, and thus large deviations from purchasing power parity are realized. The differences between prices and exchange rates were illustrated in Table 10.1. As was discussed earlier in the context of asset models of exchange rate determination, exchange rates change much more than do goods prices. Periods when many unexpected economic events occur (oil price shocks and international debt problems are two of the more obvious surprises), will be times of large, unexpected exchange rate changes and also of large deviations from PPP.

It is important to realize that the variability of the exchange rate is a result of new developments. Volatile exchange rates simply reflect turbulent times. Even with a good knowledge of the determinants of exchange rates (as discussed in this chapter), without perfect foresight exchange rates will always prove to be difficult to forecast in a dynamic world full of surprises.

Foreign Exchange Market Microstructure

The determinants of the exchange rate discussed so far identify the fundamentals that should cause changes in exchange rates. As news related to money supplies, trade balances, or fiscal policies is received by the market, exchange rates will change to reflect this news. We might think of the discussion as being macro, as such news affects the entire economy and other prices change along with exchange rates. However, there is also a micro level, at which exchange rates are determined by interactions among traders. Beyond the macro news or public information shared by all, there also exists private information from which some traders know more than others about the current state of the market. Understanding the "market microstructure" allows us to explain the evolution of the foreign exchange market in an intradaily sense, in which foreign exchange traders adjust their bid and ask quotes throughout the business day in the absence of any macro news.

A foreign exchange trader may be motivated to alter his or her exchange rate quotes in response to changes in their position with respect to orders to buy and sell a currency. For instance, suppose Helmut Smith is a foreign exchange trader at Deutsche Bank who specializes in the dollar/euro market. The bank management controls risks associated with foreign currency trading by limiting the extent to which traders can take a position that would expose the bank to potential loss from unexpected changes in exchange rates. If Smith has agreed to buy more euros than he has agreed to sell, he has a long position in the euro and will profit from euro appreciation and lose from euro depreciation. If Smith has agreed to sell more euros than he has agreed to buy, he has a short position in the euro and will profit from euro depreciation and lose from euro appreciation. His position at any point in time may be called his inventory. One reason traders adjust their quotes is in response to inventory changes. At the end of the day most traders balance their position and are said to go home "flat." This means that their orders to buy a currency are just equal to their orders to sell.

Suppose Helmut Smith has been buying and selling euros for dollars throughout the day. By early afternoon his position is as follows:

dollar purchases:	\$100,000,000
dollar sales:	\$80,000,000

In order to balance his position Smith will adjust his quotes to encourage fewer purchases and more sales. For instance, if the euro is currently trading at \$1.0250–60, then Helmut could raise the bid quote relative to the ask quote to encourage others to sell him euros in exchange for his dollars. For instance, if he changes the quote to 1.0255–60, then someone could sell him euros (or buy his dollars) for \$1.0255 per euro. Since he has raised the dollar price of a euro, he will receive more offers from people wanting to sell him euros in exchange for his dollars. When Helmut buys euros from other traders, he is selling them dollars, and this helps to balance his inventory and reduce his long position in the dollar.

This *inventory control* effect on exchange rates can explain why traders may alter their quotes in the absence of any news about exchange rate fundamentals. Richard Lyons studied the DM/dollar market before there was a euro and estimated that, on average, foreign exchange traders alter their quotes by .00008 for each \$10 million of undesired inventory. So a trader with an undesired long mark position of \$20 million would, on average, raise his quote by .00016.

In addition to the inventory control effect, there is also an *asymmetric information* effect, which causes exchange rates to change due to traders' fears that they are quoting prices to someone who knows more about current market conditions than they do. Even without news regarding the fundamentals discussed earlier in the chapter, information is being transmitted from one trader to another through the act of trading. If Helmut posts a quote of 1.0250–60 and is called by Ingrid Schultz at Citibank asking to buy \$5 million of euros at Helmut's ask price of 1.0260, Helmut then must wonder whether Ingrid knows something he doesn't. Should Ingrid's order to trade at Helmut's price be considered a signal that Helmut's price is too low? What superior information could Ingrid have? Every bank receives orders from nonbank customers to buy and sell currency. Perhaps Ingrid knows that her bank has just received a large order from Daimler Benz to sell dollars, and she is selling dollars (and buying euros) in advance of the price increase that will be caused by this nonbank order being filled by purchasing euros from other traders.

Helmut does not know why Ingrid is buying euros at his ask price, but he protects himself from further euro sales to someone who may be better informed than he is by raising his ask price. The bid price may be left unchanged because the order was to buy his euros; in such a case the spread increases, with the higher ask price due to the possibility of trading with a better-informed counterparty. Richard Lyons estimated that the presence of asymmetric information among traders resulted in the average change in the quoted price being .00014 per $10 million traded. At this average level, Helmut would raise his ask price by .00007 in response to Ingrid's order to buy $5 million.

The inventory control and asymmetric information effects can help explain why exchange rates change throughout the day, even in the absence of news regarding the fundamental determinants of exchange rates. The act of trading generates price changes among risk-averse traders who seek to manage their inventory positions to limit their exposure to surprising exchange rate changes and limit the potential loss from trading with better-informed individuals.

Summary

1. Modern exchange rate models emphasize financial asset markets.
2. Asset approach models may be divided into monetary approach models, which assume perfect substitutability of assets internationally, and portfolio-balance models, which assume imperfect substitutability.
3. Portfolio-balance models of exchange rate determination add relative asset supplies as a determinant.
4. Central bank sterilization occurs when domestic credit is changed to offset international reserve flows.
5. Since balance of trade flows are balanced by financial asset flows, changes in the trade balance have a role in asset approach views of exchange rate determination.
6. If financial asset markets clear faster relative to goods markets, then the exchange rate may overshoot the new long-run equilibrium following some shock to the system.
7. The equilibrium approach to exchange rates has exchange rates changing in response to changing tastes and technology.

8. International currency substitution will add an additional source of exchange rate variability.
9. A high degree of currency substitution breeds currency union.
10. Exchange rates are difficult to forecast because the market is continually reacting to unexpected events or news.
11. The microstructure of the foreign exchange market has exchange rates changing throughout the day due to inventory control and asymmetric information effects.

Exercises

1. Suppose Japan discovers a new technology that will result in doubling Japanese exports. As a result, Japan moves from a position of balance of trade deficits to expected long-term surpluses. How should the foreign exchange value of Japanese yen be affected? Do you expect any difference between the long run and the short run?
2. A major complaint regarding flexible exchange rates is that they are too volatile when they float. Explain how each of the topics considered in this chapter—the trade balance, currency substitution, differential speed of adjustment of asset markets versus goods markets, news, and market microstructure effects—contributes to exchange rate volatility.
3. Suppose the Canadian central bank unexpectedly lowers the Canadian money supply. In a world of exchange rate overshooting, how would the Canadian dollar/U.S. dollar spot rate, forward rate, Canadian interest rate, and Canadian price level change in response? Draw graphs representing the expected time paths. Why does your exchange rate path have the shape that it does?
4. Carefully monitor the local newspaper (better still, *The Wall Street Journal*) for news that should have an impact on the foreign exchange market. Keep a list of each news event, the effect on the value of the domestic currency you would expect (and why), and the actual effect. If you find the market moving in a different way than you expected, why do you suppose this happened?
5. Suppose the Federal Reserve in the United States wants to decrease the value of the Japanese yen against the dollar. How might the Fed intervene in the foreign exchange market to accomplish this? If the Fed wants to leave the U.S. money supply unchanged by the foreign exchange market intervention, how will it conduct a sterilized intervention?
6. Suppose a trader at Sumitomo Bank is trading yen for dollars and, near the end of the day, has bought \$300,000,000 and sold \$400,000,000 of yen. How should the trader adjust her quotes to attain a balanced inventory if the yen is currently trading against the dollar at 101.50 bid and 101.60 ask?

7. Why might governments in small developing countries worry about their citizens substituting among currencies?
8. What is the difference between the monetary approach and the portfolio-balance approach to exchange rate determination? What are the similarities between the two approaches?
9. According to the portfolio-balance to exchange rate determination, what will happen to the values of the domestic currency if the supply of foreign bonds rises relative to the supply of domestic bonds? Why?
10. Bettina is a dollar-euro trader who is currently quoting $1.0540–1.0550 for the euro. She receives a call from Helmut, a trader at a large German bank, who always seems to be well informed regarding policy changes in Europe. Helmut wants to buy euros, so Bettina now thinks there may be something happening about which she is presently uninformed. How will Bettina alter her quotes if she now has greater uncertainty about what is going on in the market?

References

Aivazian, Varouj A., Jeffrey L. Callen, Itzhak Krinsky, and Clarence C. Y. Kwan, "International Exchange Risk and Asset Substitutability," *Journal of International Money and Finance,* December 1986.

Baillie, Richard T., and William P. Osterberg, "Why Do Central Banks Intervene?" *Journal of International Money and Finance,* December 1997.

Covrig, Vicentiu, and Michael Melvin, "Asymmetric Information and Price Discovery in the FX Market: Does Tokyo Know More about the Yen?" *Journal of Empirical Finance,* August 2002.

Dominguez, Kathryn, "Central Bank Intervention and Exchange Rate Volatility," *Journal of International Money and Finance,* February 1998.

Edwards, Sebastian, "Dollarization: Myths and Realities," *Journal of Policy Modeling,* June 2001.

Levin, Jay H., "Trade Flow Lags, Monetary and Fiscal Policy, and Exchange Rate Overshooting," *Journal of International Money and Finance,* December 1986.

Lyons, Richard K., *The Microstructure Approach to Exchange Rates.* Cambridge: MIT Press, 2001.

Sarno, Lucio, and Mark P. Taylor, *New Developments in Exchange Rate Economics.* Cheltenham: Elgar, 2002.

Taylor, Mark, "The Economics of Exchange Rates," *Journal of Economic Literature,* March 1995.

APPENDIX: Technical Analysis in the Foreign Exchange Market

How do foreign exchange traders know when to buy a currency and hold a "long position," betting on currency appreciation, or sell a currency and hold a "short position," betting on currency depreciation? One popular approach is known as *technical analysis.* Technical analysis uses past exchange rate behavior to determine trading decisions. The basic idea is that an analyst can determine future movements of exchange rates in the short run by an examination of the current rates relative to their history. Scholars have typically been harsh in their judgments of technical analysis and have favored, instead, the use of fundamentals like government policy or real economic events in forecasting exchange rates. Despite the skepticism of scholars, it must be recognized that technical analysis is extremely popular among foreign exchange traders. Surveys of traders reveal that most depend upon technical analysis for short-term decision making. Mark Taylor and Helen Allen surveyed London traders in the early 1990s and found that 90 percent used technical analysis. More recent surveys confirm the important role that technical analysis plays in the market. Given the importance of such analysis in the market, this appendix provides a brief summary of the sorts of tools used.

Technical analysts believe that the past and present records of prices will provide useful trading decisions. More specifically, they believe that trends tend to continue for extended periods of time and that traders will behave in similar ways in response to similar phenomena. So analysts search for elements in the pattern of exchange rates over time that repeat past patterns that allowed profitable trades. An analyst is particularly interested in identifying major turning points in an exchange rate. This would include *troughs,* or market bottoms, where the exchange rate shifts from depreciation to appreciation, and *peaks,* or market tops, where the exchange rate shifts from appreciation to depreciation.

One popular pattern that is believed to signal a trend reversal is the *head-and-shoulders* pattern. Figure 10A.1 provides an example of a head-and-shoulders pattern. A head-and-shoulders pattern is a pattern of three successive peaks where the second is higher than the first and the third is lower than the second. In an upward-trending market, one expects to see successive peaks climbing higher and higher over time. The head-and-shoulders pattern is used as an indicator of the end of an upward trend. The "neckline" is a line drawn between the two troughs around the "head" of the pattern. When the exchange rate drops below the neckline, this is taken

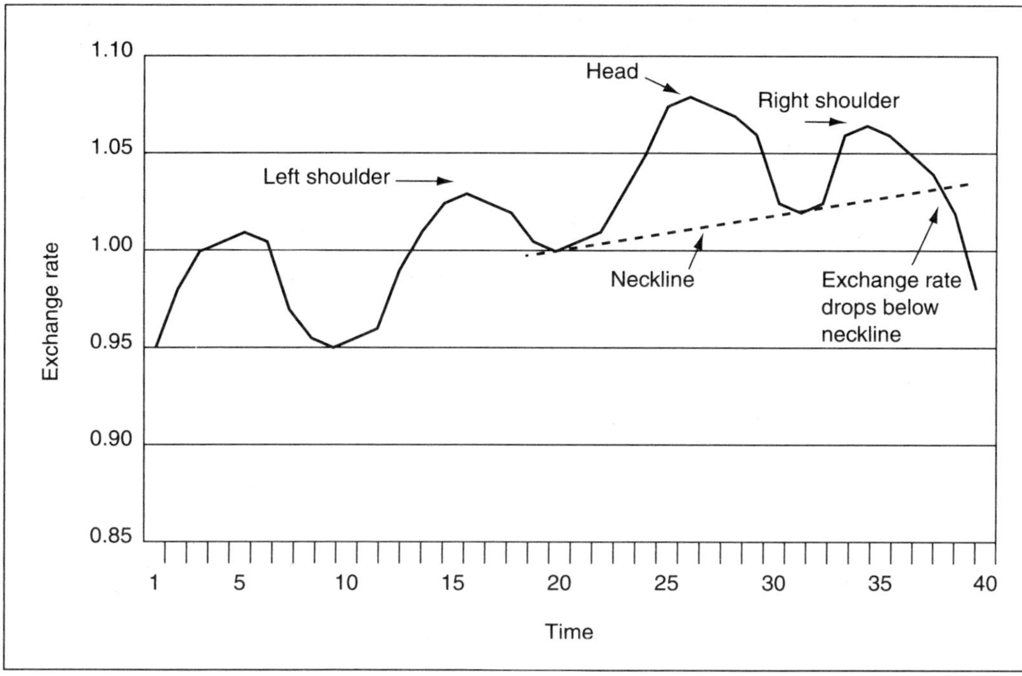

Figure 10A.1 Head-and-Shoulders Trend Reversal Pattern

as a confirmation that the upward trend has ended and a reversal toward a downward trend is under way.

Regardless of whether a head-and-shoulders pattern or some other trend reversal tool is used, a signal of a trend reversal leads traders to shift from a long or short position in a currency to the opposite position. In the example of Figure 10A.1, traders hold a long position in a currency while the currency is appreciating in value and then, once the exchange rate drops below the neckline, traders would typically sell out their long positions and shift to a short position in the currency.

In addition to trend reversal patterns distilled from charts of exchange rates over time, technical traders often use mechanical trading rules to follow trends and employ mathematical formulations to indicate when positions should change. One very popular type of mechanical rule is the *moving average rule.* A moving average is an average value of a currency over some period of time like 30 days. By averaging the value of the currency over time, the daily fluctuations are smoothed out so the analyst concentrates on the trend. An example of a moving average rule would be to calculate a 5- and

30-day moving average and then change positions when the 5-day average crosses the 30-day average. Each day, the analyst calculates the average value of the currency over the past 5 days and the past 30 days. In an upward-trending market, the shorter moving average will lie above the longer moving average. As long as the 5-day moving average is greater than the 30-day moving average, the trader holds a long position in the appreciating currency. Once the 5-day average drops below the 30-day, the trader closes out the long position. Similarly, in a downward-trending market, the shorter moving average is below the longer average. As long as this is true, the trader holds a short position in the depreciating currency. Once the shorter moving average exceeds the longer moving average, the trader closes out the short position.

Many types of technical trading rules exist. This appendix can only introduce the topic. Those interested in greater detail are referred to the references.

References

Chang, P. W. Kevin, and Carol L. Osler, "Methodical Madness: Technical Analysis and the Irrationality of Exchange-Rate Forecasts," *Economic Journal,* October 1999.

Cheung, Yin-Wong, and Menzie Chinn, "Currency Traders and Exchange Rate Dynamics: A Survey of the U.S. Market," *Journal of International Money and Finance,* August 2001.

Gehrig, Thomas, and Lukas Menkhoff, "The Use of Flow Analysis in Foreign Exchange: Exploratory Evidence," *Journal of International Money and Finance,* forthcoming.

Neely, Christopher J., "Technical Analysis in the Foreign Exchange Market: A Layman's Guide," *Federal Reserve Bank of St. Louis Review,* September/October 1997.

Taylor, Mark P., and Helen Allen, "The Use of Technical Analysis in the Foreign Exchange Market," *Journal of International Money and Finance,* June 1992.

11

Import and Export Financing

International trade, even more so than domestic trade, is carried out mostly on a credit basis. Trade across national borders involves loans, advances, and guarantees of payment that bring third parties, like banks, into a trade transaction. Besides commercial banks, governments are often involved, since low-cost financing is used as a means of stimulating exports.

Banks and governments are not the only institutions that finance international trade. Banks account for the major share of trade finance, but they specialize in short-term, unsecured loans. Other institutions specialize in higher-risk loans that must be secured by a pledge of the borrower's assets as collateral. We begin this chapter with a discussion of the institutions involved in financing trade. Then we examine exactly how trade transactions are arranged and the various alternatives available for financing.

Institutions

Let us now consider in more detail the major institutions involved in financing world trade.

Commercial Banks

Commercial banks dominate the financing of world trade. Banks have a varied assortment of financing alternatives available that allow them to compete for almost any type of financing deal. These alternatives include short-term unsecured loans with a borrowing period of up to one year; letters of credit, which are guarantees that an importer will make payment to an exporter; financing of foreign receivables, wherein exporters receive financing by pledging the money to be received from importers as collateral; and longer-term loans, wherein repayment is to be made in installments over time. We will consider these alternative financing arrangements in more detail later.

Factors

Factors are firms that buy accounts receivable from a trading firm and then assume responsibility for collecting the receivables. For instance, suppose Motorola sells $500,000 worth of computer chips to a French manufacturer with payment due in 90 days. Motorola could sell the right to collect the $500,000 to a factor. The factor will pay Motorola less than $500,000 for this right, and then the factor must collect from the French buyer. Should the French firm default on the contract, it is the factor's loss.

A factor is not a bank, although it could be a subsidiary of a bank. The factor is a specialized combination of lender and collection agency. In fact, Motorola could use the factor's collection services and not sell the receivables. In this case, the factor would collect the money owed from the French manufacturer and turn the funds over to Motorola after deducting a service charge.

To overcome the lack of credit information on foreign firms, domestic factors have foreign affiliates or cooperative agreements with foreign factors, under which the U.S. factor provides credit expertise on U.S. firms in exchange for the foreign factor's information on foreign firms.

Exporters benefit from selling their accounts receivable to a factor by transferring credit and collection problems to the factor, reducing administrative expenses related to carrying accounts receivable, and eliminating foreign exchange risk if the receivables are denominated in foreign currency. The exporter receives payment now, rather than when the importer pays, and is free to concentrate on sales and product development, allowing the financial expertise of the factor to deal with credit issues.

The price that the exporter receives from the factor for the receivables will be lower the longer the time until importer payment is due, the poorer the credit rating of the importer, and the greater the foreign exchange risk associated with the transaction.

Commercial Finance Companies

Loans that are too risky or unsuitable for banks may be made by commercial finance companies. These are secured loans—secured by assets other than the accounts receivable handled by factors.

For instance, suppose a small, financially unstable U.S. exporter, Tex's Trading Company, receives a large order for cowboy boots from a German buyer; the order is backed by a letter of credit guaranteeing importer payment from a large commercial bank. Tex's Trading Company must first buy the boots from Acme Boot Company in El Paso, Texas. The problem is that Tex's Trading Company does not have sufficient credit to cover its purchase from Acme. In fact, Acme wants a letter of credit in its favor against Tex's Trading Company. Commercial banks are not generally willing to open a letter of credit for weak exporters, so Tex's turns to a finance company. The finance company will require that Tex assign the German buyer's letter of credit to it. Then the finance company issues a letter of credit to Acme.

Finance companies specialize in such back-to-back letters of credit for firms lacking the financial strength required to deal with commercial banks. In addition, finance companies may provide exporter financing to allow production or acquisition of goods to be traded but stipulate that the goods must be stored in an independent warehouse prior to export, so that the exporter cannot have access to them. Alternatively, the finance company may require that the export contract and accounts receivable be pledged as collateral for the loan. The finance company does not collect the receivables without recourse as a factor would; it will pursue payment from the exporter should the importer default.

Finance companies generally deal with riskier loans. As a result, they charge a higher rate of interest than a bank. The example of the boot exporter could have been reversed, with a finance company providing importer financing. A weak importer can arrange for a finance company to obtain a letter of credit from a major international bank by using the assets and credit of the finance company to back up the resources of the importer.

Government Institutions

International trade financing can involve government agencies as well as private lenders. The role of government is generally one of stimulating exports. In the United States there are a few institutions of the federal government that aid the efforts of U.S. exporters.

The *Export-Import Bank,* or *Eximbank,* was established as an independent government agency in 1945. The role of the Eximbank is to provide export financing for U.S. firms that is competitive with the financing available in the other major industrial countries. The Eximbank is not in competition with other types of lending institutions. Its role is that of supplementing private credit and thus allowing U.S. firms to compete with foreign firms receiving subsidies from their governments.

The Eximbank offers several different programs to meet the financing needs of U.S. exporters and foreign importers. For large purchases requiring a long period for repayment, direct loans are made to foreign importers. In some cases, commercial banks would provide a direct loan to a foreign buyer, except when the buyer is in a high-risk region of the world or lacks sufficient credit strength to qualify for the loan. The Eximbank may guarantee the loan for either a U.S. or a foreign bank. There are several additional Eximbank programs that offer various combinations of loans and guarantees. In addition, the Eximbank provides financing for export feasibility studies, shares credit information with U.S. banks, and offers counseling and training for U.S. export firms.

The *Commodity Credit Corporation* (CCC) operates as part of the U.S. Department of Agriculture to support the export of U.S. agricultural products. As part of CCC support operations, loans to foreign buyers are made at longer terms than private lenders will provide. Since agricultural products are usually consumed in a short time, private lenders are willing to offer only short-term loans to buyers of agricultural output. The CCC has a program that allows up to 36-month financing to stimulate exports from the United States. These loans are supposed to be available only when necessary to meet certain criteria, like matching credit terms offered by competing countries.

The *Overseas Private Investment Corporation* (OPIC) is operated by the U.S. Treasury to assist U.S. investments in friendly developing countries. This occurs through direct loans, loan guarantees, and political risk insurance provided by OPIC. OPIC is not engaged principally in financing trade, although there may be some impact on international trade flows as a result of direct investment subsidized by OPIC.

The discussion of government institutions has focused on U.S. operations, but other countries also have agencies for stimulating exports. The typical arrangement is similar to that of the Eximbank in providing competitive financing to importers.

Executing Transactions

Once the importer has agreed to buy goods from an exporter, a sales contract must be written. The sales contract explicitly lists the obligations of each party and will generally include a description of the goods sold, price, method of payment, shipping date, and who must be responsible for shipping charges, insurance, and taxes. A crucial issue in a sales contract is when possession of the goods is transferred from seller to buyer. These are specified using "International Commercial Terms," or "Incoterms," as specified by the International Chamber of Commerce. The following are some of the common delivery terms used:

Ex works (EXW). The buyer takes possession of the goods at the seller's factory (works), warehouse, or some other named place where they have not been cleared for export nor loaded on any delivery vehicle. The buyer bears all costs and risks of damage from that point forward. This term involves the minimum obligation for the seller.

Free on board (FOB). The title to the goods passes to the buyer when the goods are loaded aboard ship. The seller is responsible for all costs until the goods are on board; the buyer then pays all further costs. This can only be used for waterway transport.

Free alongside ship (FAS). The seller delivers the goods alongside the ship that will transport the goods, within reach of the ship's loading apparatus. The buyer is responsible for the goods beyond this point. This can only be used for waterway transport.

Cost and freight (CFR). The seller pays for transportation to the destination point. When the goods are lifted over the rail of the ship in the destination port, the buyer is responsible. This can only be used for waterway transport.

Cost, insurance, and freight (CIF). This is similar to CFR, except the seller must also pay for insurance. Generally this means ocean marine insurance in case the ship sinks or the goods are otherwise damaged by an event other than war. War risk insurance may also be available and is generally paid for by the buyer.

Carriage paid to (CPT). The seller bears all costs of carrying the goods to some named destination. Beyond that point the costs and risks are the buyer's.

Delivered duty paid (DDP). The seller bears all costs and risks of delivering the goods to the buyer cleared for import at the named destination, including any duty levied on the import of the goods into the destination country. This term involves the maximum obligation for the seller.

In addition to the sales contract, a few other key documents are involved in international trade. One of the most important documents is the

BILL OF LADING

Shipper/Exporter	Document No. Export References
Consignee	Forwarding Agent Point and Country of Origin
Notify Party Pier or Airport	Domestic Routing Export Instructions

Exporting Carrier	Port of Loading	Onward Inland Routing
Port of Discharge	For Transshipment To	

Particulars Furnished by Shipper

Marks and Numbers	No. of Pkgs.	Description of Packages and Goods	Gross Weight	Measurement

Freight Charges Payable At — By

	Prepaid	Collect
Land Origin Charges		
Port Charges		
Subtotal		
Ocean Freight		
Subtotal		
Port Charges		
and Destination Charges		
Subtotal		
Grand Total		

Signed at (location):

Name of Carrier:

Mo./Day/Year: Signature:

Figure 11.1 Bill of lading.

bill of lading, which is illustrated in Figure 11.1. A bill of lading is issued by the shipping company to the exporter and states the agreement to carry the goods to the destination port. This is a negotiable document that serves as a receipt for the goods and can be used to transfer the title to the goods. This function of a bill of lading as a negotiable instrument is important in trade finance, since the exporter can endorse the bill of lading to a bank to obtain financing for the shipping costs by using the goods as collateral.

For goods shipped by air, the bill of lading is called an *airbill.* Airbills are rarely negotiable because the goods are received by the importer very quickly, and the exporter or bank would control the goods for only a short period.

Once the goods are received at the port of importation, a *dock receipt* is issued by the shipping company and given to the truck or railroad firm that picks up the goods at the dock. The dock receipt lists the quantity and condition of goods delivered.

Letters of Credit

A *letter of credit* (LOC) is a written instrument issued by a bank at the request of an importer that obligates the bank to pay a specific amount of money to an exporter. The time at which payment is due is specified, along with conditions regarding necessary documents to be presented by the exporter prior to payment.

The LOC may stipulate that a bill of lading be presented that evidences no damaged goods. Perhaps some minimal level of damage (like 2 percent of the boxes or crates) is stipulated. In any case, such conditions in an LOC allow the importer to retain some quality control prior to payment.

Figure 11.2 illustrates a simple letter of credit. Note that this is an *irrevocable* LOC. This means that the agreement cannot be modified without the express permission of all parties. Most letters of credit are of this type. A *revocable* LOC may be altered by the account party—the importer buying the goods. Since the importer is free to alter the LOC, we might wonder why any exporter would ever accept a revocable LOC. The exporter may interpret the issuance of the LOC as a favorable credit report on the buyer. The exporter will call the issuing bank prior to shipment to make sure that the LOC has not been altered or revoked, and then present the necessary documents and collect payment as soon as possible. The revocable LOC is still safer than shipping goods based only on the importer's promise to pay, with no bank credit backing up the transaction. Still, revocable letters of credit

[Bank Letterhead (Name & Address of Importer's Bank)]

LETTER OF CREDIT NO.
DATE:

ACCOUNT PARTY
(Buyer's Name & Address)

BENEFICIARY
(Seller's Name & Address)

TO: *(Seller's Bank & Address)*

WE HAVE OPENED AN IRREVOCABLE LETTER OF CREDIT IN FAVOR OF: *(Seller's Name)*
FOR THE AMOUNT OF: $ ______________________
(Dollar amount is written in words here)

AVAILABLE WITH US AGAINST THE FOLLOWING DOCUMENTS:
(Required documents are listed here)

TRANSSHIPMENTS: *(Permitted or not)*

PARTIAL SHIPMENTS: *(Permitted or not)*

THIS CREDIT IS VALID UNTIL *(Date)* FOR PRESENTATION OF DOCUMENTS TO US.
DOCUMENTS ARE TO BE PRESENTED WITHIN *(Number)* DAYS AFTER DATE OF ISSUANCE OF BILLS OF LADING.
PLEASE ADVISE THE BENEFICIARY OF YOUR CONFIRMATION.

THIS CREDIT IS SUBJECT TO THE UNIFORM CUSTOMS AND PRACTICE FOR DOCUMENTARY CREDITS. INTERNATIONAL CHAMBER OF COMMERCE PUBLICATION NO. 500.
THIS CREDIT IS IRREVOCABLE AND WE HEREBY ENGAGE WITH THE DRAWERS THAT DRAWINGS IN ACCORD WITH THE TERMS OF THIS CREDIT WILL BE DULY HONORED BY US.

Yours truly,

(Signature)

International Department

Figure 11.2 Letter of credit.

primarily are used only when there is no question of revocation. This form of LOC may save bank fees, which are higher with irrevocable LOCs; so if there is no chance of revocation, it may pay to use the revocable LOC.

The sales contract stipulates the method of payment. The use of LOCs is widespread, so let us assume the contract calls for payment by LOC. The importer must then apply for an LOC from a bank. The importer requests that the LOC stipulate no payment until appropriate documents are presented by the exporter to the bank. These document stipulations cannot violate the sales contract since the bank is at risk to ensure that the documents are in order at the time of payment.

If the bank considers the importer an acceptable credit risk, the letter of credit is issued and sent to the exporter. The exporter then examines the LOC to ensure that it conforms to the sales contract. If it does not, then modifications must be made before the goods are shipped. Once the exporter fulfills all obligations in delivering the goods, the documentary proof is presented to the bank for examination. If the documents conform to the LOC, payment is made, with the bank collecting from the importer and then paying the exporter.

If the importer does not pay the bank, the bank is still obligated to pay the exporter. The exporter is then satisfied, and any problems must be settled between the importer and the bank.

Banks may or may not require that the underlying goods serve as collateral for the LOC. If the bank does require an interest in the goods, then the bill of lading is consigned to the bank. With an unsecured LOC, the bank assumes the credit risk of a buyer default. With a secured LOC, the bank assumes the risk of changes in the value of the goods and the cost of disposal. Even if the importer is a sound credit risk, the bank assumes the risk that it misses a document discrepancy and that the importer refuses to pay as a result.

What are the risks for the buyer and seller? The exporter faces the risk of shipping goods without being able to meet all terms listed in the LOC. If the goods are shipped and a document discrepancy exists, then the seller will not be paid. The buyer risks fraud from the seller. The goods may not meet the specifications ordered, but the seller fraudulently prepares documents stating otherwise. The bank is not responsible for such fraudulent documents, so the risk is the buyer's.

Banks charge a flat fee for issuing and amending letters of credit. A percentage of the amount paid is also charged at the time payment is made. These charges generally apply to the importer, unless the parties agree otherwise.

Bankers' Acceptances

In the discussion of the institutions involved in financing trade, it is apparent that many alternatives exist for trade finance arrangements. Suppose an exporter needs funds now to purchase and produce goods for shipment, or to meet its obligations until payment is received from the importer. The exporter may have several alternatives for obtaining the funds. Similarly, an importer may need funds now to meet current obligations or its financial needs until the goods are received and sold. The importer may also face several financing alternatives. Often international trade will require the use of bankers' acceptances. A *bankers' acceptance* (BA) is a time draft drawn on and accepted by a particular bank to be paid at maturity.

A bank creates a BA by approving a line of credit for a customer, let's assume an importer, and then issuing a bank draft that is payable to the exporter's bank at a future date. The exporter's bank then may pay the exporter some amount less than the face value of the draft (or discount the draft) prior to maturity. Once the draft is accepted by the exporter's bank, the BA is sold in the acceptance market to an investor. The investor will pay less than the face value of the draft, but more than the amount the bank paid the exporter. At maturity, the BA is settled by the bank's receiving the full face value of the draft from the importer and paying the full value to the investor holding the BA.

Suppose an importer requires acceptance financing to meet the terms of a sales contract. The importer will agree to provide the funds needed to pay for the acceptance at least one day prior to maturity of the acceptance. The importer will use the goods purchased as security for the bank, in the event that the importer does not perform its obligation to fund the acceptance one day prior to maturity.

The Federal Reserve in the United States permits bankers' acceptances only for financing international trade in readily marketable staple products. U.S. banks issue acceptances for trade between the United States and other countries, as well as for trade between two foreign countries.

BAs generally are created only by major banks. These instruments then provide a market for safe, short-term investments for other investors. Banks do not always sell their acceptances, preferring at times to retain the BAs in their own portfolio. Usually large dollar amounts are involved when acceptances are sold, so only wealthy individuals participate and the market is dominated by institutional buyers.

The total cost of the acceptance to the importer includes the discount from the face value already mentioned. This discount is determined by the interest rate on other short-term instruments, like Treasury bills or certificates of deposit. In addition to the discount, an acceptance fee (usually 1.5 percent of the value of the draft) is charged to customers seeking acceptances. Finally, some customers may be required to hold demand deposits at the bank before a BA is created. In such cases, the forgone interest on the deposits is another cost of creating the BA.

Why use acceptance financing for international trade? During times of tight credit conditions, the acceptance market may be the only way to channel short-term funds to trade financing. The active investor market for acceptances can supplement the squeeze on loanable funds facing banks. Furthermore, bankers often prefer BAs for trade financing, because the transaction requiring the loan is clearly specified, as is the source of the loan payback.

An Example of Trade Financing

Let's consider an example that applies some of the issues covered so far. Suppose a U.S. firm, New York Wine Importers, wants to import wine from a French firm, Paris Wine Exporters. Figure 11.3 illustrates the steps involved in the transaction. First, the importer and exporter must agree on the basics of the transaction. The sales contract will stipulate the amount and kind of wine, price, shipping date, and payment method.

Following the sales contract, the importer requests a letter of credit from its bank, New York First Bank. The bank issues an LOC that authorizes Paris Wine Exporters to draw a bank draft on New York First Bank for payment. The bank draft is like a check, except that it is dated for maturity at some time in the future when payment will be made. Paris Wine Exporters ships the wine and gives its bank, Paris First Bank, the bank draft along with the necessary shipping documents for the wine. Paris First Bank then sends the bank draft, shipping documents, and LOC to New York First Bank.

When New York First Bank accepts the bank draft, a bankers' acceptance is created. At this point, Paris Wine Exporters may receive payment of a discounted value of the BA. New York First Bank discounts the BA and sends the funds to Paris First Bank for the account of Paris Wine Exporters. New York First Bank delivers the shipping documents to New York Wine Importers, and the importer takes possession of the wine.

New York First Bank is now holding the BA after paying a discounted value to Paris First Bank. Instead of holding the BA until maturity, New York First Bank sells it to an investor. Upon maturity, the investor will

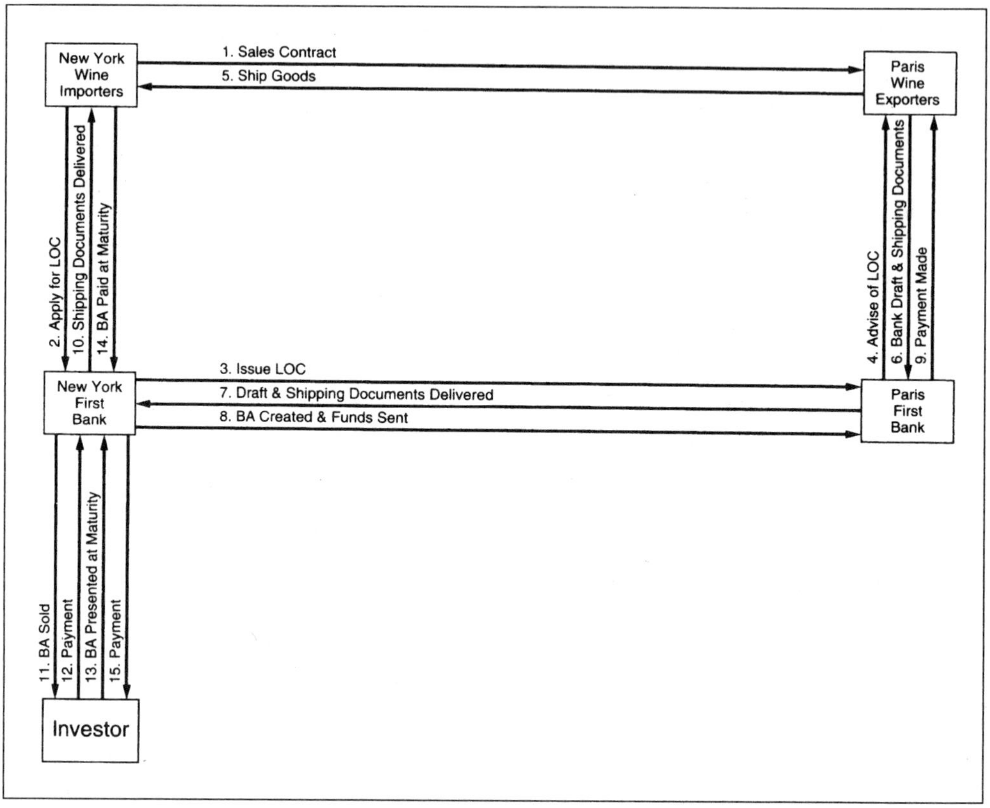

Figure 11.3 Steps involved in a U.S. import transaction.

receive the face value of the BA from New York First Bank and New York First Bank will receive the face value from New York Wine Importers.

Summary

1. Commercial banks account for most of international trade financing.
2. Factors buy accounts receivable from exporters and then are responsible for collection.
3. Commercial finance companies specialize in high-risk secured loans.
4. The Eximbank provides export financing for U.S. firms that matches the terms offered by foreign competitors.
5. The CCC provides long-term financing for U.S. agricultural exports.
6. The sales contract is the basic document of international trade.

7. A bill of lading documents the shipper's receipt and the shipment of goods.
8. A bankers' acceptance is a draft drawn on a firm and accepted by a bank as payable at maturity.
9. A letter of credit guarantees that the bank will pay the exporter the amount of money owed by the importer.
10. The letter of credit stipulates that payment will be made only upon presentation of required documents.

Exercises

1. Why would an export firm want to sell its accounts receivable to a factor?
2. Why should U.S. taxpayers fund agencies like the Eximbank that provide subsidized loans to foreign buyers? What are the costs and benefits of such agencies?
3. If you were importing toy guns from a Korean exporter, what delivery terms would you choose (FOB, CFR, and so on) if the price you paid would not be changed by your choice?
4. What is a bankers' acceptance, and why is it traded among third parties?
5. What is a letter of credit? What risks do the parties to a letter of credit take?
6. For class: Have 15 students write down one of the steps involved in an international trade deal as depicted in Figure 11.3. Then shuffle the 15 pieces of paper and hand one piece to each student. The students should then line themselves up in the proper order from step 1 to step 15.

References

Fazey, Ian, "It Pays to Be Precise," *Financial Times,* March 8, 1994.

International Standard Banking Practice. New York: International Chamber of Commerce, 2003.

Kingman-Brundage, Jane, and Susan Schulz, *The Fundamentals of Trade Finance.* New York: Wiley, 1986.

Venedikian, Harry M., and Gerald A. Warfield, *Export-Import Financing.* New York: Wiley, 1996.

12

Financial Management of the Multinational Firm

Since multinational firms are involved in payables and receivables denominated in different currencies, product shipments across national borders, and subsidiaries operating in different political jurisdictions, they face a different set of problems than firms with a purely domestic operation. The corporate treasurer and other financial decision makers of the multinational firms operate in a cosmopolitan setting that offers profit and loss opportunities never considered by the executives of purely domestic firms. This chapter looks at the unique attributes of financial management in the multinational firm. The basic issues—control, cash management, intrafirm transfers, and capital budgeting—face all firms. The problems particular to the internationally oriented firm are the ones addressed.

Financial Control

Any business firm must evaluate its operations periodically to better allocate resources and increase income. The financial management of a multinational firm involves exercising control over foreign operations. The responsible individuals at the parent office or headquarters review financial reports from foreign subsidiaries with a view toward modifying operations and assessing the performance of foreign managers.

Typical control systems are based on setting standards with regard to sales, profits, inventory, or other specific variables and then examining financial statements and reports to evaluate the achievement of such goals. There is no "correct" system of control. Methods vary across industries and even across firms in a single industry. All methods have the common goal of providing management with a means of monitoring the performance of the firm's operations, new strategies, and goals as conditions change. However, establishing a useful control system is more difficult for a multinational firm than for a purely domestic firm. For instance, should foreign subsidiary profits be measured and evaluated in foreign currency or in the domestic currency of the parent firm? The answer to this question depends on whether foreign managers are to be held responsible for currency translation gains or losses.

If top management wants foreign managers to be involved in currency management and international financing issues, then the domestic currency of the parent would be a reasonable choice. On the other hand, if top management wants foreign managers to concern themselves with production operations and behave as other managers (managers not themselves a part of a foreign multinational) in the foreign country would, then the foreign currency would be the appropriate currency for evaluation.

Some multinational firms prefer a decentralized management structure in which each subsidiary has a great deal of autonomy and makes most financing and production decisions subject only to general parent-company guidelines. In this management setting, the foreign manager may be expected to operate and think as the stockholders of the parent firm would want, so the foreign manager makes decisions aimed at increasing the parent's domestic currency value of the subsidiary. The control mechanism in such firms is to evaluate foreign managers based on their ability to increase that value.

Other firms prefer more centralized management in which financial managers at the parent make most of the decisions. They choose to move funds among divisions based on a systemwide view rather than what is best for a single subsidiary. A highly centralized system would have foreign managers evaluated on their ability to meet goals established by the parent for key variables like sales or labor costs. The parent-firm managers assume responsibility for maximizing the value of the firm, with foreign managers basically responding to directives from the top. We see then that the appropriate control system is largely determined by the management style of the parent.

Considering the discussion to this point, it is clear that managers at foreign subsidiaries should be evaluated only on the basis of things they control. Foreign managers often may be asked by the parent to follow policies and relations with other subsidiaries of the firm that the managers would never follow if they sought solely to maximize their subsidiary's profit. Actions of the parent that lower a subsidiary's profit should not result in a negative view of the foreign manager. In addition, other actions beyond the foreign manager's control—changing tax laws, foreign exchange controls, or inflation rates—could result in reducing foreign profits through no fault of the foreign manager. The message to parent-company managers is to place blame fairly where the blame lies. In a dynamic world, corporate fortunes may rise and fall because of events entirely beyond any manager's control.

Cash Management

Cash management involves using the firm's cash as efficiently as possible. Given the daily uncertainties of business, firms must maintain some liquid resources. *Liquid assets* are those that are readily spent. Cash is the most liquid asset. But since cash (and the traditional checking account) earns no interest, the firm has a strong incentive to minimize its holdings of cash. There are highly liquid short-term securities that serve as good substitutes for actual cash balances and yet pay interest. The corporate treasurer is concerned with maintaining the correct level of liquidity at the minimum possible cost.

The multinational treasurer faces the challenge of managing liquid assets denominated in different currencies. The challenge is compounded by the fact that subsidiaries operate in foreign countries where financial market regulations and institutions differ.

When a subsidiary receives a payment and the funds are not needed immediately by this subsidiary, the managers at the parent headquarters must decide what to do with the funds. For instance, suppose a U.S. multinational's Mexican subsidiary receives 500 million pesos. Should the pesos be converted to dollars and invested in the United States, or placed in Mexican peso investments, or converted into any other currency in the world? The answer depends on the current needs of the firm as well as the current regulations in Mexico. If Mexico has strict foreign exchange controls in place, the 500 million pesos may have to be kept in Mexico and invested there until a future time when the Mexican subsidiary will need them to make a payment.

Even without legal restrictions on foreign exchange movements, we might invest the pesos in Mexico for 30 days if the subsidiary faces a large payment in 30 days and we have no need for the funds in another area of the firm, and if the return on the Mexican investment is comparable to what we could earn in another country on a similar investment (which interest rate parity would suggest). By leaving the funds in pesos we do not incur any transaction costs for converting pesos to another currency now and then going back to pesos in 30 days. In any case, we would never let the funds sit idly in the bank for 30 days.

There are times when the political or economic situation in a country is so unstable that we keep only the minimum possible level of assets in that country. Even when we will need pesos in 30 days for the Mexican subsidiary's payable, if there exists a significant threat that the government could confiscate or freeze bank deposits or other financial assets, we would incur the transaction costs of currency conversion to avoid the political risk associated with leaving the money in Mexico.

Multinational cash management involves centralized management. Subsidiaries and liquid assets may be spread around the world, but they are managed from the home office of the parent firm. Through such centralized coordination, the overall cash needs of the firm are lower. This occurs because subsidiaries do not all have the same pattern of cash flows. For instance, one subsidiary may receive a dollar payment and finds itself with surplus cash, while another subsidiary faces a dollar payment and must obtain dollars. If each subsidiary operated independently, there would be more cash held in the family of multinational foreign units than if the parent headquarters directed the surplus funds of one subsidiary to the subsidiary facing the payable.

Centralization of cash management allows the parent to offset subsidiary payables and receivables in a process called *netting*. Netting involves the consolidation of payables and receivables for one currency so that only the difference between them must be bought or sold. For example, suppose Oklahoma Instruments in the United States sells C$2 million worth of car phones to its Canadian sales subsidiary and buys C$3 million worth of computer frames from its Canadian manufacturing subsidiary. If the payable and receivable both are due on the same day, then the C$2 million receivable can be used to fund the C$3 million payable, and only C$1 million must be bought in the foreign exchange market. Rather than buy C$3 million to settle the payable and sell the C$2 million to convert the receivable into dollars, incurring transaction costs twice on the full C$5 million, the firm has one foreign exchange transaction for C$1 million.

Had the two Canadian operations not been subsidiaries, the financial managers would still practice netting but on a corporatewide basis, buying or selling only the net amount of any currency required after aggregating the receivables and payables of all subsidiaries over all currencies. Effective netting requires accurate and timely reporting of transactions by all divisions of the firm.

As an example of intrafirm netting, let us consider a U.S. parent firm with subsidiaries in Canada, the United Kingdom, Germany, and Mexico. Table 12.1 sets up the report for the week of January 15. We assume that netting occurs weekly. Each division's scheduled payments and receipts are converted to dollars so that aggregation across all units can occur. Table 12.1 indicates that the Canadian subsidiary will pay $0.7 million and receive $3.2 million, so it will have a cash surplus of $2.5 million. The U.K. subsidiary will pay $1.3 million and receive $1.2 million, so it will have a cash shortage of $0.1 million. The German subsidiary will pay $3.1 million and receive $0.5 million, so it has a shortage of $2.6 million, and, finally, the Mexican subsidiary will pay $0.1 million and receive $0.3 million, so it has a surplus of $0.2 million. The parent financial managers determine the net payer or receiver position of each subsidiary for the weekly netting. Only these net amounts are transferred within the firm. The firm does not have to change $0.7 million worth of Canadian dollars into the currencies of Germany and Mexico to settle the payable of the Canadian subsidiary and then convert $3.2 million worth of pounds, euros, and pesos into Canadian dollars. Only the net cash surplus flowing to the Canadian subsidiary of $2.5 million must be converted into Canadian dollars.

So far we have considered netting when the currency flows occur at the same time. What if the payments and receipts are not for the same date?

Table 12.1 Intrafirm Payments for Netting Million-Dollar Values (Week of January 15)

	Payments				
Receipts	**Canada**	**United Kingdom**	**Germany**	**Mexico**	**Total**
Canada	—	1.2	2.0	0.0	3.2
United Kingdom	0.0	—	1.1	0.1	1.2
Germany	0.5	0.0	—	0.0	0.5
Mexico	0.2	0.1	0.0	—	0.3
Total	0.7	1.3	3.1	0.1	5.2

Suppose in our Oklahoma Instruments example that the C$3 million payable is due on October 1, and the C$2 million receivable is due September 1. Netting could still occur by *leading* or *lagging* currency flows. The sales subsidiary could lag its C$2 million payment by one month, or the C$3 million could lead one month and be paid on September 1. Leads and lags increase the flexibility of parent financial managers, but require excellent information flows between all divisions and headquarters.

Intrafirm Transfers

Since the multinational firm is made up of subsidiaries located in different political jurisdictions, transferring funds among divisions of the firm often depends on what governments will allow. Beyond the transfer of cash, as covered in the preceding section, the firm will have goods and services moving between subsidiaries. The price that one subsidiary charges another subsidiary for internal goods transfers is called a *transfer price.* The setting of transfer prices can be a sensitive internal corporate issue because it helps to determine how total firm profits are allocated across divisions. Governments are also interested in transfer pricing since the prices at which goods are transferred will determine tariff and tax revenues.

The parent firm always has an incentive to minimize taxes by pricing transfers in order to keep profits low in high-tax countries and by shifting profits to subsidiaries in low-tax countries. This is done by having intrafirm purchases by the high-tax subsidiary made at artificially high prices, while intrafirm sales by the high-tax subsidiary are made at artificially low prices.

Governments often restrict the ability of multinationals to use transfer pricing to minimize taxes. The U.S. Internal Revenue Code requires *arm's-length pricing* between subsidiaries—charging prices that an unrelated buyer and seller would willingly pay. When tariffs are collected on the value of trade, the multinational has the incentive to assign artificially low prices to goods moving between subsidiaries. Customs officials may determine that a shipment is being "underinvoiced" and may assign a value that more truly reflects the market value of the goods.

Transfer pricing may also be used for "window-dressing"—that is, to improve the apparent profitability of a subsidiary. This may be done to allow the subsidiary to borrow at more favorable terms, since its credit rating will be upgraded as a result of the increased profitability. The higher profits can be created by paying the subsidiary artificially high prices for its products in intrafirm transactions.

The firm that uses transfer pricing to shift profits from one subsidiary to another introduces an additional problem for financial control. It is important that the firm be able to evaluate each subsidiary on the basis of its contribution to corporate income. Any artificial distortion of profits should be accounted for so that corporate resources are efficiently allocated.

Table 12.2 provides an example of transfer pricing for the Waikiki Shirt Co. Waikiki Shirt Co. manufactures shirts in a low-tax country, country L, and then ships the shirts to a distribution center in a high-tax country, country H. The tax rate in L is 20 percent and the tax rate in H is 40 percent. Given these differential tax rates, Waikiki Shirt Co. increases its global profit if profits earned by the high-tax distribution operation in country H could be transferred to country L, where they would be taxed at a lower rate. The top half of the table provides the outcome if the firm uses arm's-length pricing in transferring shirts from the manufacturing operation to the distribution operation. The manufactured shirts produced in country L are sold to the distribution operation in country H at a price of $5. Since shirts cost $1 to

Table 12.2 Transfer Pricing Example.
Waikiki Shirt Co. makes T-shirts in low-tax country L (with a 20% tax rate) and ships them to a distribution center in high-tax country H (with a 40% tax rate).

	Manufacturing Country L	Distribution Country H
Arm's-Length Pricing		
Sales price	$5	$20
Cost	$1	$ 5
Pre-tax profit	$4	$15
Tax	0.2 × $4 = $ .80	0.4 × $15 = $ 6
After-tax profit	$3.20	$ 9
Global profit = $12.20		
Distorted Prices		
Sales price	$10	$20
Cost	$ 1	$10
Pre-tax profit	$ 9	$10
Tax	0.2 × $9 = $ 1.80	0.4 × $10 = $ 4
After-tax profit	$ 7.20	$ 6
Global profit = $13.20		

produce, the pre-tax profit in country L is $4 per shirt. With a tax rate of 20 percent, there is a tax of $0.80 per shirt so that the after-tax profit of the manufacturing operation is $3.20. The distribution center pays $5 per shirt and then sells the shirts for $20, earning a pre-tax profit of $15 per shirt. With a 40 percent tax rate in country H, the firm must pay $6 tax per shirt so that the after-tax profit is $9 per shirt. By summing the after-tax profit earned in countries L and H, the firm earns a global profit of $12.20 per shirt.

Now suppose the firm uses distorted transfer pricing to lower the global tax liability and increase the global profit. This involves having the manufacturing operation in the low-tax country L charge a price above the arm's-length (true market) value for the shirts it sells to the distribution operation in the high-tax country H. The bottom half of Table 12.2 illustrates how this might work. Now the manufacturing operation sells the shirts to the distribution operation for $10 per shirt. The cost of production is still the same $1 so the pre-tax profit is $9 per shirt. A 20 percent tax rate means that a tax of $1.80 per shirt must be paid, and the after-tax profit is $7.20 per shirt. The distribution operation now pays $10 for the shirt and still sells it for $20, so the pre-tax profit is $10. At 40 percent, the tax is $4 per shirt, and the after-tax profit is $6. Summing the after-tax profit of the operations in country L and country H, we find that the global profit is $13.20 per shirt.

The firm is able to increase the profit per shirt by $1 through the transfer pricing distortion of the value of the shirt transferred from country L to country H. In this manner, firms can increase profits by shifting profits from high-tax to low-tax countries. Of course, the tax authorities in country H would not permit such an overstatement of the transfer value of the shirt (and consequent underpayment of taxes in country H) if they could determine the true arm's-length shirt value. For this reason, multinational firms are frequently called upon by tax authorities to justify the prices they use for internal transfers.

Capital Budgeting

Capital budgeting refers to the evaluation of prospective investment alternatives and the commitment of funds to preferred projects. Long-term commitments of funds expected to provide cash flows extending beyond one year are called *capital expenditures.* Capital expenditures are made to acquire *capital assets,* like machines or factories or whole companies. Since such long-term commitments often involve large sums of money, careful planning is required to determine which capital assets to acquire. Plans for capital expenditures are usually summarized in a capital budget.

Multinational firms considering foreign investment opportunities face a more complex problem than do firms considering only domestic investments. Foreign projects involve foreign exchange risk, political risk, and foreign tax regulations. Comparing projects in different countries requires a consideration of how all factors will change over countries.

There are several alternative approaches to capital budgeting. A useful approach for multinational firms is the adjusted present value approach. We work with *present value* because the value of a dollar to be received today is worth more than a dollar to be received in the future, say one year from now. As a result, we must discount future cash flows to reflect the fact that the value today will fall depending on how long it takes before the cash flows are realized. The appendix to this chapter reviews present value calculations for readers unfamiliar with the concept.

For multinational firms, the adjusted present value approach is presented here as an appropriate tool for capital budgeting decisions. The *adjusted present value* (*APV*) measures total present value as the sum of the present values of the basic cash flows estimated to result from the investment (operations flows) plus all financial effects related to the investment. Or

$$APV = -I + \sum_{t=1}^{T} \frac{CF_t}{(1 + d)^t} + \sum_{t=1}^{T} \frac{FIN_t}{(1 + df)^t} \qquad (12.1)$$

where $-I$ is the initial investment or cash outlay, Σ is the summation operator, t indicates time or year when cash flows are realized (t extends from year 1 to year T, where T is the final year), CF_t represents estimated basic cash flows in year t resulting from project operations, d is the discount rate on those cash flows, FIN_t is any additional financial effect on cash flows in year t (these will be discussed shortly), and df is the discount rate applied to the financial effects.

CF_t should be estimated on an after-tax basis. Problems of estimation include deciding whether cash flows should be those directed to the subsidiary housing the project, or only to those flows remitted to the parent company. The appropriate combination of cash flows can reduce the taxes of the parent and subsidiary.

Several possible financing effects should be included in FIN_t. These may include depreciation charges arising from the capital expenditure, financial subsidies or concessionary credit terms extended to the subsidiary by a government or official agency, deferred or reduced taxes given as incentive to undertake the expenditure, or a new ability to circumvent exchange controls on remittances.

Each of the flows in Equation (12.1) is discounted to the present. The appropriate discount rate should reflect the uncertainty associated with the flow. CF_t is not known with certainty and could fluctuate over the life of the project. Furthermore, the nominal cash flows from operations will change over time as inflation changes. The discount rate, *d*, could be equal to the risk-free rate plus a risk premium that reflects the systematic risk of the project.

The financial terms in FIN_t are likely to be fixed in nominal terms over time. In this case, current market interest rates may be acceptable as discount rates, *df*.

Consider this example to illustrate the *APV* approach to capital budgeting decisions. Suppose Midas Gold Extractors has an opportunity to enter a small, developing country and apply its new gold recovery technique to some old mines that no longer yield profitable amounts of ore under conventional mining. Midas estimates that the cost of establishing the foreign operation will be \$10 million. The project is expected to last for two years, during which period the operating cash flows from the new gold extracted will be \$7.5 million per year. In addition, the new operating unit will allow Midas to repatriate an additional \$1 million per year in funds that have been tied up in the developing country by capital controls. If Midas applies a discount rate of 10 percent to operating cash flows and 6 percent to the funds that will be freed from controls, then the *APV* is:

$$
\begin{aligned}
APV &= -10 + {}^{7.5}/_{1.10} + {}^{7.5}/_{1.10^2} + {}^{1}/_{1.06} + {}^{1}/_{1.06^2} \\
&= -10 + 14.85 = 4.85
\end{aligned}
$$

So the adjusted present value of the gold recovery project equals \$4.85 million. The firm can compare this value to the *APV* of other projects it is considering in order to budget its capital expenditures in the optimum manner.

Capital budgeting is an imprecise science, and forecasting future cash flows is sometimes viewed as more art than science. The typical firm experiments with several alternative scenarios to test the sensitivity of the budgeting decision to different assumptions. One of the key assumptions in projects considered for unstable countries is the level of political risk that must be accounted for. Cash flows should be adjusted for the threat of loss resulting from government expropriation or regulation. Chapter 13 will consider the issue of political risk in detail.

Summary

1. Financial control is used to monitor the firm's operations.
2. The choice of a financial control system is determined by the management style of the firm.
3. Cash management aims to utilize the firm's liquid assets efficiently.
4. Netting is the consolidation of payables and receivables in a currency so that only the difference between them must be bought or sold.
5. A transfer price is the price paid by one subsidiary to another for goods transfers within the firm.
6. Transfer prices may be used to shift profits among subsidiaries or to try to lower tariffs paid.
7. Plans for capital expenditures are summarized in a capital budget.
8. Adjusted present value is a project-evaluation approach that separates operations cash flows from financing effects on cash flow.

Exercises

1. Suppose that the Japanese firm Sanpo will receive $1.5 million from its U.S. sales subsidiary on June 3. Moreover, on June 3 a U.S. bank is due $2.3 million from Sanpo as repayment of a loan. Explain how netting by Sanpo would apply to this example, and what the advantages are.
2. What could be done if question 1 is modified so that Sanpo owes the $2.3 million on June 13, but the $1.5 million receivable is still scheduled for June 3?
3. Give an example of how transfer pricing can be used to
   a. Shift profits to a low-tax subsidiary in Ireland.
   b. Reduce the tariff on a shipment of computer parts from a subsidiary in Taiwan to a subsidiary in Brazil.
   c. Increase profits in a French subsidiary that will soon be applying for a loan.
4. What is arm's-length pricing?
5. Why are capital budgeting decisions made using present values when the cash flows will not be realized until future periods?
6. Suppose a U.S. multinational firm estimates that a $150 million capital expenditure in a new plant in an unstable developing country will have a life of two years before it is confiscated by the foreign government. During this two-year period, the operating cash flows will be $100 million each year. In addition, the firm will be able to use the new facility to repatriate $10 million each year in funds that have been held in the country involuntarily. If the discount rate for the operations cash flows is 10 percent and the discount rate for the exchange control avoidance is 8 percent, what is the adjusted present value of the project?

References

Assef, Sherif, and Surjya Mitra, "Making the Most of Transfer Pricing," *Insurance Executive,* Summer 1999.

Dembeck, Jennifer L., and David E. Stout, "Transfer Pricing in a Global Economy," *The Small Business Controller,* Winter 1996.

Holland, John, "Capital Budgeting for International Business: A Framework for Analysis," *Managerial Finance,* 16, 1990.

Lessard, Donald R., "Evaluating Foreign Projects: An Adjusted Present Value Approach," in Donald R. Lessard, ed., *International Financial Management.* New York: Wiley, 1985.

Mitchell, Paula, "Alternative Financing Techniques in Trade with Sub-Saharan Africa," *Business America,* Jan./Feb. 1997.

APPENDIX: Present Value

What would you pay today to receive \$1,000 in one year? The answer will vary from individual to individual, but we would all want to pay less than \$1,000 today. How much less depends on the *discount rate*—a measure, like an interest rate or rate of return, that we would use to discount to the present the \$1,000 to be received in one year.

Suppose that I require a 10 percent return on all my investments. Then one way of viewing present value is as the principal amount today that when invested at 10 percent simple interest would be worth \$1,000 when the principal and interest are summed after one year. To find the required principal amount, we divide the future value (FV) of \$1,000 by 1 plus the discount rate (d) of 10 percent, or the present value (PV) formula, which is

$$PV = \frac{FV}{1 + d} = \frac{\$1{,}000}{1.10} = \$909.09 \qquad (12A.1)$$

I would pay \$909.09 for the right to receive \$1,000 in one year. Another way of stating this is to say that the present value of \$1,000 to be received in one year is \$909.09.

For amounts to be received at some year n in the future, the formula is modified to

$$PV = \frac{FV}{(1 + d)^n} \qquad (12A.2)$$

In the example just used, the \$1,000 is received in one year, so n equals 1. What if the \$1,000 is to be received in two years? Then the formula gives us

$$PV = \frac{\$1{,}000}{(1 + 0.1)^2} = \frac{\$1{,}000}{(1.10)(1.10)} \tag{12A.3}$$

$$= \frac{\$1{,}000}{1.21} = \$826.45$$

The present value of \$1,000 to be received in two years is \$826.45. The farther into the future we go, the lower the present value of any future value. Furthermore, the higher the discount rate, the lower the present value of any future value to be received.

If a capital outlay will generate a stream of earnings to be received over many years, we simply sum the present value of each individual year to obtain the present value of the future cash flows associated with the expenditure. Then we subtract the initial investment or cash outflow to find the present value of the project. If Σ is the summation operator and t denotes time (like years), then the present value of an investment of I dollars today yielding cash flows of CF_t over each year t in the future for T years is

$$PV = -I + \sum_{t=1}^{T} \frac{CF_t}{(1 + d)^t} \tag{12A.4}$$

If we can estimate the after-tax cash flows (CF_t) associated with a capital expenditure (I) today, and we can choose an appropriate discount rate (d), then the present value of the project is indicated by Equation (12A.4).

13

International Banking, Debt, and Risk

The foreign exchange market is a market in which monies are traded. Money serves as a means of paying for goods and services, and the foreign exchange market exists to facilitate international payments. Just as there exists a need for international money payments, there also is a need for international credit or deposits and loans denominated in different currencies. The international deposit and loan market is often called the *Eurocurrency market,* and banks that accept these deposits and make loans are often called *Eurobanks.*

The use of the prefix *Euro,* as in Eurocurrency or Eurobank, is misleading since the activity described is related to *offshore banking* (providing foreign currency borrowing and lending services) in general and is in no way limited to Europe. For instance, the Eurodollar market originally referred to dollar banking outside the United States. But now Eurodollar banking also occurs in the United States. The Euroyen market involves yen-denominated bank deposits and loans outside Japan. Similarly, there are Euroeuros and Eurosterling.

The distinguishing feature of the Eurocurrency market is that the currency used in the banking transaction generally differs from the domestic currency of the country in which the bank is located. However, this is not strictly the case, as some international banking activity in domestic currency may exist. Where such international banking occurs, it is segregated from other domestic currency banking activities in regard to regulations applied to such transactions. As we learn in the next section, offshore banking activities have grown rapidly because of a lack of regulation, which allows greater efficiency in providing banking services.

Reasons for Offshore Banking

The Eurodollar market began in the late 1950s. Why and how the market originated have been subjects of debate, but there is agreement upon certain elements. Given the reserve currency status of the dollar, it was only reasonable that the first external money market to develop would be for dollars. Some argue that the Communist countries were the source of early dollar balances held in Europe, since these countries needed dollars from time to time but did not want to hold these dollars in U.S. banks for fear of reprisal should hostilities flare up. Thus, the dollar deposits in U.K. and French banks owned by the Communists would represent the first Eurodollar deposits.

Aside from political considerations, the Eurobanks developed as a result of profit considerations. Since costly regulations are imposed on U.S. banks, banks located outside the United States could offer higher interest rates on deposits and lower interest rates on loans than their U.S. competitors. For instance, U.S. banks are forced to hold a fraction of their deposits in the form of non-interest-bearing reserves. Because Eurobanks are essentially unregulated and hold much smaller reserves than their U.S. counterparts, they can offer narrower spreads on dollars. The *spread* is the difference between the deposit and loan interest rate. Besides lower reserve requirements, Eurobanks also benefit from having no government-mandated interest rate controls, no deposit insurance, no government-mandated credit allocations, no restrictions on entry of new banks (thus encouraging greater competition and efficiency), and low taxes. This does not mean that the countries hosting the Eurobanks do not use such regulations. What we observe in these countries are two sets of banking rules: various regulations and restrictions apply to banking in the domestic currency, whereas offshore banking activities in foreign currencies go largely unregulated.

Figure 13.1 portrays the standard relationship between the U.S. domestic loan and deposit rates and the Euroloan and Eurodeposit rates. The figure shows that U.S. spreads exceed Eurobank spreads. Eurobanks are able to offer a lower rate on dollar loans and a higher rate on dollar deposits than their U.S. competitors. Without these differences the Eurodollar market would likely not exist, since Eurodollar transactions, lacking deposit insurance and government supervision, are considered to be riskier than are

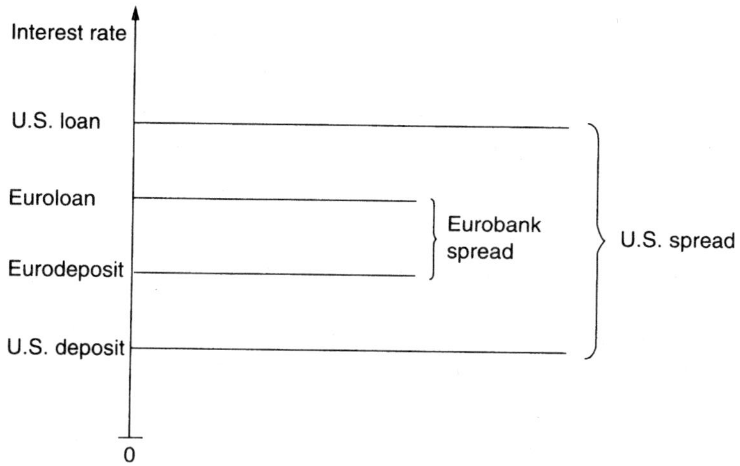

Figure 13.1 Comparison of U.S. and Eurodollar spreads.

domestic dollar transactions in the United States. This means that with respect to the supply of deposits to Eurobanks, the U.S. deposit rate provides an interest rate floor for the Eurodeposit rate, since the supply of deposits to Eurobanks is perfectly elastic at the U.S. deposit rate (this means that if the Eurodeposit rate fell below this rate, Eurobanks would have no dollar deposits). With respect to the demand for loans from Eurobanks, U.S. loan rates provide a ceiling for Euroloan rates because the demand for dollar loans from Eurobanks is perfectly elastic at the U.S. loan rate (any Eurobank charging more than this would find the demand for its loans falling to zero).

LIBOR

When comparing actual loan and deposit interest rates in the United States with those in the Eurobank market, there is a problem of determining which interest rates to compare. In the Eurodollar market, loan interest rates are usually quoted as percentage points above LIBOR. *LIBOR* stands for "London interbank offered rate" and is the interest rate at which a group of large London banks would deposit or lend to each other each morning. The U.S. commercial paper rate is considered the most comparable domestic interest rate. The Eurodollar deposit rate is best compared to the large certificate of deposit (CD) rate in the United States.

Interest Rate Spreads and Risk

The British Bankers' Association (BBA) fixes a value for LIBOR each day at 11:00 A.M. London time for each major currency. LIBOR is the key rate for fixing interest rates around the world. For instance, a variable interest rate loan in some currency may be priced at 2 percentage points above LIBOR and adjusted annually. Once a year, the interest rate on the loan would be adjusted to the currency value of LIBOR plus 2 percentage points.

The daily value of LIBOR is drawn from a panel of contributing banks chosen based upon their reputation, level of activity in the London market, and perceived expertise in the currency concerned. Shortly before 11:00 A.M. each business day, each bank reports the rate at which it could borrow funds of a reasonable market size by accepting interbank offers from banks other than the LIBOR panel of contributing banks. The contributed rates are ranked in order and only the middle two quartiles are averaged in determining LIBOR.

LIBOR is fixed daily for the following seven currencies: the British pound (GBP), Canadian dollar (CAD), euro (EUR), U.S. dollar (USD), Australian dollar (AUD), Japanese yen (JPY), and Swiss franc (CHF). The maturities for which LIBOR is set each day are: overnight, 2 days, 1 week, 2 weeks, and 1 to 12 months.

We have seen that the external interest rates on a particular currency will be constrained by the domestic spread. With capital controls, this may no longer be true. Controls on international capital flows could include quotas on foreign lending and deposits or taxes on international capital flows. For instance, if Switzerland limits inflows of foreign money, then we could have a situation where the domestic Swiss deposit interest rate exceeds the external rate on Swiss franc deposits in other nations. Although foreigners would prefer to have their Swiss franc deposits in Swiss banks in order to earn the higher interest, the legal restrictions on capital flows might prohibit such a response.

It is also possible that a perceived threat to private property rights could lead to seemingly perverse interest rate relations. If the United States threatens to confiscate foreign deposits, the funds would tend to leave the United States and shift to the external dollar market. This could result in the Eurodollar deposit rate falling below the U.S. deposit rate.

In general, risk contributes to the domestic spread exceeding the external spread. In domestic markets government agencies help ensure the sound performance of domestic financial institutions, whereas the Eurocurrency markets are largely unregulated, with no central bank ready to come to the rescue. There is an additional risk in international transactions in that investment funds are subject to control by the country of currency denomination (when it is time for repayment) as well as the country of the deposit bank. For instance, suppose a U.S. firm has a U.S. dollar bank deposit in Hong Kong. When the firm wants to withdraw those dollars—say, to pay a debt in Taiwan—not only is the transaction subject to control in Hong Kong (the government may not let foreign exchange leave the country freely), but the United States may control outflows of dollars from the United States, so that the Hong Kong bank may have difficulty paying back the dollars. It should be recognized that even though domestic and external deposit and loan rates differ, primarily because of risk, all interest rates tend to move together. When the domestic dollar interest rate is rising, the external rate will also tend to rise.

The growth of the Eurodollar market is the result of the narrower spreads offered by Eurobanks. We would expect the size of the market to grow as the total demand for dollar-denominated credit increases and as dollar banking moves from the United States to the external market. The shift of dollar intermediation would occur as the Eurodollar spread narrows relative to the domestic spread or as individual responsiveness to the spread differential changes.

Over time, important external markets have developed for the other major international currencies (euro, pound, yen, Canadian dollar, and Swiss franc). But the value of activity in Eurodollars (which refers to offshore banking in U.S. dollars) dwarfs the rest. In 2002, the Bank for International Settlements estimated the currency composition of the Eurocurrency market to be: U.S. dollar, 63%; euro, 19%; yen, 5%; British pound, 4%; with other currencies taking the remainder.

Figure 13.2 illustrates the foreign assets held by banks of different nations. The major role of the United Kingdom and the United States in international banking is obvious. Note that the figure distinguishes between bank assets, including interbank claims and credit extended to nonbanks. Interbank claims are deposits held in banks in other countries. If we want to know the actual amount of credit extended to nonbank borrowers, we must remove the interbank activity. Figure 13.2 illustrates the huge size of the interbank market in international finance. An example of interbank deposits versus credit extended to nonbanks is provided later in the chapter.

International Banking Facilities

In December 1981, the Federal Reserve permitted U.S. banks to engage in Eurobanking activity on U.S. soil. Prior to this time, U.S. banks engaged in international banking by processing loans and deposits through their offshore

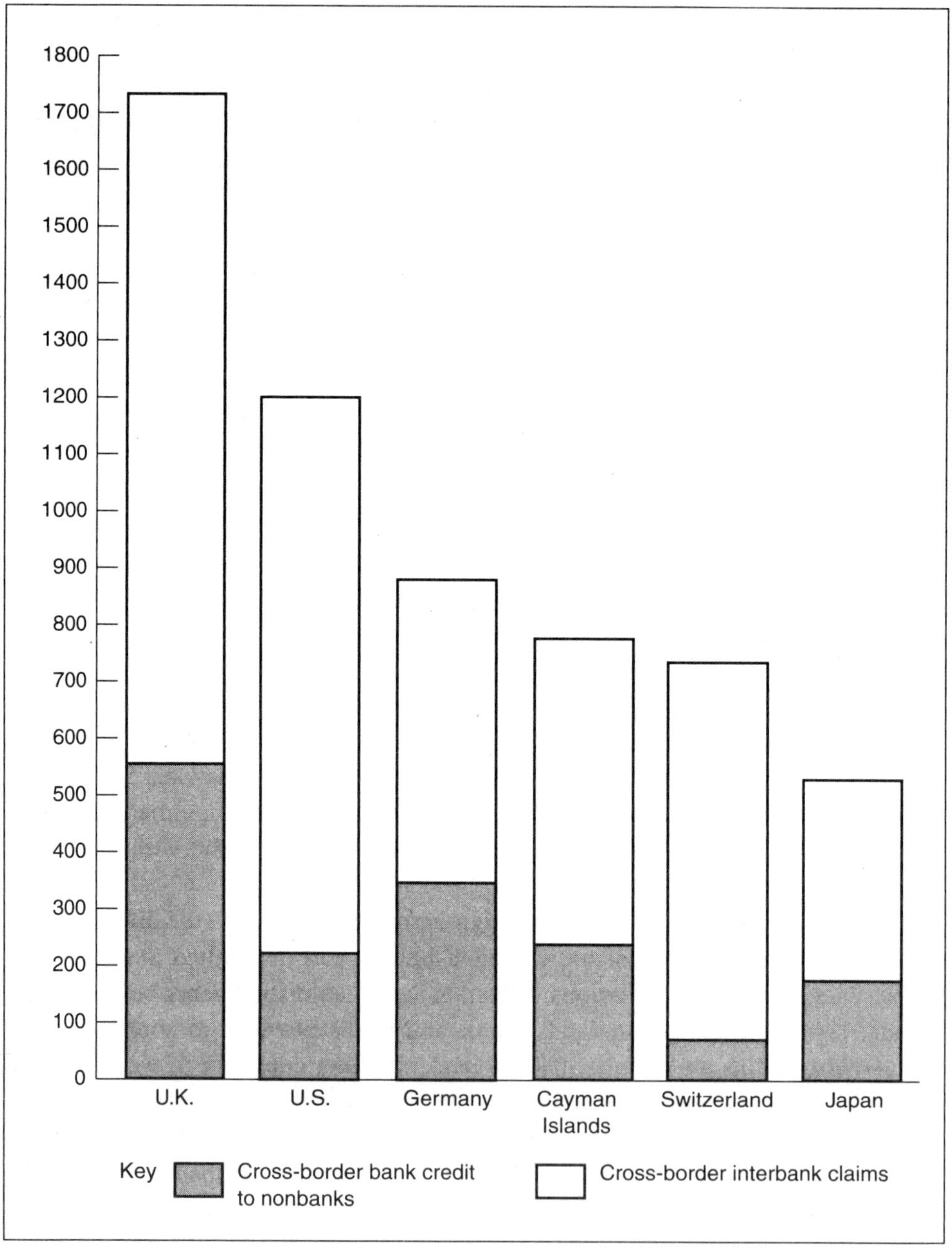

Figure 13.2 Deposit banks' foreign assets, by country. (Data are for June 2002 and are from Bank for International Settlements, Basle [http://www.bis.org/publ/].)

branches. Many "shell" bank branches in places like the Cayman Islands or the Bahamas really amounted to nothing more than a small office and a telephone. Yet by using these locations for booking loans and deposits, U.S. banks could avoid the reserve requirements and interest rate regulations that applied to normal U.S. banking.

In December 1981, international banking facilities, or *IBFs,* were legalized. IBFs did not involve any new physical presence in U.S. bank offices. Instead, they simply required a different set of books for an existing bank office to record the deposits and loans permitted under the IBF proposal. IBFs are allowed to receive deposits from, and make loans to, nonresidents of the United States or other IBFs. These loans and deposits are kept separate from the rest of the bank's business because IBFs are not subject to reserve requirements, interest rate regulations, or Federal Deposit Insurance Corporation deposit insurance premiums applicable to normal U.S. banking.

The goal of the IBF plan was to allow banking offices in the United States to compete with offshore banks without having to use an offshore banking office. The location of IBFs reflects the location of banking activity in general. It is not surprising that New York State, as the financial center of the country, has over 75 percent of IBF deposits. Aside from New York, California and Illinois are the only states with a significant IBF business. After IBFs were permitted, several states encouraged their formation by granting low or no taxes on IBF business. The volume of IBF business that resulted mirrored the preexisting volume of international banking activity, with New York dominating the level of activity found in other states.

Since IBFs grew very rapidly following their creation, we may ask where the growth came from. Rather than new business that was stimulated by the existence of IBFs, it appears that much of the growth was a result of shifting business from Caribbean shell branches to IBFs. After the first month of IBF operation, $29.1 billion in claims on foreign residents existed. During this same period, the claims existing at Caribbean branches of U.S. banks fell $23.3 billion. Since this time, IBF growth has continued with growth of Eurodollar banking in general.

Offshore Banking Practices

The Eurocurrency market handles a tremendous volume of funds. Because of the importance of interbank transactions, the gross measure overstates the actual amount of activity regarding total intermediation of funds between nonbank savers and nonbank borrowers, as Figure 13.2 shows. To measure the amount of credit actually extended through the Eurobanks, we use the net size of the market—subtracting interbank activity from total deposits or total loans existing. To understand the difference between the gross and net volume of Eurodollar activity, consider the following example.

Suppose that a U.S. firm, IBM in New York, shifts $1 million from its U.S. bank to a Eurobank, Eurobank A, to receive a higher return on its deposits. Table 13.1 shows the T accounts recording this transaction. The U.S. bank now has a liability (recorded on the right-hand side of its balance sheet) of $1 million owed to Eurobank A, since the ownership of the $1 million deposit has shifted from IBM to Eurobank A. Eurobank A records the transaction as a $1 million asset in the form of a deposit it owns in U.S. Bank, plus a $1 million liability from the deposit it has accepted from IBM. Now suppose that Eurobank A does not have a borrower waiting for $1 million (U.S.), but another Eurobank, Eurobank B, does have a borrower. Eurobank A will deposit the $1 million with Eurobank B, earning a fraction of a percent more than it must pay IBM for the $1 million. Table 13.2 shows that after Eurobank A deposits in Eurobank B, U.S. Bank now owes the U.S. dollar deposit to Eurobank B, which is shown as an asset of Eurobank B, matched by the deposit liability of $1 million from Eurobank B to Eurobank A.

Finally, in Table 13.3, Eurobank B makes a loan to BMW in Munich. Now U.S. Bank has transferred the ownership of its deposit liability to BMW. (Whenever dollars are actually spent following a Eurodollar transaction, the actual dollars must come from the United States—only the United States creates U.S. dollars; the Eurodollar banks simply act as inter-

Table 13.1 IBM-New York Deposits $1 Million in Eurobank A

U.S. Bank

Assets	Liabilities
	$1 million due Eurobank A

Eurobank A

Assets	Liabilities
$1 million deposit in U.S. Bank	$1 million Eurodollar deposit due IBM

Table 13.2 Eurobank A Deposits $1 Million in Eurobank B

U.S. Bank

Assets	Liabilities
	$1 million due Eurobank B

Eurobank A

Assets	Liabilities
$1 million Eurodollar deposit in Eurobank B	$1 million Eurodollar deposit due IBM

Eurobank B

Assets	Liabilities
$1 million deposit in U.S. Bank	$1 million Eurodollar deposit due Eurobank A

mediaries.) The gross size of the market is measured as total deposits in Eurobanks, or $2 million ($1 million in Eurobank A and $1 million in Eurobank B). The net size of the market is found by subtracting interbank deposits, and thus is a measure of the actual credit extended to nonbank users of dollars. In the example, Eurobank A deposited $1 million in Eurobank B. If we subtract this interbank deposit of $1 million from the total Eurobank deposits of $2 million, we find the net size of the market to be $1 million. This $1 million is the value of credit actually intermediated to nonbank borrowers.

Since the Eurodollar market deals with such large magnitudes, it is understandable that economists and politicians are concerned about the effects the Eurodollar market can have on domestic markets. In the United States, Eurodollar deposits are counted in the M3 definition of the money supply. Measures of the U.S. money supply are used by economists to evaluate the resources available to the public for spending. Eurodollars are not spendable money but, instead, are money substitutes like time deposits in a domestic bank. Because Eurodollars do not serve as a means of payment, Eurobanks are not able to create money as banks can in a domestic setting. Eurobanks are essentially intermediaries; they accept deposits and then loan these deposits.

Table 13.3 Eurobank B Loans $1 Million to BMW

U.S. Bank

Assets	Liabilities
	$1 million due BMW

Eurobank A

Assets	Liabilities
$1 million Eurodollar deposit in Eurobank B	$1 million Eurodollar deposit due IBM

Eurobank B

Assets	Liabilities
$1 million loan to BMW	$1 million Eurodollar deposit due Eurobank A

BMW-Munich

Assets	Liabilities
$1 million deposit in U.S. Bank	$1 million loan owed to Eurobank B

Even though Eurodollars do not provide a means of payment, they still may have implications for domestic monetary practice. For countries without efficient money markets, access to the very efficient and competitive Eurodollar market may reduce the demand for domestic money.

The efficiency of the Eurodollar market may also have encouraged international capital flows and thus led to a greater need for sterilization on the part of central banks. In Chapter 10 we defined sterilization as a change in the domestic component of base money aimed at offsetting a change in the foreign reserve component. Thus, if international reserve flows are greater due to the international capital flows encouraged by Eurodollar market efficiency, then central banks must engage in larger and more frequent sterilization operations to achieve a given domestic money growth policy.

All banks are interested in maximizing the spread between their deposit and loan interest rates. In this regard, Eurobanks are no different from domestic banks. All banks are also concerned with managing risk, the risk associated with their assets and liabilities. Like all intermediaries, Eurobanks tend to borrow short term and lend long term. Thus, if the deposit liabilities were reduced greatly, we would see deposit interest rates rise very rapidly in the short run. The advantage of matching the term structures of deposits and loans is that deposits and loans are maturing at the same time, so that the bank is better able to respond to a change in demand for deposits or loans.

Deposits in the Eurocurrency market are for fixed terms, ranging from days to years, although most are for less than six months. Certificates of deposit are considered to be the closest domestic counterpart to a Eurocurrency deposit. Loans in the Eurocurrency market can range up to ten or more years. The interest rate on a Eurocurrency loan is usually stated as some spread over LIBOR and is adjusted at fixed intervals, like every three months. These adjustable interest rates serve to minimize the interest rate risk to the bank. Although LIBOR is the dominant pricing tool, the second most popular pricing mechanism is the U.S. prime rate.

Large loans are generally made by syndicates of Eurobanks. The syndicate will be headed by a lead or managing bank; other banks wishing to participate in the loan will join the syndicate and help fund the loan. By allowing banks to reduce their level of participation in any loan, syndicates can participate in more loans, so the diversification reduces their risk of loss.

International Lending and Crisis

In many ways, international lending is similar to domestic lending. Lenders care about the risk of default and the expected return from making loans whether they are lending across town or across international borders. However, international lending has had recurrent horror stories where regional financial crises have imposed large losses on lenders. In the 1980s, there was a Latin American debt crisis in which many countries were unable to service the international debts they had accumulated. In 1994 to 1995 there was the Mexican financial crisis, when Mexico devalued the peso dramatically and required a large loan from the IMF and the U.S. Treasury to avoid defaulting on international debts. More recently is the Asian financial crisis of 1997 to 1998, when a devaluation of the Thai baht in July 1997 was followed by financial panic that spread to Malaysia, Indonesia, the Philippines, and, to a lesser extent, South Korea.

All of these crises imposed large losses on international investors and led to banks turning inward for a while, devoting fewer resources to international lending, particularly in developing countries. Table 13.4 illustrates the commitment of U.S. banks to lending in each of the crisis areas. The table indicates that the situation from the perspective of U.S. banks was

Table 13.4 U.S. Bank Loans in Financial Crisis Countries as a Percentage of U.S. Bank Capital

Latin America in 1982	
Argentina	12%
Brazil	26%
Chile	9%
Mexico	37%
Mexico in 1994	11%
Asia in 1997	
Indonesia	2%
Korea	3%
Thailand	1%

Source: Steve Kamin, "The Asian Financial Crisis in Historical Perspective: A Review of Selected Statistics," Working Paper, Board of Governors of the Federal Reserve System, 1998.

much more dire in the 1982 Latin American crisis than in the more recent cases. The 1980 debtor nations owed so much money to international banks that a default would have wiped out the biggest banks in the world. As a result, debts were *rescheduled* rather than allowed to default. A debt rescheduling postpones the repayment of interest and principal so that banks can claim the loan as being owed in the future rather than in default now. This way, banks do not have to write off the debt as a loss—which would have threatened the existence of many large banks due to the large size of the loans relative to the capitalization of the bank. For instance, the Mexican debt to U.S. banks in 1982 was equal to 37 percent of U.S. bank capital. Banks simply could not afford to write off as bad debt a loss of this magnitude. By rescheduling the debt, banks would avoid this alternative.

In contrast to the heavy exposure of international banks to Latin American borrowers in 1982, the Asian financial crisis of 1997 involved a much more manageable debt position. Many international investors lost money in the Asian crisis, but the crisis did not threaten the stability of the world banking system to the extent the 1980s crisis did. However, the debtor countries required international assistance to recover from the crisis in all recent crisis situations. This recovery involves new loans from governments, banks, and the IMF. The next section considers the role of the IMF in more detail. First, it is useful to think about what causes financial crises.

The causes of the recent Asian financial crisis are still being debated. Yet, it is safe to say that certain elements are essential in any explanation, including external shocks, domestic macroeconomic policy, and domestic financial system flaws. Let's consider each of these in turn.

1. *External shocks.* Following years of rapid growth, the East Asian economies faced a series of external shocks in the mid-1990s that may have contributed to the crisis. The Chinese renminbi and the Japanese yen were both devalued, making other Asian economies with fixed exchange rates less competitive relative to China and Japan. Because electronics manufacturing is an important export industry in East Asia, another factor contributing to a drop in exports and national income was the sharp drop in semiconductor prices. As exports and incomes fell, loan repayment became more difficult and property values started to fall. Since real property is used as collateral in many bank loans, the drop in property values made many loans of questionable value so that the banking systems were facing many defaults.

2. *Domestic macroeconomic policy.* The most obvious element of macroeconomic policy in most crisis countries was the use of fixed exchange rates. Fixed exchange rates encouraged international capital flows into the countries, and many debts incurred in foreign currencies were not hedged because of the lack of exchange rate volatility. Once pressures for devaluation began, countries defended the pegged exchange rate by central bank intervention—buying domestic currency with dollars. Because each country has a finite supply of dollars, countries also raised interest rates to increase the attractiveness of investments denominated in domestic currency. Finally, some countries resorted to capital controls, restricting foreigners access to domestic currency to restrict speculation against the domestic currency. For instance, if investors wanted to speculate against the Thai baht, they could borrow baht and exchange them for dollars, betting that the baht would fall in value against the dollar. This increased selling pressure on the baht could be reduced by capital controls limiting foreigners' ability to borrow baht. However, ultimately the pressure to devalue is too great, as even domestic residents are speculating against the domestic currency and the fixed exchange rate is abandoned. This occurs with great cost to the domestic financial market. Because international debts are denominated in foreign currency and most are unhedged because of the prior fixed exchange rate, the domestic currency burden of the debt is increased in proportion to the size of the devaluation. To aid in the repayment of the debt, countries turn to other governments and the IMF for aid.

3. *Domestic financial system flaws.* The Asia crisis countries were characterized by banking systems in which loans were not always made on the basis of prudent business decisions. Political and social connections were often more important than expected return and collateral when applying for a loan. As a result, many bad loans were extended. During the boom times of the early to mid-1990s, the rapid growth of the economy covered such losses. However, once the growth started to falter, the bad loans started to adversely affect the financial health of the banking system. A related issue is that banks and other lenders expected the government to bail them out if they ran into serious financial difficulties. This situation of implicit government loan guarantees created a *moral hazard* situation. A moral hazard exists when one does not have to bear the full cost of bad decisions. This creates excessive risk taking as the institution or individual taking the risk is assured of not being held liable if a bad decision results. So if banks believe that the government will cover any significant losses from loans to political cronies that are not repaid, they will be more likely to extend such loans.

Considerable resources have been devoted to understanding the nature and causes of financial crises in hopes of avoiding future crises and forecasting those crises that do occur. Forecasting is always difficult in economics, and it is safe to say that there will always be surprises that no economic forecaster foresees. Yet there are certain variables that are so obviously related to past crises that they may serve as warning indicators of potential future crises. The list includes the following:

1. *Fixed exchange rates.* Countries involved in recent crises, including Mexico in 1993 to 1994, the Southeast Asian countries in 1997, and Argentina in 2002, all utilized fixed exchange rates prior to the onset of the crisis. Generally, macroeconomic policies were inconsistent with the maintenance of the fixed exchange rate and when large devaluations ultimately occurred, domestic residents holding unhedged loans denominated in foreign currency suffered huge losses.

2. *Falling international reserves.* The maintenance of fixed exchange rates may be no problem. One way to tell if the exchange rate is no longer an equilibrium rate is to monitor the international reserve holdings of the country (largely the foreign currency held by the central bank and treasury).

If the stock of international reserves is falling steadily over time, that is a good indicator that the fixed exchange rate regime is under pressure and there is likely to be a devaluation.

3. *Lack of transparency.* Many crisis countries suffer from a lack of transparency in governmental activities and in public disclosures of business conditions. Investors need to know the financial situation of firms in order to make informed investment decisions. If accounting rules allow firms to hide the financial impact of actions that would harm investors, then investors may not be able to adequately judge when the risk of investing in a firm rises. In such cases, a financial crisis may appear as a surprise to all but the "insiders" in a troubled firm. Similarly, if the government does not disclose its international reserve position in a timely and informative manner, investors may be caught by surprise when a devaluation occurs. The lack of good information on government and business activities serves as a warning sign of potential future problems.

This short list of warning signs provides an indication of the sorts of variables an international investor must consider when evaluating the risks of investing in a foreign country.

Once a country finds itself with severe international debt repayment problems, it has to seek additional financing. Because international banks are not willing to commit new money where prospects for repayment are slim, the IMF becomes an important source of funding.

IMF Conditionality

The IMF has been an important source of loans for debtor nations experiencing repayment problems. The importance of an IMF loan is more than simply having the IMF "bail out" commercial bank and government creditors. The IMF requires borrowers to adjust their economic policies to reduce balance of payments deficits and improve the chance for debt repayment. Such IMF-required adjustment programs are known as *IMF conditionality.*

Part of the process of developing a loan package includes a visit to the borrowing country by an IMF mission. The mission comprises economists who review the causes of the country's economic problems and recommend solutions. Through negotiation with the borrower, a program of conditions attached to the loan is agreed to. The conditions usually involve targets for macroeconomic variables, such as money supply growth or the government deficit. The loan is disbursed at intervals, with a possible cutoff of new disbursements if the conditions have not been met.

The importance of IMF conditionality to creditors can now be understood. Loans to sovereign governments involve risk management from the lenders' point of view just as loans to private entities do. Although countries cannot go out of business, they can have revolutions or political upheavals leading to a repudiation of the debts incurred by the previous regime. Even without such drastic political change, countries may not be able or willing to service their debt due to adverse economic conditions. International lending adds a new dimension to risk since there is neither an international court of law to enforce contracts nor any loan collateral aside from assets that the borrowing country may have in the lending country. The IMF serves as an overseer that can offer debtors new loans if they agree to conditions. Sovereign governments may be offended if a foreign creditor government or commercial bank suggests changes in the debtor's domestic policy, but the IMF is a multinational organization of over 180 countries. The members of the IMF mission to the debtor nation will be of many different nationalities, and their advice will be nonpolitical. However, the IMF is still criticized at times as being dominated by the interests of the advanced industrial countries. In terms of voting power, this is true.

Votes in the IMF determine policy, and voting power is determined by a country's quota. The quota is the financial contribution of a country to the IMF and it entitles membership. Each country receives 250 votes, plus one additional vote for each SDR100,000 of its quota. (At least 75 percent of the quota may be contributed in domestic currency, with less than 25 percent paid in reserve currencies or SDRs.) The United States has the most votes, since the U.S. quota accounts for almost 20 percent of the total fund. Then come Japan and Germany, each with about 6 percent of the total, followed by the U.K. and France, each with about 5 percent of the total. These five developed countries contribute more than 40 percent of the IMF quotas and dominate voting accordingly.

The IMF has been criticized for imposing conditions that restrict economic growth and lower living standards in borrowing countries. The typical conditionality involves reducing government spending, raising taxes, and restricting money growth. For example, in July 1986, Mexico signed a $1.6 billion loan agreement with the IMF that included the following conditions: the budget deficit would fall by 3 percentage points over the next 18 months, monetary growth would be restricted to reduce capital flight, nominal interest rates would exceed the inflation rate, and the deductibility of business expenses would fall to increase the tax base. Such policies may be interpreted as austerity imposed by the IMF, but the austerity is intended for the borrowing government in order to permit the productive private sector to play a larger role in the economy.

The view of the IMF is that adjustment programs are unavoidable in debtor countries facing repayment difficulties. The adjustments required are those that promote long-run growth. While there may indeed be short-run costs of adjusting to a smaller role for government and fewer and smaller government subsidies, in the long run the required adjustments should stimulate growth to allow debt repayment.

The Role of Corruption

Corrupt practices by government officials have long reduced economic growth. Payment of money or gifts in order to receive a government service or benefit is quite widespread in many countries. Research shows that there is a definite negative relationship between the level of corruption in a country and both investment and growth.

Research shows that corruption thrives in countries where government regulations create distortions between the economic outcomes that would exist with free markets and the actual outcomes. For instance, a country where government permission is required to buy or sell foreign currency will have a thriving black market in foreign exchange where the black market exchange rate of a U.S. dollar costs much more domestic currency than the "official rate" offered by the government. This distortion allows government officials an opportunity for personal gain by providing access to the official rate.

Generally speaking, the more competitive a country's markets are, the fewer the opportunities for corruption. So policies aimed at reducing corruption typically involve reducing the discretion that public officials have in granting benefits or imposing costs on others. This may include greater transparency of government practices and the introduction of merit-based competitions for government employment. Due to the sensitive political nature of the issue of corruption in a country, the IMF has only recently begun to include this issue in its advisory and lending functions. When loans from the IMF or World Bank do not go to the purposes intended but, instead, are siphoned off by corrupt politicians, the industrial countries providing the major support for such lending are naturally concerned and pressure the international organizations to include anticorruption measures in loan conditions. In the late 1990s, both the IMF and World Bank began explicitly including anticorruption policies as part of the lending process to countries when severe corruption is ingrained in the local economy.

Country Risk Analysis

International financial activity involves risks that are missing in domestic transactions. There are no international courts to enforce contracts and a bank cannot repossess a nation's collateral, because typically no collateral is pledged. Problem loans to sovereign governments have received most of the publicity, but it is important to realize that loans to private firms can also become nonperforming because of capital controls or exchange rate policies. In this regard, even operating subsidiary units in foreign countries may not be able to transfer funds to the parent multinational firm if foreign exchange controls block the transfer of funds.

It is important for commercial banks and multinational firms to be able to assess the risks involved in international deals. Country risk analysis has become an important part of international business. *Country risk analysis* refers to the evaluation of the overall political and financial situation in a country and the extent to which these conditions may affect the country's ability to repay its debts. In determining the degree of risk associated with a particular country, we should consider both qualitative and quantitative factors. The qualitative factors include the political stability of the country. Certain key features may indicate political uncertainty:

1. Splits between different language, ethnic, and religious groups that threaten to undermine stability.
2. Extreme nationalism and aversion to foreigners that may lead to preferential treatment of local interests and nationalization of foreign holdings.
3. Unfavorable social conditions, including extremes of wealth.
4. Conflicts in society evidenced by frequency of demonstrations, violence, and guerrilla war.
5. The strength and organization of radical groups.

Besides the qualitative or political factors, we also want to consider the financial factors that allow an evaluation of a country's ability to repay its debts. Country risk analysts examine factors such as these:

1. *External debt.* Specifically, this is the debt owed to foreigners as a fraction of GDP or foreign exchange earnings. If a country's debts appear to be relatively large, then the country may have future repayment problems.
2. *International reserve holdings.* These reserves indicate the ability of a country to meet its short-term international trade needs should its export earnings fall. The ratio of international reserves to imports is used to rank countries according to their liquidity.
3. *Exports.* Exports are looked at in terms of the foreign exchange earned as well as the diversity of the products exported. Countries that depend largely on one or two products to earn foreign exchange may be more susceptible to wide swings in export earnings than countries with a diversified group of export products.
4. *Economic growth.* Measured by the growth of real GDP or real per capita GDP, economic growth may serve as an indicator of general economic conditions within a country.

Although no method of assessing country risk is foolproof, by evaluating and comparing countries on the basis of some structured approach, international lenders have a base on which they can build subjective evaluations of whether to extend credit to a particular country.

Euromoney magazine ranks countries' creditworthiness twice a year. Rankings are based on loan officers opinions of country risk, debt levels, forecasted economic performance, and current access to credit. Countries are ranked on a scale from zero (for least creditworthy) to 100 (for most creditworthy). Table 13.5 provides the results from a recent survey. We should not make too much out of who is ranked number 1 or 2. It is more useful to think of groups of countries. For instance, all the countries at the top of the list are good risks to which banks readily extend new credit. Those countries at the bottom would find new commercial bank lending impossible to attract.

Summary

1. The international bank deposit and loan market is called the Eurocurrency market.
2. Eurobanking grew because it is less regulated and permits greater efficiency.
3. International banking facilities (IBFs) are departments of U.S. banks that are permitted to engage in Eurocurrency banking.

Table 13.5 *Euromoney* Magazine Country Credit Ratings

Rank (Sept. 02)	Country	Rank (Sept. 02)	Country
1	Luxembourg	47	Malaysia
2	Switzerland	48	Macau
3	Norway	49	Oman
4	Denmark	50	Mexico
5	United States	51	Croatia
6	Sweden	52	South Africa
7	Finland	53	Latvia
8	Netherlands	54	Mauritius
9	Ireland	55	Trinidad & Tobago
10	Austria	56	Slovak Republic
11	United Kingdom	57	Tunisia
12	France	58	China
13	Germany	59	Thailand
14	Canada	60	Lithuania
15	Belgium	61	India
16	Australia	62	Morocco
17	Singapore	63	El Salvador
18	Japan	64	Costa Rica
19	Spain	65	Panama
20	Italy	66	Philippines
21	Iceland	67	Egypt
22	New Zealand	68	Bulgaria
23	Bermuda	69	Kazakhstan
24	Portugal	70	Colombia
25	Taiwan	71	Dominican Republic
26	Greece	72	Peru
27	Hong Kong	73	Romania
28	United Arab Emirates	74	Iran
29	Kuwait	75	Vietnam
30	Slovenia	76	Jordan
31	Cyprus	77	Russia
32	Qatar	78	Guatemala
33	Malta	79	Bolivia
34	Korea South	80	Turkey
35	Hungary	81	Uruguay
36	Bahamas	82	Azerbaijan
37	Bahrain	83	Brazil
38	Israel	84	Jamaica
39	Saudi Arabia	85	Algeria
40	Czech Republic	86	Sri Lanka
41	Botswana	87	Fiji
42	Poland	88	Venezuela
43	Chile	89	Lebanon
44	Brunei	90	Honduras
45	Estonia	91	Pakistan
46	Barbados	92	Bangladesh

(Continued)

Table 13.5 (Continued)

Rank (Sept. 02)	Country	Rank (Sept. 02)	Country
93	Senegal	140	Mali
94	Uganda	141	Nepal
95	Papua New Guinea	142	Guinea
96	Indonesia	143	Benin
97	Paraguay	144	Cambodia
98	Ghana	145	Bhutan
99	Syria	146	Argentina
100	Kenya	147	Mongolia
101	Seychelles	148	Djibouti
102	Macedonia (FYR)	149	Namibia
103	Ukraine	150	Moldova
104	Tanzania	151	Zambia
105=	Yemen	152	Solomon Islands
105=	Turkmenistan	153	Vanuatu
107	Antigua & Barbuda	154	Congo
108	St Lucia	155	Guyana
109	Swaziland	156	Sudan
110	Lesotho	157	Kyrgyz Republic
111	Georgia	158	Mauritania
112	Grenada	159	Nigeria
113	Armenia	160	Suriname
114	Mozambique	161	Bosnia-Herzegovina
115	Uzbekistan	162	Laos
116	Albania	163	Libya
117	Gabon	164	Angola
118	Tajikistan	165	Haiti
119	Maldives	166	Chad
120	The Gambia	167	Central African Republic
121	Belize	168	Guinea-Bissau
122	Cape Verde	169	Zimbabwe
123	Nicaragua	170	Entrea
124	Niger	171	Myanmar
125	Ecuador	172	Sierra Leone
126	Burkina Faso	173	São Tomé & Príncipe
127	Côte d'Ivoire	174	Burundi
128	Belarus	175	Rwanda
129	Yugoslavia (Fed. Republic)	176	New Caledonia
130	Cameroon	177	Micronesia (Fed. States)
131	Ethiopia	178	Somalia
132	Dominica	179	Liberia
133	Samoa	180	Dem. Rep. of the Congo (Zaire)
134	St Vincent & the Grenadines	181	Marshall Islands
135	Malawi	182	Cuba
136	Equatorial Guinea	183	Iraq
137	Togo	184	Afghanistan
138	Madagascar	185	Korea North
139	Tonga		

4. The net size of the Eurodollar market measures the amount of credit actually extended to nonbanks.
5. Large Eurocurrency loans are made by bank syndicates.
6. Recent international financial crises have resulted in debt and rescheduling rather than default.
7. The recent Asian financial crisis resulted from a combination of external shocks, domestic macroeconomic policy, and domestic financial system flaws.
8. IMF loans come with conditions that require the debtor country to adjust its economy to increase the likelihood of repayment.
9. Corruption reduces economic growth and is now included in IMF loan conditions.
10. Country risk analysis involves a consideration of both economic and political factors.

Exercises

1. Why must Eurobanks operate with narrower spreads than domestic banks? What would happen if the spreads were equal in both markets?
2. Use T-accounts to explain the difference between the gross and net size of the Eurodollar market.
3. Why would a debtor nation prefer to borrow from a bank rather than the IMF, other things being equal? Can "other things" ever be equal between commercial bank and IMF loans?
4. Pick three developing countries and create a country risk index for them. Rank them ordinally in terms of factors that you can observe (like exports, GDP growth, reserves, etc.) by looking at *International Financial Statistics* published by the IMF. Based on your evaluation, which country appears to be the best credit risk? How does your ranking compare to that found in the most recent *Institutional Investor* survey?
5. How did each of the following contribute to the Asian financial crisis of the late 1990s: external shocks, domestic macroeconomic policy, and domestic financial system flaws?
6. Create an example of $10 million being deposited in the Eurodollar market by a U.S. manufacturing firm, Motorola. Your example should include at least one interbank transaction before the dollars are borrowed by a French public utility firm, Paris Electric. How is the gross size of the Eurodollar market affected by your example? What about the net size?
7. Imagine yourself in a job interview for a position with a large international bank. The interviewer mentions that, recently, the bank has experienced some problem loans to foreign governments. The interviewer asks you what factors you think the bank should consider when evaluating a loan proposal involving a foreign governmental agency. How do you respond?

References

Bird, Graham, Mumtaz Hussain, and Joseph P. Joyce, "Many Happy Returns? Recidivism and the IMF," *Journal of International Money and Finance,* June 2004.

Brealey, R. A., and E. Kaplanis, "The Impact of IMF Programs on Asset Values," *Journal of International Money and Finance,* June 2004.

Schadler, Susan, Adam Bennett, Maria Carkovic, Louis Dicks-Mireaux, Mauro Mecagni, James H. J. Morsink, and Miguel A. Savastano, *IMF Conditionality: Experience under Stand-By and Extended Arrangements,* International Monetary Fund Occasional Paper 128, September 1995.

Somerville, R. A., and R. J. Taffler, "Banker Judgment versus Formal Forecasting Models: The Case of Country Risk Assessment," *Journal of Banking and Finance,* May 1995.

14

Macroeconomic Policy in the Open Economy

An economy open to international trade and payments will face different problems than an economy closed to the rest of the world. The typical introductory economics presentation of macroeconomic equilibrium and policy is a closed-economy view. Discussions of economic adjustments required to combat unemployment or inflation do not consider the rest of the world. Clearly, this is no longer an acceptable approach in an increasingly integrated world.

In the open economy, we can summarize the desirable economic goals as being the attainment of internal and external balance. *Internal balance* means a steady growth of the domestic economy consistent with a low unemployment rate. *External balance* is the achievement of a desired trade balance or desired international capital flows. In principles of economics classes, the emphasis is on internal balance. By concentrating solely on internal goals like inflation, unemployment, and economic growth, simpler-model economies may be used for analysis. A consideration of the joint pursuit of internal and external balance calls for a more detailed view of the economy. The slight increase in complexity yields a big payoff in terms of a more realistic view of the problems facing the modern policy maker. It is no longer a question of changing policy to change unemployment or inflation at home. Now the authorities must also consider the impact on the balance of trade, capital flows, and exchange rates.

Internal and External Macroeconomic Equilibrium

The major tools of macroeconomic policy are fiscal policy (government spending and taxation) and monetary policy (central bank control of the money supply). These tools are used to achieve macroeconomic equilibrium. We assume that macroeconomic equilibrium requires equilibrium in three major sectors of the economy:

Goods market equilibrium. The quantity of goods and services supplied is equal to the quantity demanded. This is represented by the *IS* curve.

Money market equilibrium. The quantity of money supplied is equal to the quantity demanded. This is represented by the *LM* curve.

Balance of payments equilibrium. The current account deficit is equal to the capital account surplus, so that the official settlements definition of the balance of payments equals zero. This is represented by the *BP* curve.

We will analyze the macroeconomic equilibrium with a graph that summarizes equilibrium in each market. Figure 14.1 displays the *IS-LM-BP* diagram. This graph illustrates various combinations of the domestic interest rate (i) and domestic national income (Y) that yield equilibrium in the three markets considered here.

The *IS* Curve

First, let's look at the *IS curve,* which represents combinations of i and Y that provide equilibrium in the goods market when everything else (like the price level) is held constant. Equilibrium occurs when the output of goods and services is equal to the quantity of goods and services demanded. In principles of economics classes, macroeconomic equilibrium is said to exist when the "leakages equal the injections" of spending in the economy. More precisely, domestic saving (S), taxes (T), and imports (IM) represent income received that is not spent on domestic goods and services—the leakages from spending. The offsetting injections of spending are represented by investment spending (I), government spending (G), and exports (X). Investment spending is the spending of business firms for new plants and equipment.

Equilibrium occurs when

$$S + T + IM = I + G + X \tag{14.1}$$

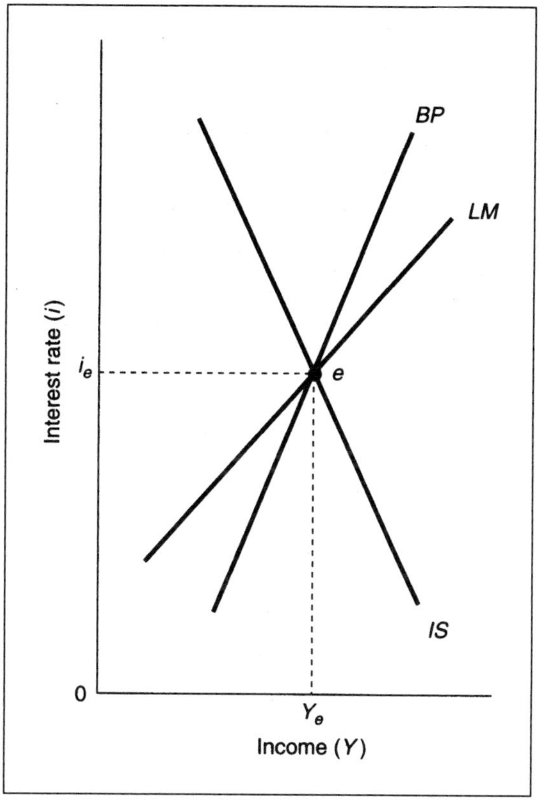

Figure 14.1 Equilibrium in the goods market (*IS*), in the money market (*LM*), and in the balance of payments (*BP*).

When the leakages from spending equal the injections, then the value of income received from producing goods and services will be equal to total spending, or the quantity of output demanded. The *IS* curve in Figure 14.1 depicts the various combinations of *i* and *Y* that yield the equality in Equation (14.1). We now consider why the *IS* curve is downward sloping.

We assume that *S* and *IM* are both functions of income and that taxes are set by governments independent of income. The higher that domestic income, the more domestic residents want to save and the more they spend on imports. In the bottom panel of Figure 14.2, the $S + T + IM$ line is upward sloping. This illustrates that the higher domestic income rises, the greater are saving plus taxes plus imports. Investment is assumed to be a function of the domestic interest rate and so does not change as current domestic income changes. Similarly, exports are assumed to be determined by foreign income (they are foreign imports) and so do not change as domestic income changes. Finally, government spending is set independent of income. Since I, G, and X are all independent of current domestic income, the $I + G + X$ line in the bottom panel of Figure 14.2 is drawn as a horizontal line.

Equation (14.1) indicated that equilibrium occurs at that income level where $S + T + IM = I + G + X$. In the bottom panel of Figure 14.2, point A represents an equilibrium point with an equilibrium level of income Y_A. In the upper panel of the figure, Y_A is shown to be consistent with point A on the IS curve. This point is also associated with a particular interest rate i_A.

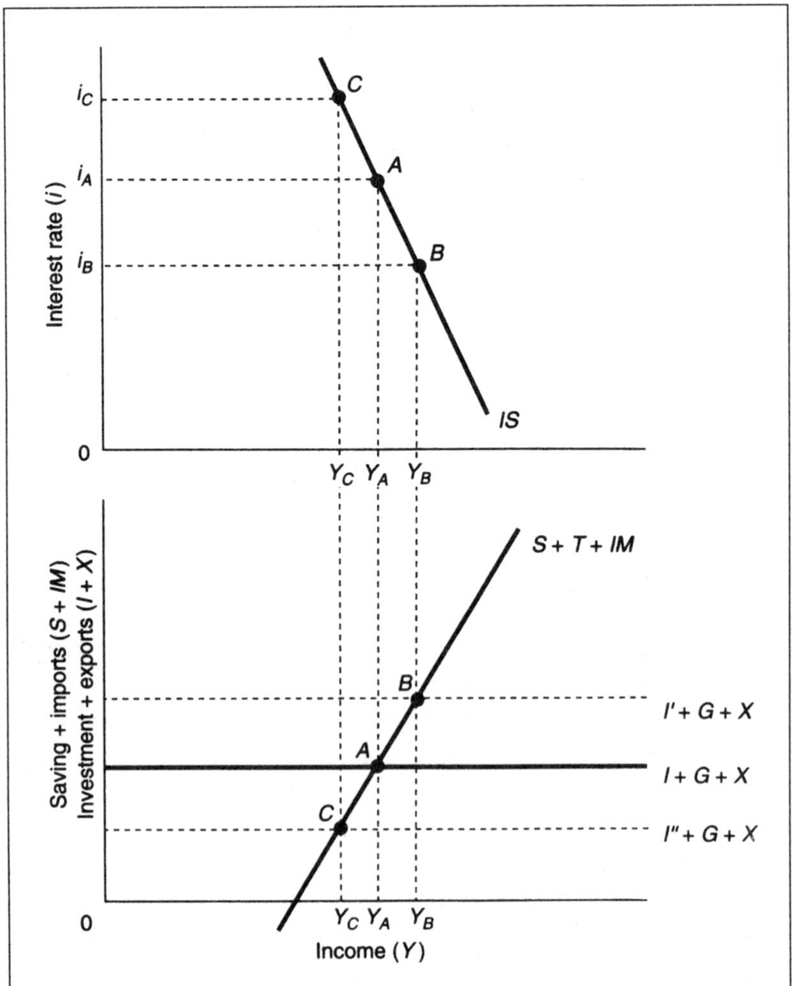

Figure 14.2 Derivation of the *IS* curve.

To understand why the *IS* curve slopes downward, consider what happens as the interest rate varies. Suppose the interest rate falls. At the lower interest rate, more potential investment projects become profitable (firms will not require as high a return on investment when the cost of borrowed funds falls), so investment increases as illustrated in the move from $I + G + X$ to $I' + G + X$ in Figure 14.2. At this higher level of investment spending, equilibrium income increases to Y_B. Point *B* on the *IS* curve depicts this new goods market equilibrium, with a lower equilibrium interest rate i_B and higher equilibrium income Y_B.

Finally, consider what happens when the interest rate rises. Investment spending will fall, because fewer potential projects are profitable as the cost of borrowed funds rises. At the lower level of investment spending, the $I + G + X$ curve shifts down to $I'' + G + X$ in Figure 14.2. The new equilibrium point *C* is consistent with the level of income Y_C. In the *IS* diagram in the upper panel we see that point *C* is consistent with equilibrium income level Y_C and equilibrium interest rate i_C. The other points on the *IS* curve are consistent with alternative combinations of income and interest rate that yield equilibrium in the goods market.

We must remember that the *IS* curve is drawn holding the domestic price level constant. A change in the domestic price level will change the price of domestic goods relative to foreign goods. If the domestic price level falls with a given interest rate, then investment, government spending, taxes, and saving don't change; but, since domestic goods are now cheaper relative to foreign goods, exports increase and imports fall. The rise in the $I + G + X$ curve and the fall in the $S + T + IM$ curve would both increase income. Because income increases with a constant interest rate, the *IS* curve shifts to the right. A rise in the domestic price level would cause the *IS* curve to shift left.

The *LM* Curve

The *LM curve* in Figure 14.1 displays the alternative combinations of *i* and *Y* at which the demand for money equals the supply. Figure 14.3 provides a derivation of the *LM* curve. The left panel shows a money demand curve labeled M^d and a money supply curve labeled M^s. The horizontal axis measures the quantity of money and the vertical axis measures the interest rate. Note that the M^s curve is vertical. This is so because the central bank can choose any money supply it wants, independent of the interest rate. The actual value of the money supply chosen is M_0. The money demand curve slopes

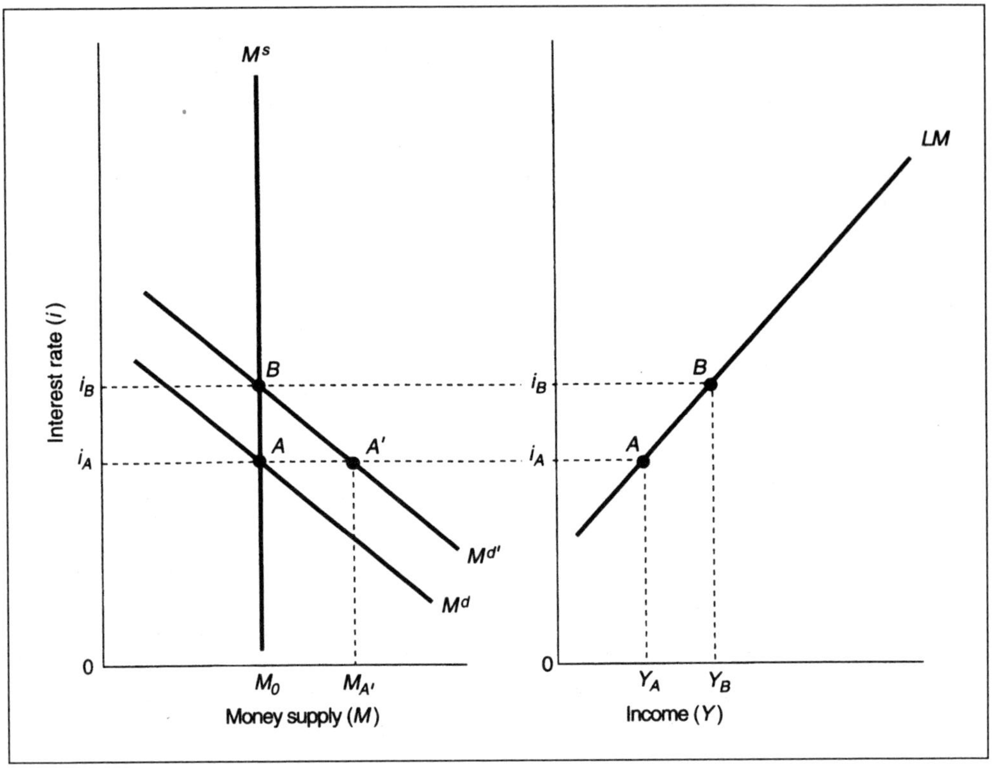

Figure 14.3 Derivation of the *LM* curve.

downward, indicating that the higher the interest rate, the lower the quantity of money demanded.

The inverse relationship between the interest rate and quantity of money demanded is a result of the role of interest as the opportunity cost of holding money. Since money earns no interest, the higher the interest rate, the more you must give up to hold money, so less money is held.

The initial money market equilibrium occurs at point *A* with interest rate i_A. The initial money demand curve, M^d, is drawn for a given level of income. If income increased, then the demand for money would increase, as seen in the shift from M^d to $M^{d'}$. Money demand increases because, at the higher level of income, people want to hold more money to support the increased spending on transactions.

Now let's consider why the *LM* curve has a positive slope. Suppose initially there is equilibrium at point *A* with the interest rate at i_A and income at Y_A in Figure 14.3. If income increases from Y_A to Y_B, money demand increases from M^d to $M^{d'}$. If the interest rate remains at i_A, there will be an excess demand for money. This is shown in the left panel of Figure 14.3, as the quantity of money demanded is now $M_{A'}$. With the higher income, money demand is given by $M^{d'}$. At i_A, point A' on the money demand curve is consistent with the higher quantity of money demanded, $M_{A'}$. Since the money supply remains constant at M_0, there will be an excess demand for money given by $M_{A'} - M_0$. The attempt to increase money balances above the quantity of money outstanding will cause the interest rate to rise until a new equilibrium is established at point *B*. This new equilibrium is consistent with a higher interest rate i_B and a higher income Y_B. Points *A* and *B* are both indicated on the *LM* curve in the right panel of Figure 14.3. The rest of the *LM* curve reflects similar combinations of equilibrium interest rates and income.

The *LM* curve is drawn for a specific money supply. If the supply of money increases, then money demand will have to increase to restore equilibrium. This requires a higher *Y* or lower *i*, or both, so the *LM* curve will shift right. Similarly, a decrease in the money supply will tend to raise *i* and lower *Y*, and the *LM* curve will shift to the left.

The *BP* Curve

The final curve portrayed in Figure 14.1 is the *BP* curve. The *BP curve* gives the combinations of *i* and *Y* that yield balance of payments equilibrium. The *BP* curve is drawn for a given domestic price level, a given exchange rate, and a given net foreign debt. Equilibrium occurs when the current account surplus is equal to the capital account deficit. Figure 14.4 illustrates the derivation of the *BP* curve. The lower panel of the figure shows a *CS* line, representing the current account surplus, and a *CD* line, representing the capital account deficit. Realistically, the current account surplus may be negative, which would indicate a deficit. Similarly, the capital account deficit may be negative, indicating a surplus. The *CS* line is downward sloping because as income increases, domestic imports increase and the current account surplus falls. The capital account is assumed to be a function of the interest rate and is, therefore, independent of income and a horizontal line. Equilibrium occurs when the current account surplus equals the capital account deficit, so that the official settlements balance of payments is zero. Initially, equilibrium occurs at point *A* with income level Y_A and interest rate i_A. If the interest rate increases, then domestic financial assets are more attractive to foreign buyers and the capital account deficit falls to CD'. At the old income level Y_A, the current account surplus will exceed the capital account deficit, and income must increase to Y_B to provide a new equilibrium at point *B*.

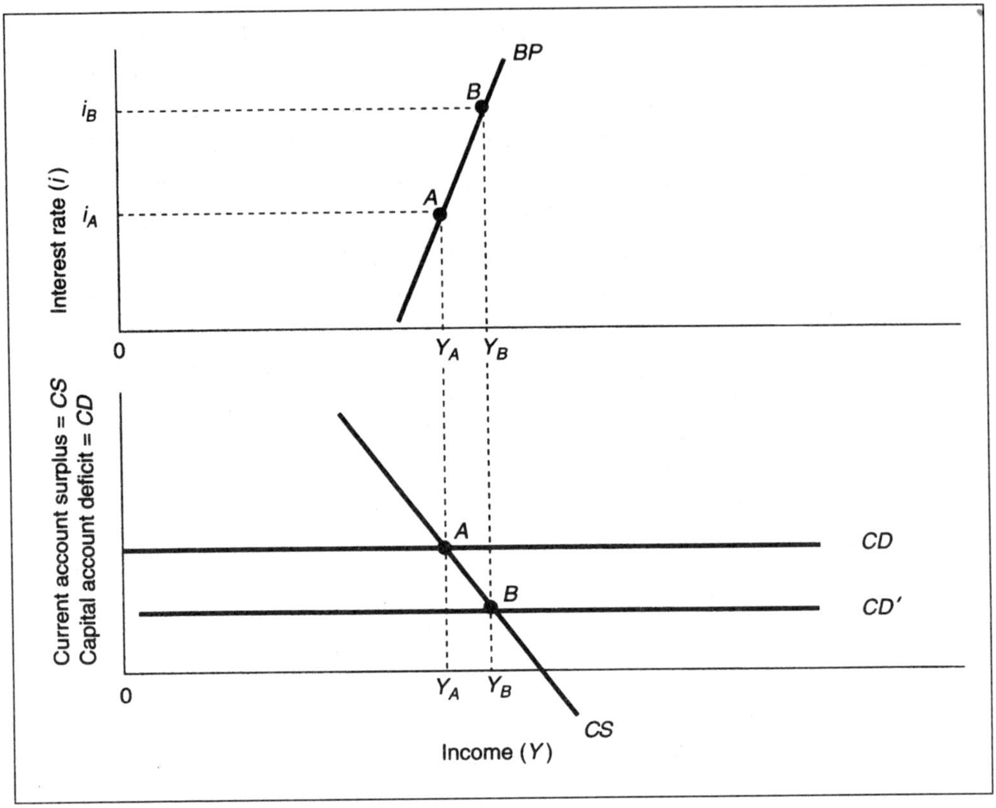

Figure 14.4 Derivation of the BP curve.

Points *A* and *B* on the *BP* curve in Figure 14.4 illustrate that, as *i* increases, *Y* must also increase to maintain equilibrium. Only an upward-sloping *BP* curve will provide combinations of *i* and *Y* consistent with equilibrium.

Equilibrium

Equilibrium for the economy requires that all three markets—the goods market, the money market, and the balance of payments—be in equilibrium. This occurs when the *IS, LM,* and *BP* curves intersect at a common equilibrium level of the interest rate and income. In Figure 14.1, point *e* is the equilibrium point that occurs at the equilibrium interest rate i_e and the equilibrium income level Y_e. Until some change occurs that shifts one of the curves, the *IS-LM-BP* equilibrium will be consistent with all goods produced being sold, money demand equal to money supply, and a current account surplus equal to a capital account deficit that yields a zero balance on the official settlements account.

Monetary Policy under Fixed Exchange Rates

In deriving the *BP* curve, we assumed that higher interest rates in the domestic economy would attract foreign investors and decrease the capital account deficit. With fixed exchange rates, the domestic central bank is not free to conduct monetary policy independent of the rest of the world. In the discussion of sterilization in Chapter 10, it was argued that, in the short run, the central bank could exercise some control over the money supply if domestic and foreign financial assets were imperfect substitutes. If assets are perfect substitutes, then they must yield the same return to investors. With fixed exchange rates, this means that the domestic interest rate will equal the foreign interest rate. If capital is perfectly mobile, then any deviation of the domestic interest rate from the foreign rate would cause investors to attempt to hold only the high return assets. Clearly, in this case there is no room for central banks to conduct an independent monetary policy under fixed exchange rates.

Figure 14.5 illustrates this situation. With perfect asset substitutability, the *BP* curve is a horizontal line at the domestic interest rate i, which equals the foreign interest rate i_F. Any rate higher than i_F results in large (infinite) capital inflows, while any lower rate yields large capital outflows. Only at i_F is the balance of payments equilibrium obtained.

Suppose the central bank increases the money supply so that the *LM* curve shifts from *LM* to *LM*′. The *IS-LM* equilibrium is now shifted from e to e'. While e' results in equilibrium in the money and goods market, there will be a large capital outflow and large official settlements balance deficit. This will pressure the domestic currency to depreciate on the foreign exchange market. To maintain the fixed exchange rate, the central bank must intervene and sell foreign exchange to buy domestic currency. The foreign exchange market intervention will decrease the domestic money supply and shift the *LM* curve back to *LM* to restore the initial equilibrium at e. With perfect capital mobility, this would all happen instantaneously, so that no movement away from point e is ever observed. Any attempt to lower the money supply and shift the *LM* curve to the left would have just the reverse effect on the interest rate and intervention activity.

With less than perfect capital mobility, the central bank has some opportunity to vary the money supply. Still, the maintenance of the fixed

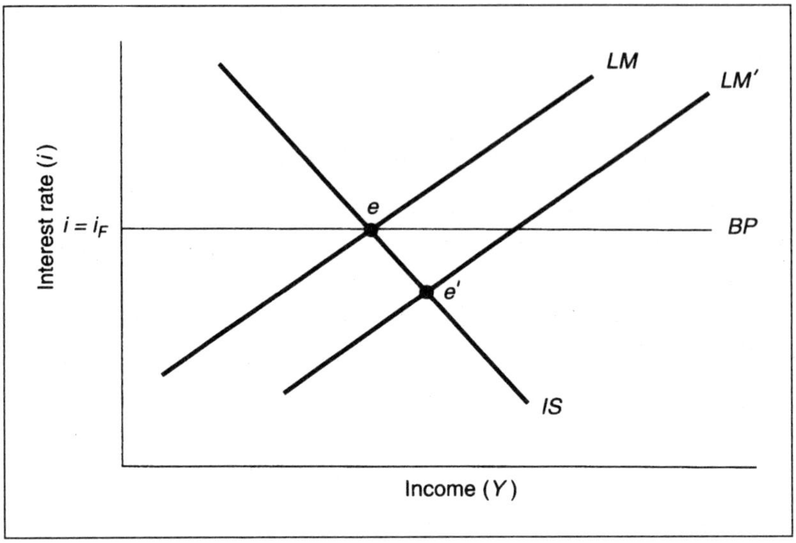

Figure 14.5 Monetary expansion with fixed exchange rates.

exchange rate will require an ultimate reversal of policy in the face of a constant foreign interest rate. The process is essentially just drawn out over time rather than occurring instantly.

Fiscal Policy under Fixed Exchange Rates

A change in government spending or taxes will shift the *IS* curve. Suppose an expansionary fiscal policy is desired. Figure 14.6 illustrates the effects. With fixed exchange rates, perfect asset substitutability, and perfect capital mobility, the *BP* curve is a horizontal line at $i = i_F$. An increase in government spending shifts the *IS* curve right to *IS*′. The domestic equilibrium shifts from point e to e', which would mean a higher interest rate and higher income. Since point e' is above the *BP* curve, the official settlements balance of payments moves to a surplus because of a reduced capital account deficit associated with the higher domestic interest rate. To stop the domestic currency from appreciating, the central bank must increase the money supply and buy foreign exchange with domestic money. The increase in the money supply shifts the *LM* curve to the right. When the money supply has increased enough to move the *LM* curve to *LM*′ in Figure 14.6, equilibrium is restored at point e''. Point e'' has the interest rate back at $i = i_F$, and yet income has increased.

This result is a significant difference from the monetary policy expansion considered in the preceding section. With fixed exchange rates and per-

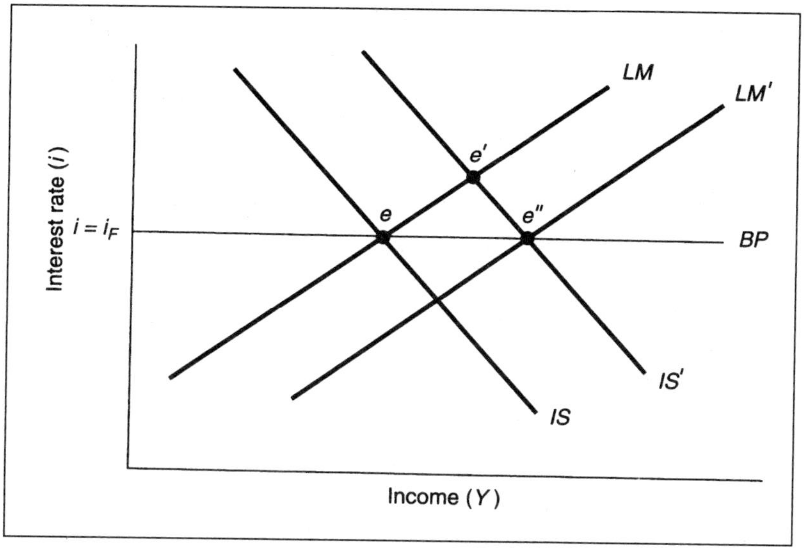

Figure 14.6 Fiscal expansion with fixed exchange rates.

fect capital mobility, monetary policy was seen to be ineffective in changing the level of income. This was so because there was no room for independent monetary policy with a fixed exchange rate. In contrast, fiscal policy will have an effect on income and can be used to stimulate the domestic economy.

Monetary Policy under Floating Exchange Rates

We now consider a world of flexible exchange rates and perfect capital mobility. The notable difference between the analysis in this section and the fixed exchange rate stories of the previous two sections is that with floating rates the central bank is not obliged to intervene in the foreign exchange market to support a particular exchange rate. With no intervention, the current account surplus will equal the capital account deficit so that the official settlements balance equals zero. In addition, since the central bank does not intervene to fix the exchange rate, the money supply can change to any level desired by the monetary authorities. This independence of monetary policy is one of the advantages of flexible exchange rates according to proponents of a float.

The assumptions of perfect substitutability of assets and perfect capital mobility will result in $i = i_F$ as before. Once again, the *BP* curve will be a horizontal line at $i = i_F$. Only now, equilibrium in the balance of payments will mean a zero official settlements balance.

Changes in the exchange rate will cause shifts in the *IS* curve. With fixed domestic and foreign goods prices, depreciation of the domestic currency will make domestic goods relatively cheaper and will stimulate domestic exports. Since net exports are part of total spending, the *IS* curve will shift rightward. A domestic currency appreciation will decrease domestic net exports and cause the *IS* curve to shift to the left.

Figure 14.7 illustrates the effects of an expansionary monetary policy. The increase in the money supply shifts the *LM* curve to the right to *LM'*. The interest rate and income existing at point *e'* would yield equilibrium in the money and goods markets but would cause a larger capital account deficit (and official settlements deficit) since the domestic interest rate would be less than i_F. Since this is a flexible exchange rate system, the official settlements deficit is avoided by adjusting the exchange rate to a level that restores equilibrium. Specifically, the pressure of the official settlements deficit will cause the domestic currency to depreciate. This depreciation is associated with a rightward shift of the *IS* curve as domestic exports increase. When the *IS* curve shifts to *IS'*, the new equilibrium is obtained at *e''*. At *e''*, income has increased and the domestic interest rate equals the foreign rate.

Had there been a monetary contraction instead of an expansion, the story would have been reversed. A temporarily higher interest rate would decrease the capital account deficit, causing pressure for the domestic currency to appreciate. As domestic net exports are decreased, the *IS* curve

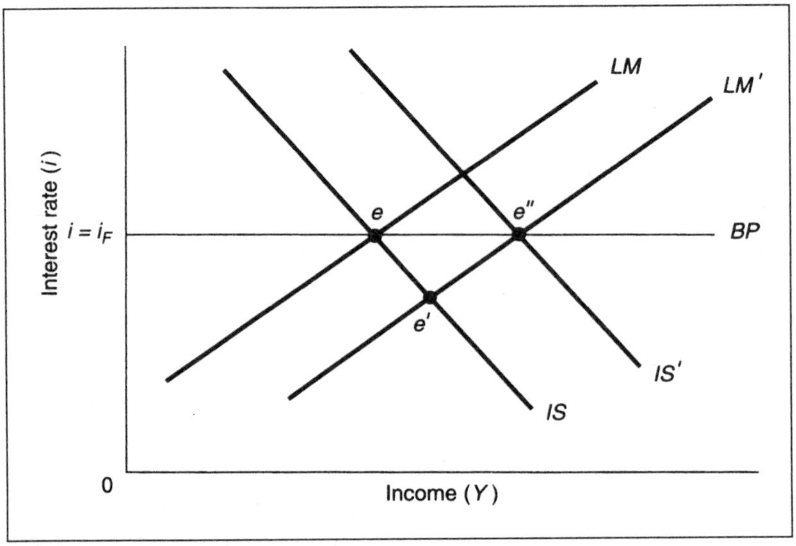

Figure 14.7 Monetary expansion with floating exchange rates.

shifts to the left until a new equilibrium is established at a lower level of income and the original $i = i_F$ is restored.

In contrast to the fixed exchange rate world, monetary policy can change the level of income with floating exchange rates. Since the exchange rate adjusts to yield balance of payments equilibrium, the central bank can choose its monetary policy independent of other countries' policies. This world of flexible exchange rates and perfect capital mobility is often called the *Mundell–Fleming model* of the open economy. (Robert Mundell and Marcus Fleming were two early researchers who developed models along the lines of those presented here.)

Fiscal Policy under Floating Exchange Rates

An expansionary fiscal policy caused by a tax cut or increased government spending will shift the *IS* curve to the right. Earlier it was shown that with fixed exchange rates, such a policy would result in a higher domestic income level. With flexible exchange rates we will see that the story is much different.

In Figure 14.8, the expansionary fiscal policy shifts the *IS* curve right, from *IS* to *IS'*. This shift would result in an intermediate equilibrium at point e'. At e', the goods market and money market will be in equilibrium, but there will be an official settlements surplus because of the lower capital account deficit induced by the higher interest rate at e'. Since the exchange

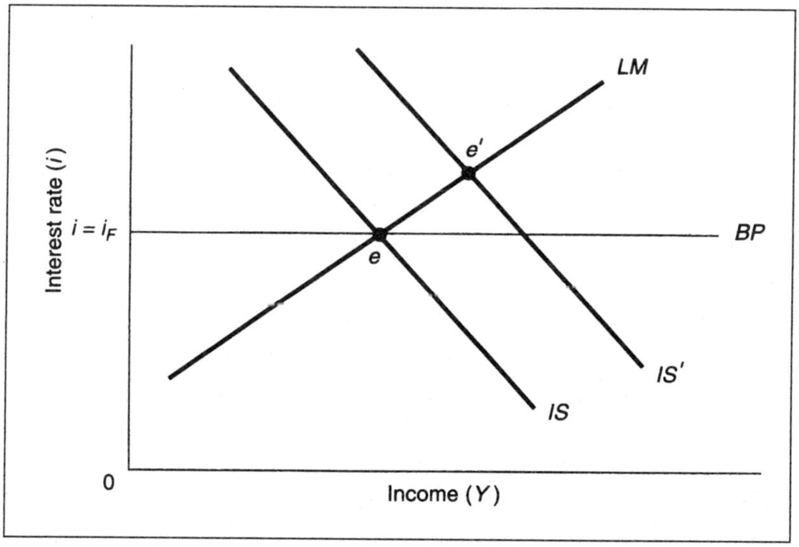

Figure 14.8 Fiscal expansion with floating exchange rates.

rate is free to adjust to eliminate the balance of payments surplus, the intersection of the *IS* and *LM* curves cannot remain above the *BP* curve.

The official settlements surplus causes the domestic currency to appreciate. This appreciation will reduce domestic exports and increase imports. As net exports fall, the *IS* curve shifts left. When the *IS* curve has returned to the initial equilibrium position that passes through point *e*, equilibrium is restored in all markets. Note that the final equilibrium occurs at the initial level of *i* and *Y*. With floating exchange rates, fiscal policy is ineffective in shifting the level of income. When an expansionary fiscal policy has no effect on income, complete *crowding out* has occurred. This crowding out occurs because the currency appreciation induced by the expansionary fiscal policy reduces net exports to a level that just offsets the fiscal policy effects on income.

The New Open-Economy Macroeconomics

In recent years, new macroeconomic models of open economies have been developed to take us beyond the *IS-LM-BP* framework just presented. While these new models are too complex to be covered in detail here, we should realize where economic thought is moving and the implications of this new thinking. The New International Macroeconomics carefully considers the details of the economy to the level of individual firms and households and how their actions aggregate to macroeconomic phenomena.

The *IS-LM-BP* model focused on one country and abstracted from the rest-of-the-world, which is in the background. The New International Macroeconomics typically examines two countries (you might think of one as the rest-of-the-world) and the determination of key macroeconomic variables like incomes, prices, and the exchange rate. The predictions of this type of model would include the following effects of a surprising increase in the domestic money supply: consumer spending increases at home and abroad; domestic income increases by more than foreign income; the domestic currency depreciates and purchasing power parity is maintained continuously.

The *IS-LM-BP* model was developed holding the price level constant. In many New International Macroeconomic models the price level is held fixed for a short run and then allowed to change in the long run. So the short-run fixed price is like the old model, but the long run allows for a dynamic adjustment of prices over time that is missing from the static models of the *IS-LM-BP* type. In many New International Macroeconomic models, if prices were perfectly flexible, then money supply shocks would have no effects on real variables like income or consumption due to the assumption of purchasing power parity. In this case, prices would change in proportion to changes in the money supply and the exchange rate would change to leave relative prices at home and abroad unchanged (the "law of one price") so that there is no inducement for changes in consumption or production. So the assumption of "sticky prices" is important to generate changes in spending and output.

Since there is much evidence against the law of one price, some research has focused on a modified version of a New International Macroeconomic model that allows for *pricing to market.* This occurs when local currency pricing reflects local market conditions in each country and allows for price discrimination across countries. In this case, purchasing power parity does not hold and so changes in the money supply of one country may result in bigger exchange rate changes due to the relative lack of responsiveness of price levels across countries. This is an important change since we observe real-world exchange rates having much greater volatility than relative prices across countries.

International Policy Coordination

This chapter has so far demonstrated the effects of fiscal and monetary policy under fixed and floating exchange rates. From the early 1970s on, the major developed nations have generally operated with floating exchange rates. In this framework, fiscal and monetary policy can generate large swings in exchange rates. The high degree of capital mobility existing among the developed countries suggests that fiscal actions that lead to a divergence of the domestic interest rate from the given foreign interest rate will quickly be undone by the influence of exchange rate changes on net exports, as was illustrated in Figure 14.8. Many economists argue that the sharp reduction in U.S. net exports in the mid-1980s was due to the expansionary fiscal policy followed by the U.S. government.

How could such a reduction in net exports be minimized? If all nations coordinated their domestic policies and simultaneously stimulated their economies, the world interest rate would rise and the pressure for exchange rate change and net export adjustment would fall. The problem illustrated in Figure 14.8 was that of a single country attempting to follow an expansionary policy while the rest of the world retained unchanged policies, so that i_F remains constant. If i_F increased at the same time that i increased, the *BP* curve would shift upward and the balance of payments equilibrium would be consistent with a higher interest rate.

Similarly, changes in exchange rates and net exports induced by monetary policy can be lessened if central banks coordinate policy so that i_F shifts with i. There have been instances of coordinated foreign exchange market intervention when a group of central banks jointly followed policies aimed at a depreciation or appreciation of the dollar. These coordinated interventions, intended to achieve a target value of the dollar, also work to bring domestic monetary policies more in line with each other. If the United States has been following an expansionary monetary policy relative to Japan, U.S. interest rates may fall relative to the other country's rates, so that a larger capital account deficit is induced and pressure for a dollar depreciation results. If the central banks decide to work together to stop the dollar depreciation, the Japanese will buy dollars on the foreign exchange market with their domestic currencies, while the Federal Reserve must sell foreign exchange to buy dollars. This will result in a higher money supply in Japan and a lower money supply in the United States. The coordinated intervention works toward a convergence of monetary policy in each country.

The basic argument in favor of international policy coordination is that such coordination would stabilize exchange rates. Whether exchange rate stability offers any substantial benefits over freely floating rates with independent policies is a matter of much debate. Some experts argue that coordinated monetary policy to achieve fixed exchange rates or to reduce exchange rate fluctuations to within narrow target zones would reduce the destabilizing aspects of international trade in goods and financial assets when currencies become overvalued or undervalued. This view emphasizes that in an increasingly integrated world economy, it seems desirable to conduct national economic policy in an international context rather than by simply focusing on domestic policy goals without a view of the international implications.

An alternative view is that most changes in exchange rates result from real economic shocks and should be considered permanent changes. In this view, there is no such thing as an overvalued or undervalued currency because exchange rates always are in equilibrium given current economic conditions. Furthermore, governments cannot change the real relative prices of goods internationally by driving the nominal exchange rate to some particular level through foreign exchange market intervention, because price levels will adjust to the new nominal exchange rate. This view, then, argues that government policy is best aimed at lowering inflation and achieving governmental goals that contribute to a stable domestic economy.

The debate over the appropriate level and form of international policy coordination has been one of the livelier areas of international finance in recent years. Many leading economists have participated, but a problem at the practical level is that different governments emphasize different goals and may view the current economic situation differently. Ours is a more complex world in which to formulate international policy agreements than is typically viewed in scholarly debate, where it is presumed that governments agree on the current problems and on the impact of alternative policies on those problems. Nevertheless, the research of international financial scholars offers much promise in contributing toward a greater understanding of the real-world complexities government officials must address.

The Open-Economy Multiplier

We can use the macroeconomic model developed in this chapter to analyze the effects of changes in spending on the equilibrium level of national income, assuming the interest rate is unchanged. We begin with the basic macroeconomic equilibrium conditions seen in the bottom half of Figure 14.2:

$$S + T + IM = I + G + X \tag{14.2}$$

In equilibrium, the planned level of saving plus taxes plus imports must equal the planned level of investment plus government spending plus exports. To find the equilibrium levels of national income (Y) and net exports ($X - IM$), we must make some assumptions regarding the variables in Equation (14.2). Specifically, we assume that saving and imports both depend on the level of national income. The greater the domestic income, the more people want to save, and the more they want to spend on imports. The fraction of any extra income that people want to save is called the *marginal propensity to save,* which we will denote as s. The fraction of any extra income that people want to spend on imports is called the *marginal propensity to import,* which we will denote as m. So, $S = sY$ and $IM = mY$. The rest of the variables in Equation (14.2)—T, I, G, and X—are assumed to be exogenously determined by factors other than domestic income.

With these assumptions, we can substitute the new specifications of S and IM and rewrite Equation (14.2) as

$$sY + T + mY = I + G + X \tag{14.3}$$

Gathering our Y terms and subtracting T from each side of the equation, we have $(s + m)\,Y = I + G + X - T$. Solving for the equilibrium level of Y yields

$$Y = (I + G + X - T)/(s + m) \tag{14.4}$$

If I, G, or X increased by \$1, the equilibrium level of Y would increase by $1/(s + m)$ times \$1. An increase in T would cause Y to fall. The value of $1/(s + m)$ is known as the *open-economy multiplier.* This multiplier is equal to the reciprocal of the marginal propensity to save (s) plus the marginal propensity to import (m). Since s and m will both be some fraction less than 1, we expect this multiplier to exceed 1, so that an increase in I, G, or X spending would cause the equilibrium level of national income to rise by more than the change in spending.

Let's consider an example of this multiplier effect. Suppose that we return to the model of Figure 14.2 as redrawn in Figure 14.9. In this model economy, the marginal propensity to save is .3, the marginal propensity to import is .2, taxes equal 20, and investment, government spending, and exports each equal 10 (assume the units are billions of dollars). In this case, the macroeconomic model is given by

$$S + T + IM = .3Y + 20 + .2Y = .5Y + 20 \qquad (14.5)$$

and

$$I + G + X = 10 + 10 + 10 = 30 \qquad (14.6)$$

These two equations are drawn in Figure 14.9 as the $S + T + IM$ line and the $I + G + X$ line. The point of intersection occurs at e, where the equilibrium level of national income equals \$20 billion.

The equilibrium level of income could have been found by using Equation (14.4) and substituting the values given for each variable:

$$Y = (I + G + X - T)/(s + m) = 10/.5 = 20 \qquad (14.7)$$

Whether we solve for the equilibrium level of Y algebraically or graphically, we find the value of \$20 billion.

What would happen if exports increased? For instance, suppose exports increase from \$10 to \$20 billion. In Figure 14.9, the $I + G + X$ line shifts up by the amount of the increase in exports to $I + G + X'$. The two lines are parallel because they differ by a constant \$10 billion, the increase in exports, at each level of income. The new equilibrium level of income is found by the new point of intersection e' at an income level of \$40 billion. Note that exports increase by 10, yet income increases by 20, from the original equilibrium level of 20 to the new level of 40. Since the increase in equilibrium national income is twice the increase in exports, the open-economy multiplier must equal 2. Algebraically, the multiplier is $1/(s + m)$, which, in the example,

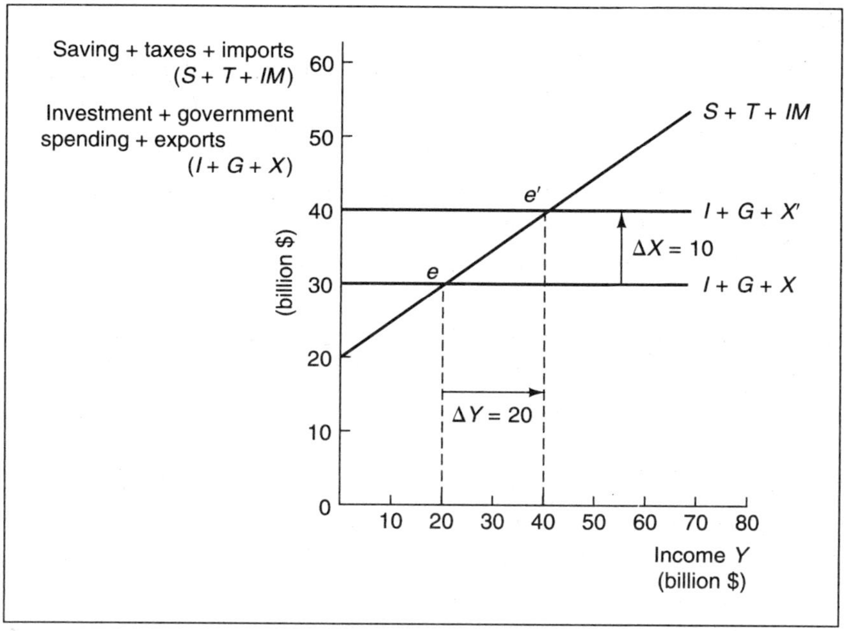

Figure 14.9 The effect of an increase in exports.

is $1/(.3 + .2) = 1/.5 = 2$. An increase in *I, G,* or *X* would increase *Y* by twice the increase in spending in our example.

The intuition behind the multiplier effect is taught in principles of economics courses. If spending, such as export spending, rises in some industry, then there is an increase in the income of factors employed in that industry. These employed resource owners, such as laborers, will increase their spending on goods and services and further stimulate production, which further raises income and spending. This "multiplier effect" has a finite value because not all of the increased income is spent in the domestic economy. Some is saved and some is spent on imports. Saving and imports act as leakages from domestic spending that serve to limit the size of the multiplier. The larger the marginal propensity to save and the marginal propensity to import, the smaller the multiplier.

In the real world, such multiplier effects will be more complex due to the presence of taxes and feedback effects from the rest of the world. However, the essential point—that changes in spending may create much larger changes in the national income—remains. Stable growth of the economy requires stable growth of spending.

Summary

1. Internal balance is a domestic rate of growth consistent with a low unemployment rate.
2. External balance is a desired level of trade or capital flows.
3. Macroeconomic equilibrium requires equilibrium in the goods market, money market, and balance of payments.
4. The *IS* curve presents combinations of i and Y that yield goods market equilibrium.
5. The *LM* curve presents combinations of i and Y that yield money market equilibrium.
6. The *BP* curve presents combinations of i and Y that yield balance of payments equilibrium.
7. With perfect asset substitutability and perfect capital mobility, the domestic interest rate is equal to the foreign interest rate.
8. With fixed exchange rates, a country cannot conduct an independent monetary policy to shift domestic income.
9. Fiscal policy is effective in changing domestic income with fixed exchange rates.
10. With floating exchange rates, monetary policy is effective in changing domestic income.
11. With floating exchange rates, fiscal policy changes tend to be offset by the balance of payments, so that crowding out occurs and income is unaffected.
12. The New International Macroeconomics emphasizes modeling economies down to the level of the firm and household and provides an alternative to the *IS-LM-BP* model.
13. International policy coordination is viewed as a way to stabilize exchange rates.
14. The open-economy multiplier is equal to the reciprocal of the marginal propensity to save plus the marginal propensity to import.

Exercises

1. How would the pursuit of internal balance be different in a closed economy, where there is no concern over external balance, than in an open economy?
2. Derive the *IS, LM,* and *BP* curves. Carefully label and explain each diagram you use.
3. If a nation has a surplus balance of payments, what is the appropriate government policy to induce balance of payments equilibrium? What effects might this have on income and employment?

4. Why do central banks have to formulate monetary policy differently under fixed exchange rates than under floating exchange rates?
5. Draw an initial *IS-LM-BP* equilibrium. Now put four additional points on the graph: one is directly above the equilibrium, one is to the right of the equilibrium, one is directly below the equilibrium, and one is directly to the left of the equilibrium. Label these points *A, B, C,* and *D.* For each point, explain the nature of the disequilibrium that would exist if income and the interest rate were at levels consistent with each point rather than with their equilibrium levels.
6. Why would macroeconomic policy coordination help stabilize exchange rates?

References

Canzoneri, Matthew, Robert E. Cumby, and Behzad T. Diba, "The Need for International Policy Coordination: What's Old, What's New, What's Yet to Come?" *NBER Working Paper* 8765.

Fleming, Marcus, "Domestic Financial Policies under Fixed and under Floating Exchange Rates," *IMF Staff Papers,* November 1962.

Ghosh, Atish, "International Policy Coordination in an Uncertain World," *Economics Letters,* 3, 1986.

Lane, Philip R., "The New Open Economy Macroeconomics: A Survey," *Journal of International Economics,* August 2001.

Mundell, Robert A., "Capital Mobility and Stabilization Policy under Fixed and Flexible Exchange Rates," *Canadian Journal of Economics,* November 1963.

Obstfeld, Maurice, and Kenneth Rogoff, "Exchange Rate Dynamics Redux," *Journal of Political Economy,* June 1995.

Sarno, Lucio, and Mark P. Taylor, *New Developments in Exchange Rate Economics, Volume I.* Cheltenham, U.K.: Edward Elgar, 2002.

Stockman, Alan C., "The Equilibrium Approach to Exchange Rates," *Federal Reserve Bank of Richmond Economic Review,* April 1987.

Glossary

absorption approach to the balance of trade A theory based on domestic spending for domestic goods (absorption) relative to domestic output.
adjustable peg A system of fixed exchange rates, with periodic devaluations allowed when conditions warrant.
adjusted present value The value today of future cash flows from operations plus related financial effects.
adjustment mechanism The method by which the international economy reacts to remove a disequilibrium.
airbill A bill of lading for goods shipped by air.
American depositary receipts (ADRs) Negotiable instruments certifying shares of a foreign stock held by a foreign custodian.
arbitrage Buying in a market where the price is low and then selling in a market with a higher price.
arm's-length pricing Prices that an unrelated buyer and seller would willingly pay.
asymmetric information Causes exchange rates to change due to traders' fear that they are quoting prices to someone who knows more about current market conditions than they do.
autocorrelation The errors from a regression equation are related over time.

balance of payments A balance sheet recording a nation's international transactions.
balance of payments equilibrium When credits equal debits on some sub-account of the balance of payments.
balance of trade Merchandise exports minus merchandise imports.
bankers' acceptance A time draft drawn on and accepted by a particular bank, to be paid at maturity.
bank notes Actual paper currency.
base money Currency plus commercial bank reserves held against deposits.
basic balance The sum of the balances on the merchandise, services, unilateral transfers, and long-term capital accounts.
basis point One-hundredth of a percent, or 0.0001.
basket pegger A country that maintains a fixed exchange rate with a composite or weighted average of foreign currencies rather than against a single foreign currency.
beta A measure of the portfolio risk associated with an individual asset.
bill of lading Agreement issued by a shipping company to carry goods to a destination port.

bimetallism Two metals, like gold and silver, serving as backing for the money supply.
black market An illegal market in foreign exchange.
broker An intermediary in the foreign exchange market.

call option The right to buy currency at a stated price on or before a future date.
capital account That part of the balance of payments that records trade in financial assets.
capital budgeting Evaluating prospective investment alternatives in order to fund preferred projects.
capital controls Restrictions on international capital flows, like taxes or quotas.
capital flight Large investment outflows associated with increased risk in a country.
central bank The official bank of a government, like the Federal Reserve in the United States.
chartists Forecasters who use the past history of exchange rates to predict future movements.
closed economy An economy with little or no economic activity involving the rest of the world.
commodity money standard Money has a fixed value relative to some commodity.
comparative advantage A determinant of the pattern of world trade in terms of which country exports which goods.
compensating balances Bank deposits that must be held as a form of compensation to the bank.
country risk analysis An evaluation of the potential for default or rescheduling on loans made to a particular country.
covariance A measure of the degree to which two variables move together.
covered interest arbitrage Buying or selling assets internationally and using the forward market to eliminate exchange risk in order to take advantage of return differentials.
crawling peg A system in which the exchange rate is held fixed in the short run but is adjusted at regular intervals to reflect supply and demand pressures.
cross rate The implied third exchange rate, given two exchange rates involving three currencies.
currency board A government institution that exchanges domestic currency for foreign currency at a fixed rate of exchange.
currency contract period The period immediately following a devaluation when contracts negotiated prior to the devaluation come due.
currency swap Where two counterparties exchange streams of interest payments in different currencies for an agreed period of time and exchange principal amounts in the respective currencies at an agreed exchange rate at maturity.
currency union A region within which exchange rates are fixed.
current account In the balance of payments the sum of the merchandise, services, and unilateral transfers accounts.

debt-equity swaps An exchange of debt for the debtor's domestic currency, which is then used to buy equity positions in the debtor country.
deep market A market with a large number of buyers and sellers, and assets traded, so that trading occurs at all times.
depreciation A decrease in a currency's value.
destabilizing speculation Speculation causing exchange rates to fluctuate more than they would in the absence of such speculation.
direct foreign investment Expenditures related to the establishment of foreign operating units.

discount The forward pricing of a currency at less than the spot price.
discount rate Rate of interest used to determine present value of future cash flow.
diversified portfolio A mix of investments that lowers an investors risk.
dock receipt A document issued by a shipping company listing the quantity and quality of the goods delivered to the dock.
domestic credit The domestic component of base money.
durable goods Goods with useful lives of more than one year.

economic exposure The exposure of the value of the firm to changes in exchange rates.
effective return The foreign interest rate of a foreign investment plus the forward premium or discount.
efficient market A market in which prices reflect all available information.
elasticities approach to the balance of trade An analysis that addresses the conditions necessary for a devaluation to improve the trade balance.
elasticity The responsiveness of quantity to changes in price.
endogenous Determined by factors within a model.
equation of exchange An equation stating that the money supply times the velocity of money is equal to the price level times the quantity of transactions.
equilibrium approach An approach that says that changes in exchange rates are largely due to changing tastes or technology.
Eurobank A bank that accepts deposits and makes loans in foreign currencies.
Eurobond market The market engaging in direct offshore borrowing and lending through the sale of bonds denominated in one currency yet sold in many countries.
Eurocurrency market The offshore banking market where commercial banks accept deposits and make loans in foreign currencies.
European currency unit (ECU) An average of the values of EMS currencies.
European Monetary System (EMS) A monetary union within which exchange rates were fixed, since the countries involved floated jointly against the rest of the world.
exchange rate The price of one nation's currency in terms of another nation's currency.
exchange rate index A measure of the average value of a currency.
exchange risk The risk arising from uncertainty regarding future exchange rates.
exogenous Determined by factors given to a model, outside of or independent of other variables in the model.
external balance A desired trade balance or desired international capital flows.

factors Firms that buy accounts receivable and assume responsibility for collection.
Fisher effect The expected effect of inflation on the nominal interest rate.
Fisher equation An equation stating that the nominal interest rate is equal to the real rate plus expected inflation.
fixed exchange rates When central banks set exchange rates at particular levels.
flexible exchange rates Free market supply and demand determine the exchange rate.
foreign exchange Bank deposits and currency denominated in foreign monetary units.
foreign exchange market A market mostly comprising large commercial banks buying and selling foreign exchange from and to each other.
foreign exchange swap The simultaneous exchange of two currencies on a specific date at a rate agreed at the time of the contract and a reverse exchange of the same two currencies at a date further in the future at a rate agreed at the time of contracting.
forward discount A forward rate at less than the spot rate.
forward exchange market A market for trading currencies among banks where delivery occurs at a future date.
forward exchange rate The price of a currency to be delivered sometime in the future.

forward premium A forward rate in excess of the spot rate.
fundamental model Forecasts exchange rates based on variables that are believed to be important determinants of exchange rates.
futures Contracts to buy and sell currency for future delivery that are traded on organized exchanges.

gold exchange standard A standard whereby a currency is valued in terms of a gold equivalent and every other currency is to maintain fixed exchange rates against that currency.
gold standard Currencies maintain a fixed price relative to gold.
Gresham's law A law stating that cheap money drives out good money.

hedging Taking a position to reduce risk.

IBFs International banking facilities—units of banks located in the United States that conduct Eurocurrency business.
IMF conditionality Economic adjustments imposed on a country by the IMF (International Monetary Fund) before loans will be made.
inflation-adjusted exchange rate The exchange rate minus the inflation differential between two countries.
interest rate parity The equivalence of the interest differential between two currencies to the forward premium or discount.
internal balance Domestic economic growth consistent with a low unemployment rate.
International Monetary Fund (IMF) An international organization that provides loans to countries experiencing balance of payments problems.
international reserves The international component of base money, primarily foreign exchange.
intervention The buying and selling of currencies by central banks to affect the exchange rate.
inventory control Effect on exchange rates when traders alter quotes to maintain a balance between amount of currency bought and sold.

J-curve effect Following a devaluation, an initial decrease in the trade balance followed by an increase.

law of one price A law stating that all goods sell for the same price worldwide when converted to a common currency.
letter of credit A letter issued by a bank that obligates the bank to pay a specific amount of money to an exporter.
LIBOR London interbank offer rate—the interest rate on interbank deposits among the large London banks.
liquid assets Things that can be easily spent, like cash or checking account money.
long position Buying a currency to be delivered in the future.

managed float The floating of exchange rates with central bank intervention.
margin Money deposited with a broker to finance futures trading.
marginal propensity to import The change in imports given a change in income.
Marshall-Lerner condition The necessary international demand elasticities that will ensure an improvement in the trade balance following a devaluation.
monetary approach to the balance of payments (MABP); monetary approach to the exchange rate (MAER) An analysis emphasizing money demand and

money supply as determinants of the balance of payments under fixed exchange rates and of the exchange rate under floating rates.

money multiplier The ratio of the money supply to base money.

moral hazard An inducement to greater risk taking that occurs when the decision maker does not expect to bear the full cost of bad decisions.

multinational firm A business firm operating in more than one country.

Mundell-Fleming model A model of an economy with flexible exchange rates and perfect capital mobility.

netting Consolidating payables and receivables in a currency so that only the difference must be bought or sold.

nominal interest rate The interest rate actually observed in the market.

nonsystematic risk Risk unique to an individual asset, which can be diversified away.

official settlements balance The balance of payments account measuring the change in short-term capital held by foreign monetary authorities and official reserve asset transactions.

offshore banking Accepting deposits and making loans in foreign currency—the Eurocurrency market.

open economy An economy actively involved in international trade.

opportunity cost The next-best alternative when undertaking some activity.

optimum currency area The best area within which exchange rates are fixed among currencies in the area and between which exchange rates are flexible among areas.

options Contracts that give the right to buy or sell a certain amount of currency at a stated price on or before a future date.

parallel market A free foreign exchange market that exists as an alternative to a regulated official market.

Paris Club An arrangement whereby creditor governments meet with debtor nations in Paris to restructure debts.

pass-through The effects of a devaluation on prices—the devaluing country sees its import prices rise while export prices to foreign buyers fall.

percent per annum The percentage return on a 12-month basis.

perfect capital mobility The free flow of capital between nations because there are no significant transactions costs or capital controls.

petrodollars Dollars earned by the export of oil, generally the earnings of the Organization of Petroleum Exporting Countries (OPEC).

portfolio-balance approach A theory of exchange rate determination that considers relative supply and demand for bonds.

premium The forward pricing of a currency at more than the spot price.

present value The value today of some amount to be received in the future.

pricing to market Adjusting domestic currency prices in response to exchange rate changes in order to maintain market share.

purchasing power parity *Absolute:* the equivalence of the exchange rate to the ratio of the foreign and domestic price levels. *Relative:* the equivalence of the percentage change in the exchange rate to the inflation differential between two nations.

put option The right to sell currency at a stated price on or before a future date.

real exchange rate The nominal exchange rate for two currencies divided by the ratio of their price levels.

real interest rate The nominal interest rate minus the rate of inflation.

regression analysis A statistical technique for estimating the relationship between a dependent variable and one or more independent variables.
relative price The price of one good relative to the price of another good.
risk aversion The degree to which people wish to avoid risk.
risk premium The difference between the forward exchange rate and the expected future spot rate.

seigniorage The difference between the cost of issuing money and the real resources acquired by the money issuer.
short position Selling a currency forward for future delivery.
Smithsonian agreement A December 1971 proclamation that the dollar was officially devalued and that currencies would now be allowed to fluctuate within ±2.25 percent of the new parity values.
special drawing right (SDR) An international reserve asset created by the IMF.
spot exchange rate The price of a currency for current delivery.
spot market Buying and selling currency for immediate delivery.
spread The difference between the buying and selling price of a currency or the differential between the interest rate on loans and deposits.
stable-valued money A currency with a stable and low inflation rate.
statistical significance A concept that allows one to relate estimated values to a hypothesized true value.
sterilization The offsetting of international reserve flows with domestic credit.
sterilized intervention Using open-market operations to offset the effect of intervention on the domestic money supply.
strike price The price at which currency may be bought or sold in an option contract.
swap The trade of one currency for another currency, combining a spot and forward transaction (or two forwards) in one deal.
systematic risk The risk common to all assets.

technical trading model Uses the past history of exchange rates to predict future movements.
term structure of interest rates The return on an asset over different maturity dates.
thin market A market with a small number of buyers and sellers, and assets traded.
tiered exchange rates Different exchange rates applied to different classes of transactions.
transaction costs The costs associated with buying and selling activity.
transaction exposure The foreign exchange risk associated with a particular transaction to be completed sometime in the future.
transfer price The price charged to a subsidiary for internal goods transfers.
translation The conversion of monetary values from one currency to another.
translation exposure The difference between a firm's foreign-currency-denominated assets and its foreign-currency-denominated liabilities.
triangular arbitrage Infer cross rate from two currencies to compare with another then buying where price is low and selling where price is high.

unbiased The property of being correct on average.

variance A measure of how a variable changes in value about its mean.

Index